MERCHANTS AND RULERS IN GUJARAT

M.N. PEARSON

MERCHANTS AND RULERS IN GUJARAT

THE RESPONSE TO THE PORTUGUESE
IN THE SIXTEENTH CENTURY

UNIVERSITY OF CALIFORNIA PRESS
BERKELEY • LOS ANGELES • LONDON

UNIVERSITY OF CALIFORNIA PRESS
Berkeley and Los Angeles, California

University of California Press, Ltd.
London, England

Copyright © 1976, by
The Regents of the University of California

ISBN 0-520-02809-0
Library of Congress Catalog Card Number: 74-81438

TO THE MEMORY OF
my father and mother

CONTENTS

Abbreviations Used in Footnotes	ix
Acknowledgments	xi
Introduction	1
I. The Setting	7
II. The Portuguese	30
III. The State	57
IV. The Merchants	92
V. Merchants and Their State	118
VI. Rulers and Subjects	133
Appendices:	
Money and Values	155
Glossary	157
Bibliographical Essay	161
Index	175

MAPS

1. Sixteenth-century Asia	9
2. Sixteenth-century Gujarat	59

ABBREVIATIONS USED IN FOOTNOTES

AHU	Arquivo Histórico Ultramarino, Lisbon.
ANTT	Arquivo Nacional da Torre do Tombo, Lisbon.
ANTTCC	Corpo Chronologico, ANTT.
ANTTDR	Documentos Remetidos da India, ANTT.
ANTTSL	Colecção de São Lourenço, ANTT.
ANTTSV	Colecção de São Vicente, ANTT.
APOCR	*Archivo Português Oriental*, ed. J.H. da Cunha Rivara, 6 vols. (Nova Goa, 1857-77).
Arabic History	Abdullah Muhammad al-Makhi al-Asafi al-Ulughkhani Hajji ad-dabir, *Zafar ul Walih bi Muzaffar wa Alihi*, trans. M.F. Lokhandwalla, vol. I (Baroda, 1970).
Assentos	*Assentos do Conselho do Estado*, ed. P.S.S. Pissurlencar, 5 vols. (Bastorá, Goa, 1953-57).
Barreto de Rezende	"Descripçõens das Cidades e Fortalezas da India Oriental" by Pedro Barreto de Rezende, 2 vols, in Biblioteca da Academia das Ciências, Lisbon.
Barros	João de Barros, *Asia,* 4 vols. (Lisbon, 1945-46).
Bocarro, Decada	António Bocarro, *Década 13 da História da India* (Lisbon, 1876).
Bocarro, Livro	António Bocarro, *Livro das plantas de todas as fortalezas, cidades e povações do Estado da India Oriental*, published in *Arquivo Português Oriental,* ed. A.B. de Bragança Pereira (Bastorá, Goa, 1937-40), tome IV, vol. II, parts 1-3.
B. Mus.	British Museum Library, London.
Castanheda	Fernão Lopes de Castanheda, *História do descobrimento e conquista da India pelos Portugueses,* 9 vols. (Coímbra, 1924-33).
Correa	Gaspar Correa, *Lendas da India,* 4 vols. (Lisbon, 1858-64).

ABBREVIATIONS USED IN FOOTNOTES

Couto	Diogo do Couto, *Da Asia,* 15 vols. (Lisbon, 1778-88).
Descrição	"Descrição das terras da India Oriental, e dos seus usos, costumes, ritos e leis," in Biblioteca Nacional, Lisbon.
DI	*Documenta Indica,* ed. J. Wicki, 10 vols. (Rome, 1948-).
DUP	*Documentação Ultramarina Portuguesa,* 5 vols. (Lisbon, 1960-67).
Factories	*The English Factories in India, 1618-1684,* ed. W. Foster and C. Fawcett, 17 vols. (London, 1904-54).
Fazenda	"Assentos do Conselho de Fazenda" in HAG, 10 vols.
Gavetas	*As Gavetas da Torre do Tombo,* 7 vols. (Lisbon, 1960-70).
HAG	Historical Archives of Goa, Panaji, Goa.
I.O.	India Office Records, London.
LM	"Livros das Monções do Reino," HAG.
LMBP	*Documentos Remettidos da India ou Livros das Monções,* ed. R.A. de Bulhão Pato, 5 vols. (Lisbon, 1880-1935).
Mirat	Ali Muhammad Khan, *Mirat-i Ahmadi,* trans. C.N. Seddon, S.N. Ali, M.F. Lokhandwalla (Baroda, 1928, 1965).
Sikandar	*The Mirat-i Sikandari,* ed. S.C. Misra and M.L. Rahman (Baroda, 1961).

In references to the chronicles by Barros, Couto, and Castanheda, I have followed the usual custom of quoting only década, book, and chapter numbers. Thus "Couto, VII, vi, 8" is: Couto, década VII, book vi, chapter 8. It should also be noted that for Couto's *Da Asia* I used the Lisbon edition of 1778-88 in 15 vols. except for the fifth decade. For this I used the fuller version, edited by Marcus de Jonge as *The Fifth Decada* (Coímbra, 1937).

Earlier versions of parts of this monograph appeared in the *Proceedings of the Indian History Congress,* in the *Indian Economic and Social History Review,* and in *South Asia* (Perth).

ACKNOWLEDGMENTS

In Mughal times an emperor's tutors were sometimes rewarded by being weighed against gold. The favored scholars thus received a weight of gold equal to the weights of their bodies. Times change; but my thanks to those who have helped me with this monograph are sincere, even if less auriferous.

John Broomfield guided my graduate studies at the University of Michigan, and directed the dissertation which formed a first draft of this work. His friendship, advice, criticism, and encouragement were invaluable during these years. The other readers of the dissertation, Rhoads Murphey, K. Allin Luther and Thomas R. Trautmann, all gave my early work the benefit of much more than routine evaluation.

My research in Singapore, India, Portugal, Edinburgh and London was aided by the cooperation of the staffs of the various archives and libraries in which I worked. I remember with particular gratitude the helpfulness of V. T. Gune and his staff at the Historical Archives of Goa in Panaji, and the many kindnesses my family and I received from S. C. Misra during our all too short stay at the M. S. University of Baroda. Other debts are legion: to Jean Aubin of the Sorbonne, and Surendra Gopal of Patna, for hospitality and advice; to Peter Reeves, now of the University of Western Australia, who introduced me to South Asian studies; to Holden Furber, Tom Kessinger, and David Washbrook, three past or present colleagues at the University of Pennsylvania who read different drafts of this study; to Ashin Das Gupta and Howard Spodek for critical evaluations; to C. R. Boxer, Irfan Habib, and Bernard S. Cohn for direct advice and for the helpfulness of their many publications; to Kathleen and David Ludden for the maps; above all to my wife Margot, who has borne with this work in its various incarnations, and at the same time raised a family and pursued her own career.

My research and writing in Singapore, London and India in 1968-70 was financed by a Commonwealth Fellowship from the Government of India, and grants from the Center for South and Southeast

Asian Studies, and the Horace H. Rackham School of Graduate Studies, both of the University of Michigan. The Calouste Gulbenkian Foundation supported a most useful eight months in Portugal in 1970. Research in Edinburgh for three weeks in 1972-73 was financed by a generous grant from the American Philosophical Society. Writing in the summer of 1971 was supported by a Summer Research Fellowship from the University of Pennsylvania. I am grateful for all this advice and support from these people and agencies, but responsibility for the final form of this monograph remains entirely mine.

Philadelphia, June, 1974   M. N. Pearson

INTRODUCTION

Among historians of South Asia it is generally recognized that we know little about the activities of the Portuguese in the sixteenth century, and still less about the effects of their activities on the local population. An occasional plea is heard: "Why doesn't someone learn Portuguese and work in the Goa archives?" Yet it is ironic that most historians probably also feel that they can live with this lacuna. There are other gaps of more pressing significance in our knowledge. The general attitude is that the Portuguese never ruled large areas in India anyway. It is generally known that they failed to achieve control of the spice trade to Europe; if they failed here, where they tried hardest, then why bother with them at all? We can give them credit for being the first Europeans to sail to India via the Cape of Good Hope (though we all know that it was a Gujarati Muslim pilot who guided them across from East Africa to Calicut), but their real significance ends here. It was the people who followed them, the Dutch and the British, who were really important because they initiated the colonial period of Indian history. The beginnings of this momentous period are usually found in Surat in the early seventeenth century, or perhaps in the dynamics of Western European history in the late sixteenth century.

This monograph argues that neglect of the Portuguese is unfortunate for two reasons. Portuguese activities in the sixteenth century were not just an anachronistic "renaissance" prelude to the arrival of the "modern" British and Dutch. It is indeed arguable that the Portuguese in the sixteenth century had more "impact" on India than did the Dutch and British in the seventeenth century. During their first century in India, the northern Europeans simply merged into an existing commercial framework as two more groups of foreign merchants; there were ample precedents for such activities, for India had always been hospitable to foreigners come to trade. The Portuguese, however, were not like this. They had no intention of trading peacefully alongside the dominant Muslim merchants in the Indian ocean. They tried to monopolize some items of Asian trade, and direct and tax trade in all other products. Obviously they failed to enforce their grandiose design, but in one area, Gujarat, they came close to success: for most of the sixteenth century they did control and tax most sea trade from the Gulf of Cambay. The setting in which the Portuguese operated, the mechanics of their system, and the nature of contacts between Portuguese and Gujaratis, are set out in the first four chapters of this monograph.

To the historian of India the Portuguese presence is not of interest only because of their trade control system. When the angle of focus is reversed, the response to the Portuguese from Gujarat provides a fascinating case study of the nature of political connections in this medieval Indian society. It is argued that this response to a new phenomenon of trade control cannot be explained in strictly economic or military terms. In fact, the rulers of Gujarat could, with an extremely good chance of success, have pressured the Portuguese to end their system. But this they never wanted to do, because normally rulers did not care what merchants did.

In analyzing the success of the Portuguese system, the key factor is therefore not Portuguese valor nor the timidity of Gujarat's merchants. Nor ultimately is it logistics or economics. Rather, it is the lack of political connections between ruler and merchant in Gujarati society which is crucial. Chapter V. elaborates on the nature of this relationship.

Finally, it would be dodging an important issue to conclude by saying that the explanation of Gujarati acquiescence in the Portuguese system is to be found in the nature of merchant-ruler relations in this medieval state. From the viewpoint of Indian history the prime contribution of this monograph lies in chapter VI. Here relations between the rulers and other social groups are elaborated. The conclusion is that what the response to the Portuguese reveals about relations between the rulers and one social group, the merchants, is not unique. Rather, it is a paradigm of the negligible contact and lack of communication between social groups in general, and the state, in medieval Gujarat. The detail on the Portuguese system and its workings is a contribution to both colonial historiography and to the maritime history of sixteenth-century Asia, but in terms of Indian history it is the nature of the Gujarati response which is most interesting, for this tells us important things about political relationships in one medieval Indian society.

The problem was where to stop. Students of other premodern societies will probably find parallels in their own areas to my findings; indeed, the work of non-Indianists such as H. A. R. Gibb and W. Eberhard, and of non-historians, notably Talcott Parsons, Max Weber, and Clifford Geertz, have influenced my thinking considerably. Yet this monograph was clearly not the place in which to attempt a comparative or theoretical study of political systems in premodern states. At most, chapter VI is a modest contribution of data for such a study.

There are available a large number of studies of court politics and administrative systems in medieval India.[1] One can thus follow rather closely the activities of a sultan of Gujarat and his nobles. But in trying to describe the doings of lower social groups, the task becomes much more difficult. This is because of the nature of the sources; it is appropriate to say something here about this problem.

Sylvia Thrupp, in her *The Merchant Class of Medieval London*, has two appendices covering sixty-seven pages in which she lists details on members of aldermanic families and London landowners in 1436.[2] This is precisely the sort of material we need and do not have for premodern Gujarat. All too often the merchants remain disembodied figures, dimly seen through the swirling mists created by the preconceptions of the chroniclers. More generally, it has usually been impossible to "disaggregate the data," to talk in terms of categories more specific than "nobles" or "merchants" or "sufis." Clearly within all of these rubrics different people had different interests, and acted in different ways at different times. These subtleties are usually hidden from us by the nature and extent of the sources.

The limitations of these sources (which are more fully described in the bibliographic essay) dictated that I take my evidence from a very long period, roughly 1500-1650, and especially from 1600 onward when the comparatively voluminous English and Dutch records on Gujarat start. Critics will say that such a procedure is invalid; but I have tried to be honest and not read back from 1660 to the early

---

[1] Ibn Hasan, *The Central Structure of the Mughal Empire* (London, 1936); P. Saran, *The Provincial Government of the Mughals* (Allahabad, 1941); S. R. Sharma, *Mughal Government and Administration* (Bombay, 1965); I. H. Qureshi, *The Administration of the Mughal Empire* (Karachi, 1966); J. N. Sarkar, *History of Aurangzeb*, 5 vols. in 4 (Calcutta, 1925-30); Bani Prasad, *History of Jahangir* (Allahabad, 1940); U. N. Day, *The Mughal Government* (New Delhi, 1970).

[2] Sylvia Thrupp, *The Merchant Class of Medieval London* (Chicago, 1948), pp. 321-88.

sixteenth century. In essence, I have used the fuller seventeenth-century records to elaborate on hints, indications, partial descriptions, from the sixteenth century. If the slightly later source has more detail on what is clearly a parallel sixteenth century process, then I feel justified in using the former as well as the latter.

It is true that this sort of procedure can disguise change over time; if this has happened, it is indeed a serious fault in an historical study. But as regards relations between merchants and rulers, and wider ruler-subject relations, it does not appear that there were important changes over the period from which my evidence is taken. In general, one of the crucial characteristics of the society I am describing is that it changed very slowly. This is to be expected; the continuity of the Confucian system in China has been stressed by many writers,[3] with structural changes occurring only in the later nineteenth century. Similarly, B. S. Cohn's and A. M. Shah's descriptions of the eighteenth-century Indian political system, especially in Benares and Gujarat, make it clear that at least up to this time fundamental changes had not taken place in the nature of relations between ruler and subject which are described in this monograph.[4]

For many historians, Akbar's conquest of Gujarat in 1572, or the arrival of the Dutch and English in Surat in the early seventeenth century, make decisive watersheds. The former event was in fact of little moment as regards my main concerns, as will become clear later. Nor did the latter affect politics or society in Gujarat, at least until the eighteenth century. Even in economic terms the presence of the Dutch and English meant little. They settled in Gujarat as simply two more groups of foreign merchants. The English especially were often heavily in debt to local merchants, and were bullied by them because of their financial weakness.[5] As a trade center Surat remained vastly more important than the new English possession of Bombay until the 1720s at least.[6] The average capital employed on the 165 ships sent to the east by the English East India Company from 1601 to 1640 was only about Rs. 2,00,000. In the 1620s the Dutch had Rs. 5,00,000

[3]For example, John K. Fairbank, Edwin O. Reischauer, and A. N. Craig, *East Asia: The Modern Transformation* (Boston, 1965), p. 5.

[4]B. S. Cohn, "Political Systems in Eighteenth Century India," *Journal of the American Oriental Society* 82 (1962); A. M. Shah, "Political System in Eighteenth Century Gujarat," *Enquiry* n.s. 1 (Spring 1964).

[5]Irfan Habib, "Usury in Medieval India," *Comparative Studies in Society and History* VI (July 1964); Factories, 1624-29, p. 94; 1633-36, p. 24; 1642-45, p. 108.

[6]Holden Furber, *Bombay Presidency in the Mid-Eighteenth Century* (Bombay, 1965), pp. 6, 9.

invested in all of India, according to the head of their Surat factory. He considered this to be a large sum.[7] Some Gujarati ships trading to the Red Sea in the late sixteenth century were worth more than Rs. 10,00,000 *each.*[8] The Europeans were poor relations. Nor, in the seventeenth century, were they capable of teaching new commercial or manufacturing techniques to the locals. The two seem to have been on much the same level of development.

What is at issue here are two biases in historical writing on India: "Whiggishness" and "Euro-centricity," the former reading back from the present to find the significance of the past, the latter looking at things Indian through European spectacles. P. E. Roberts finds the British Empire in India stemming inevitably from the arrival of Hawkins in Surat in 1608: "From the Eastern aspect it [the first century of the British in India] affords a wonderful spectacle of the advance of a Western civilization into the vast dominions of an Oriental empire—an advance as gradual, yet as irresistible, as the surging-in of the ever-moving ocean through the tidal creeks and lagoons of the Indian shore."[9] At the risk of belaboring the obvious, this sort of perspective ignores the fact that the British conquest of India was facilitated, if not made possible, by the decline of the Mughal Empire, and in this decline the English played no role. One example of the latter bias is the unpromising start to a book on the French in India: "L'Asie, berceau du genre humain, n'a pas tenu dans l'histoire de la civilisation du monde la place éminente que lui promettait ce début."[10] Such gross prejudice, dismissing in a cavalier way great world religions

---

[7] K. N. Chaudhuri, *The English East India Company* (New York, 1965), pp. 22, 226-30; *Recueil des voyages qui ont servi à l'établissement et aux progrez de la Compagnie des Indes Orientales formée dans les Provinces-Unies des Pais-Bas*, 12 vols. (Rouen, 1725), VII, 565.

[8] See p. 101, and footnotes.

[9] P. E. Roberts' introduction to W. W. Hunter, *A History of British India*, 2 vols. (London, 1899-1900), II, 8.

[10] Henri Weber, *La Compagnie Française des Indes (1604-1875)* (Paris, 1904), p. 1. For these biases, see Herbert Butterfield, *The Whig Interpretation of History* (London, 1931); J. C. van Leur, *Indonesian Trade and Society* (The Hague, 1955), pp. 145-56; John R. W. Smail, "On the Possibility of an Autonomous History of Modern Southeast Asia," *Journal of Southeast Asian History* II (July 1961). The perceptive reader will have already noticed that I occasionally use the term "medieval." To a purist it is invalid to use a European term relating to a period in European history, and loaded with a freight of associations from a European context, when writing about India. There is, however, no alternative word to refer to the period of the sixteenth and seventeenth centuries in Gujarat. "Medieval" is used simply to refer to this period; there are not necessarily any parallels between Gujarat at this time and medieval Europe.

and the fact that Western dominance is in world historical terms very recent, is today less frequently met with. Yet many modern writers still, by their use of terms and general attitudes, betray at least vestiges of a European stance in their writing on Asia. The general point is simply that the arrival of the Dutch and English, and Akbar's conquest of Gujarat, were important events for the Dutch and English, and for Akbar. But they were not of much significance for the merchants of Gujarat, nor did they affect the nature of merchant-state relations in Gujarat. Thus, I contend, *not* to use material from the seventeenth century would be to show the influence of these two historiographical biases.

CHAPTER I

THE SETTING

Gujarat and Asian Trade

Even today the economy of South and Southeast Asia is largely dependent on the arrival of the monsoon winds, and the amount of rain they bring with them. These monsoons were, and to a large extent are, the governing factor controlling shipping in the surrounding seas. They largely determined when a particular route could be sailed, when a market would be high or low, and when a punitive naval expedition could be undertaken.

In the area with which this monograph is most concerned, from East Africa to Indonesia, the northeast monsoon prevails from about October to March, and the southwest from May or June to September. Trade was regulated in accordance with these winds: for example, the "season" for trade from Gujarat to Aden was from September to May, for Aden to Malabar from October to February. A further refinement may be noted, of particular importance to western Indian trade. A ship coming across the Arabian Sea from East Africa, the Cape of Good Hope, or the Red Sea had to adjust its voyage so that it reached the Indian coast as the southwest monsoon was slackening, in September, for with the full force of the wind behind it a ship would have great difficulty in entering the poor harbors of western India. If, however, it reached western Indian waters too late, it would not reach the coast at all in the face of the beginning northeast monsoon. Similarly, a ship bound for the Cape of Good Hope had to leave western India as soon as possible in the new calendar year in order to round the Cape before the northeast monsoon slackened.[1]

By 1500 the ships trading in these seas on long-distance routes were

---

[1]On the importance of the monsoons in Asia, see Eric Axelson, *The Portuguese in Southeast Africa, 1600-1700* (Johannesburg, 1960), p. 2; W. H. Moreland, *India at the Death of Akbar* (Delhi, 1962), pp. 213-15; Bocarro, Livro, part 1, pp. 119-20; Barros, II, vi, 1. For a detailed description of Diu's monsoons, see Barreto de Rezende, I, 60-60v.

all of the Arab type. A century earlier Chinese junks had come to western India and far beyond, and Arab ships had called regularly at Canton.[2] Now there was a fairly strict dividing line at Malacca, with junks going no further west, and no Muslim ships sailing to China. These Muslim ships were single-masted, with very large rudders worked by two cords on either side of the boat. They were primarily held together by cords, but nails and glue were also sometimes used in their construction. One large latteen sail was used, and they were not fitted with keels. The ships were not decked, which increased the carrying capacity; huts were provided for the passengers and some of the cargo. These ships were dominant on all the international routes of South and Southeast Asia, whether in Gujarat, the Red Sea, Malabar, or Malacca.[3] In capacity the largest seem to have at least equalled contemporary Portuguese ships. The early sixteenth-century records speak of Muslim ships of between 375 and 800 tons capacity.[4] A list of 1525 describes thirty-six Portuguese ships in India, the biggest of which was 550 tons. It was not until 1558 that the Portuguese sent a ship of 1,000 tons to India.[5] Both locals and Portuguese used increasingly larger ships during the century. In the early seventeenth century the sultan of Bijapur owned a monster of 2,000 tons, but the average for local ships was 300-400 tons.[6]

[2]Barros, II, ii, 9; G. F. Hourani, *Arab Seafaring* (Princeton, 1951), for early Arab trade; for Arab trade to Southeast Asia, see articles by R. R. Di Meglio and M. A. P. Meilink Roelofsz in D. S. Richards, ed., *Islam and the Trade of Asia* (Philadelphia, 1970); for the China trade in the early Islamic period, see articles by M. Rogers, G. T. Scanlon, N. Chittick, and G. F. Hudson, in *ibid*.

[3]Correa, I, 122-24; Castanheda, III, cxxx. For a detailed study of navigational methods and cartography around 1500, see A. Teixeira da Mota, "Methodes de Navigation et Cartographie Nautique dans l'Ocean Indien avant le XVIe Siècle," *Studia* 11 (January 1963): 49-91.

[4]*Commentaries of Afonso Albuquerque*, 4 vols. (London, 1875-84), II, 122; ANTTSV, XIV, lv; Descrição, f. 36v. The ship of 800 tons belonged to the sultan of Gujarat, and was captured by the Portuguese at Hurmuz in 1510. It "was the biggest ship that used to sail in that Gulf [of Cambay] and in many parts was famous for its size." (Castanheda, III, xxxv.) It should be noted that a ton of capacity meant a quantity of goods sufficient to occupy 60 cubic feet. The 800-ton ship thus had a capacity of 48,000 cubic feet.

[5]ANTTSV, XI, 12v-15v; Bernando Gomes de Brito, *História Trágico-Maritima*, 6 vols. (Porto, 1942-43), II, 53.

[6]A. Jan Qaisar, "Shipbuilding in the Mughal Empire during the Seventeenth Century," *Indian Economic and Social History Review* V (June 1968): 65-66; "Consultas do serviço de partes," HAG, III, 47v; Bocarro, Livro, part 1, p. 124. See also a second excellent article by Qaisar, "Merchant Shipping in India during the Seventeenth Century," *Medieval India: A Miscellany*, vol. II (Aligarh Muslim University, 1972), pp. 195-220.

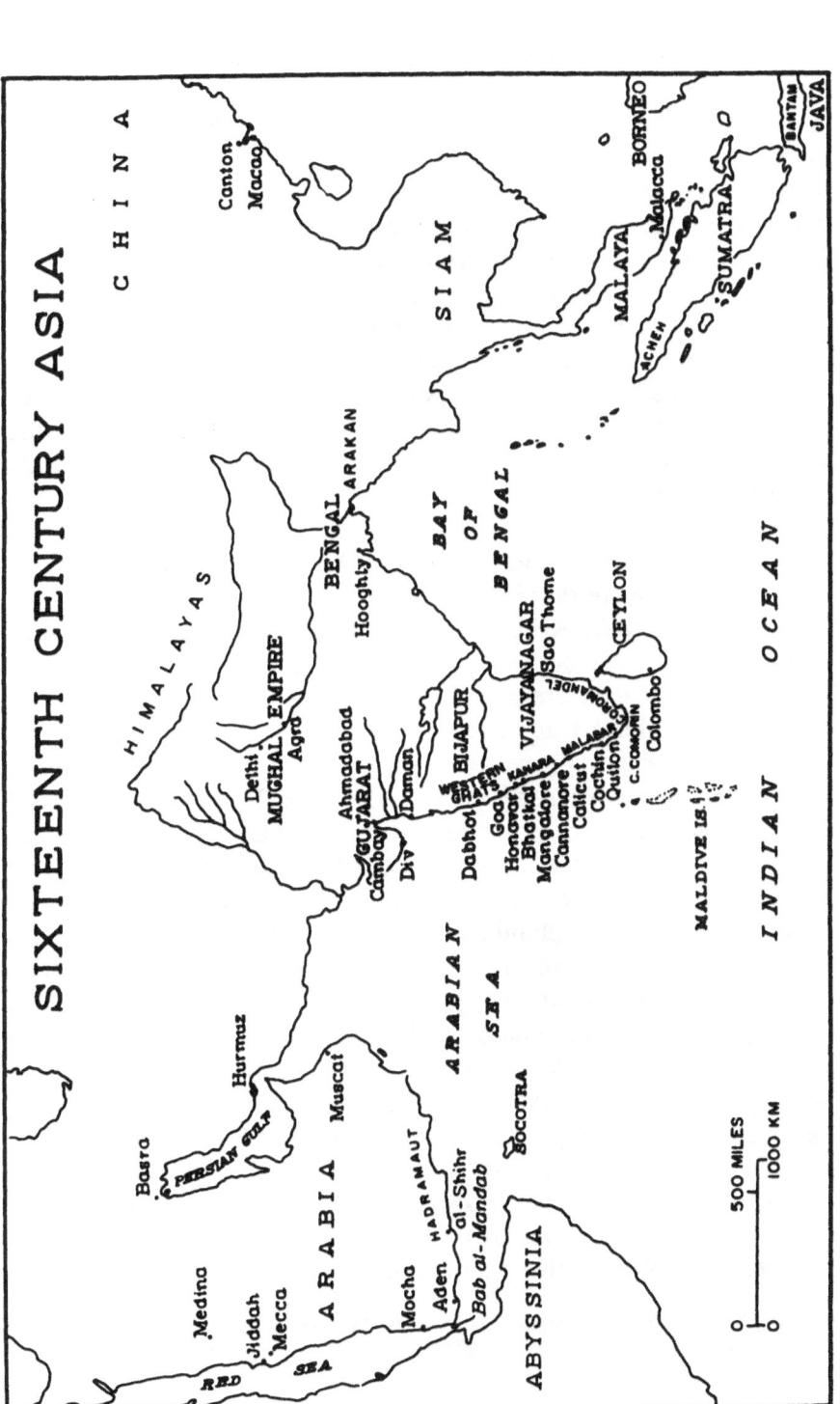

Descriptions of Asian trade around 1500 have tended to focus on the long-distance trade in spices from Indonesia via Calicut to the Red Sea and Europe. There is no doubt that this was an important trade, and that Calicut was a great emporium when the Portuguese first reached India, but it is necessary to be careful of the sources here. Asia's main export to Europe for at least a century on either side of da Gama's voyage was spices; these were what the Portuguese came to India to get, and so Malabar was the area best known to their early writers. Similarly, one can admit the importance of the trade in spices to Europe, at least to Europeans, to the Mamluks of Egypt, and to the Arab merchants who carried the pepper from Malabar. Nevertheless, one does not need to go so far as the early Portuguese chronicles and later W. H. Moreland[7] in elevating spices and Arabs into the dominant products and merchants in Asian trade. This Euro-centric stress on trade to Europe ignores the vast bulk of Asian trade, that which was *not* bound for Europe. And in this inter-Asian trade it was Gujaratis, not Arabs, who were dominant.

Around 1500 there were in Asia a number of well-defined "international" routes, the most important of which were: from China and Indonesia to Malacca; from Malacca to Gujarat; from Gujarat to the Red Sea; from Malabar to the Red Sea; from Gujarat to Malabar and intermediate ports on the western coast; from Aden to Hurmuz; from East Africa to Gujarat; from Gujarat to Hurmuz. Various feeder routes linked areas such as Ceylon, Bengal, Siam, and Coromandel to the great centers of Malacca, Calicut, Cambay, Hurmuz and the Red Sea. Despite the complexity of this network of routes, one fact stands out: the most important merchants on all these "international" routes, with only two exceptions, were Gujaratis, carrying not only their own cloths, indigo, and opium, but also the goods of others, especially spices.

The greatest port in Gujarat in 1500 was Cambay, or more strictly Gandhar. Cambay itself was, as a result of the silting of the Gulf of Cambay, now one mile inland. Yet this great city, despite its advantages as the best-sited port to serve the most fertile area in Gujarat, faced serious difficulties, first from the continual problem of the silting up of the upper reaches of the gulf, and second from the dreaded tidal bore in the gulf, which by repute could put even a man on horseback in danger.[8] For these reasons, ocean-going ships usually put in

---

[7]W. H. Moreland, "The Ships of the Arabian Sea about A.D. 1500," *Journal of the Royal Asiatic Society* (April 1939): 174-75.

[8]Barros, IV, v, 1.

at either Div or Gogha, and their goods were off-loaded into smaller coastal craft which took them to Gandhar. The inconvenience of this method was apparently such that in 1500 Div was increasing greatly in importance, as more and more commodity exchanges, not just transshipment, took place there rather than in Cambay. The other two great Gujarati ports were Surat and Rander, on the left and right banks of the Tapti River. The former rose to preeminence during the century, the latter was destroyed by the Portuguese. The ports south of Surat and west of Div were of less importance in "international" trade.[9]

Gujarat's most important trade was that linking Aden and Malacca via her own great ports. As the most acute contemporary observer said, "Cambay [i. e. Gujarat] chiefly stretches out two arms, with her right arm she reaches out towards Aden and with the other towards Malacca, as the most important places to sail to, and the other places are held to be of less importance."[10] Goods and money from Italy, Greece, and Damascus were brought down the Red Sea by the merchants of Cairo and Jiddah to Aden. There they were either exchanged for goods brought to Aden in local or Gujarati ships, or else the goods from west Asia and Europe continued on in Arab ships to Gujarat. These cargoes included gold and silver, quicksilver, vermilion, copper, rosewater, wools, and brocades. In the great ports of the Gulf of Cambay they were exchanged for local goods, preeminently cotton cloths, and imports, especially spices from Malacca. The trade between Gujarat and Malacca was handled almost entirely in Gujarati ships. European and Gujarati products were imported to this great Southeast Asian entrepôt, and exchanged for Chinese goods, especially silks and porcelains, for rubies and lacre from Pegu, for Bengal and Coromandel cloths, and for the cloves, nutmeg, and mace of the Molucca and Banda Islands. The ships sailing this Gujarat-Malacca route were based on Gujarat, but the merchants were various. The majority were Gujarati, but there were many others from countries in west Asia.[11]

Apart from this blue-ribbon Aden to Malacca route, one inevitably

[9] Descrição, f. 22; *Cartas de Affonso de Albuquerque*, 7 vols. (Lisbon, 1884-1935), I, 135-36; Barros, II, ii, 9; Couto, IV, vii, 5; Marechal Gomes da Costa, *Descobrimentos e Conquistas*, 3 vols. (Lisbon, 1927-30), III, 256; Tomé Pires, *The Suma Oriental of Tomé Pires*, 2 vols. (London, 1944), I, 34-35.

[10] Pires, I, 42. See an account of 1500 in *Arquivo Português Oriental*, ed. A. B. de Bragança Pereira, 10 vols. (Bastorá, Goa, 1936-40), tome I, vol. 1, part 1, p. 128.

[11] Pires, I, 43; II, 269-70; Descrição, f. 6v; Barros, I, viii, 1; Stephano's account in R. H. Major, ed., *India in the Fifteenth Century* (London, 1857), p. 9.

found Gujaratis with their ubiquitous cloths in many other parts of seaborne Asia. They traded to points east of Aden in the Hadramaut, as far as Hurmuz. They went to Bengal, Pegu, and Sumatra, as well as collecting products from these places in Malacca. They virtually monopolized overseas trade in East Africa, collecting gold and ivory and slaves in exchange for their cloths, for the people of Sofala, like those of Melinde and Mombasa, "want nothing but the cloths of Cambay."[12] Gujaratis also operated in the coastal trade of western India, in Dabhol, Chaul, Goa, and the Malabar ports, from which last they took pepper back to the Deccan ports and their own homeland. "The best house of the area" in Calicut in 1500 was owned by a Muslim from Gujarat.[13]

It has been noted that the spices of Southeast Asia—mace, nutmeg, and cloves—were carried by Gujarati ships, though the merchants concerned were heterogeneous. Pepper also was carried by Gujaratis to central and north India, but the pepper trade from Malabar to the Red Sea, and secondarily from Malabar to Hurmuz, was handled by Arab merchants in their own ships. These merchants were based on Cairo or Jiddah, the port of Mecca. To Malabar, and especially to the great entrepôt of Calicut, they brought the same goods as went to Gujarat. In return, they took the local pepper and ginger, and cinnamon from Ceylon. Some of the goods from Malacca, as spices and Chinese goods, came via Calicut also, but most of them went direct from Malacca to Gujarat.[14]

In terms of total Asian trade, and even in terms of total Asian trade in spices, the carriage of spices up the Red Sea to Suez, Cairo, Alexandria, and Venice was of less than major importance. In the sixteenth century only a tiny part of Asia's total production of spices was used in Europe, the rest being used within Asia.[15] Nevertheless, to the merchants of Venice, and to the Mamluk rulers of Egypt, this trade to Europe was vital. The later medieval prosperity of Venice

[12]*Alguns Documentos do Archivo nacional da Torre de Tombo* (Lisbon, 1892), p. 205; Descrição, ff. 1-1v, 22; Castanheda, I, x; *Commentaries of Afonso Albuquerque* I, 44, 105.

[13]A. B. de Bragança Pereira, *op. cit.*, p. 134; Descrição, f. 55v.

[14]Pires, *op. cit.*, I, 78, 82; Bragança Pereira, *op. cit.*, p. 140; Descrição, ff. 36v-37; *The Itinerary of Ludovico di Varthema* (London, 1928), p. 61; Conti's account in R. H. Major, ed., *op. cit.*, p. 20; Nikitin's account in *ibid.*, p. 20.

[15]This is based on production figures, and figures for exports to Portugal, in Barros, IV, i, 12; F. Mendes da Luz, *O Conselho da India* (Lisbon, 1952), p. 514; C. R. Boxer, *The Portuguese Seaborne Empire* (London, 1969), p. 59; F. C. Lane, "The Mediterranean Spice Trade. Further Evidence of its revival in the sixteenth century," *American Historical Review* XLV (April 1940): 581-85.

was based on it, and so were the revenues of Mamluk Egypt. The latter collected taxes at Jiddah, Suez, and Alexandria, at each of which places the spices were transshipped, so that from the time when spices entered Jiddah to when they left Alexandria, they would pay taxes of at least 30 percent.[16]

Many other products and routes could be distinguished, but a mention of the last of the great Asian trade centers, Hurmuz, must suffice. From this entrepôt came goods from Persia, the Persian Gulf, Afghanistan, and the Oxus River valley, especially pearls, seed pearls, horses, and silks. To this port came merchandise from Aden, Gujarat, and Malacca. The most important item traded to India was undoubtedly horses, for although horses were bred in Kathiawar they were of poor quality, and the best horses were desired in all the Indian states of the fifteenth century both for show and for war. They came in to Vijayanagar at the rate of 3,000-4,000 a year via the Kanara ports of Honavar and Bhatkal, to the Deccan sultanates through Goa and Chaul, to Gujarat through her own ports and also overland, and overland via Qandahar to the sultanate of Delhi.[17]

It is sometimes assumed, with Gibbon, that the products of Asian trade in 1500 were "splendid and trifling." The role of overseas commerce in the economy of the very wealthy state of sultanate Gujarat will be considered later, but meanwhile I may note that this view is based at least partly on the belief that India in particular was virtually self-sufficient in all essential commodities. This was broadly true of the subcontinent in 1500, but India was only a geographical expression; coastal trade was thus as much "international" trade as was that from Jiddah to Cambay. And on the coastal routes basic foodstuffs were carried. Calicut imported nearly all her staple of rice,[18] as did the rest of Malabar, from the Kanara area. Goa, then as now, was a deficit rice area. In the seventeenth century, and presumably in the sixteenth, Gujarat imported grains from Malwa and Ajmer.[19] Malacca imported rice from Siam and Bengal. Further, cloths, horses, and even spices can be categorized as necessities. Basic raw materials were traded. Gujarat imported copper, and *madder*, a red dye.[20]

Later in this chapter the composition of the merchant class of

[16]Castanheda, II, lxxv.
[17]*Ibid.*, II, xvi, lviii; Barros, I, vii, 10; II, v, 2; Bragança Pereira, *op. cit.*, p. 127; Marechal Gomes da Costa, *op. cit.*, II, 149; Sikandar, pp. 144, 404.
[18]Castanheda, I, xii.
[19]Irfan Habib, *The Agrarian System of Mughal India* (Bombay, 1963), pp. 73-74.
[20]Descrição, f. 6v.

sultanate Gujarat will be investigated. At this point, however, it is necessary to consider who were the dominant overseas traders in Asia at this time. Chinese traders had, for internal political reasons, disappeared from the seas west of Malacca during the fifteenth century. For the rest of the area, it is clear that Muslims were dominant on most of the long-distance routes, but this does not mean that one can talk of a Muslim period, let alone of Moreland's "Arab" one.[21] Certainly Arabs were in control of the trade between Calicut and the Red Sea, and Calicut was dominated by them. They participated in the trade from the Red Sea to Malacca via Gujarat, but were dominant in it only as far as Aden. On the rest of this route they were outnumbered by other Muslims—Gujaratis, Persians, Turks, and others—and by Gujarati *vanias*.[22] Hurmuz had an enormous variety of merchants resident during the trading season, but again mostly Muslims. Trade in the western Indian ports of Goa, Dabhol, and Chaul was dominated by Muslims.[23] Non-Muslims, especially Gujaratis, also traded to Calicut, though not from there to the Red Sea,[24] and Malacca was far from being such a Muslim-dominated town as was Aden or Hurmuz. The bulk of the merchants on the great Aden-Gujarat-Malacca route were Muslims, but the feeder trades from Coromandel, Bengal, Indonesia, and China were handled largely by non-Muslims.[25] The less important trade to East Africa was controlled by Gujaratis, both Muslim and Hindu.[26]

The long-distance "international" trade of Asia around 1500 was thus largely handled by Muslims of various origins. On what was this dominance based? It is possible that caste prohibitions concerning travel by sea played some part in discouraging Hindus from trading, although in fact such a claim has not been found in any contemporary source, and Gujarat's *vanias* were certainly not affected by any such theoretical prohibition. A more likely explanation is that the Arabs,

[21] W. H. Moreland, "The Ships of the Arabian Sea," pp. 174-75.

[22] *The Itinerary of Ludovico di Varthema*, p. 61; Pires, I, 82; Stephano's account in R. H. Major, ed., *op. cit.*, p. 9; Bragança Pereira, *op. cit.*, p. 140. It seems that Arabs had been important in Cambay trade circles, but by the fifteenth century had been replaced by local Muslims and *vanias*. For their importance in the early fourteenth century, see S. C. Misra. *The Rise of Muslim Power in Gujarat* (London, 1963), pp. 63-64, 67, 96.

[23] Abd-er-Razzak's account in R. H. Major, ed., *op. cit.*, pp. 5-6; Nikitin's account in *ibid.*, p. 19; Castanheda, III, vii; *The Itinerary of Ludovico di Varthema*, p. 47.

[24] Bragança Pereira, *op. cit.*, p. 139; Descrição, f. 56.

[25] *Alguns Documentos do Archivo nacional da Torre de Tombo*, p. 224.

[26] Castanheda, I, x; Descrição, ff. 1-3v.

as they erupted south and east in the early years of the *hijrah,* tended to convert mostly people who lived on the coasts and so were most accessible. This was certainly the case in Gujarat and Indonesia,[27] and among such people would be a high proportion of the previously non-Muslim merchants. It is clear that Muslims from different areas combined with their countrymen to discourage competition; this was done by the Arabs on the Calicut-Red Sea route. Muslims from particular areas tended to live together under their own headmen in the great trade centers, but so did Gujarat's *vanias,* at least in Calicut.[28] Whatever the reason for this partial dominance, there is no evidence extant that it was gained or kept by force. There is no mention in the sources that merchants of any kind were prohibited from trading to a particular area, or in a particular product. Certainly outsiders could be, and no doubt were, discouraged from breaking into an area dominated by another group, but apparently the only sanctions used were commercial; this of course does not mean they were ineffective.

Nor is there any evidence that in fifteenth century South and Southeast Asia rulers of ports tried to compel merchants to call and pay duties; merchants called at the great entrepôts of their own free will. There are, however, three scattered instances where compulsion was used. As background for the sixteenth-century Portuguese trade control policies, it is necessary to consider whether there were precedents for their actions.

In the seventh and eighth centuries the southeast Sumatran state of Srivijaya controlled and taxed trade to China, apparently by force.[29] In 1344 Ibn Batuta found the ruler of the port of Fakaner in south Kanara compelling passing ships to put in and pay duties.[30] It is, however, more significant that Ibn Batuta visited virtually every other major port in south Asia, and does not mention any element of compulsion in any of them, except Fakaner.[31] No fifteenth-century account

---

[27]Castanheda, II, cxi; III, cxxx.
[28]W. H. Moreland, "The Ships of the Arabian Sea," p. 174; Descrição, f. 56.
[29]O. W. Wolters, *Early Indonesian Commerce: A Study of the Origins of Srivijaya* (Ithaca, 1967), pp. 238-39, 248-49.
[30]Ibn Batuta, *The Rehla of Ibn Batuta. (India, Maldive Islands and Ceylon),* trans. Mahdi Husain (Baroda, 1953), pp. 184-85.
[31]*Ibid.,* pp. 150-242. Leeds, however, uses the sole case of Fakaner to construct a general rule of compulsion in pre-sixteenth century Asian trade so that this area fits his preconceived definition of a "port of call." Anthony Leeds, "The Port-of-Call in Pre-European India as an Ecological and Evolutionary Type," in Viola E. Garfield, ed., *Proceedings of the 1961 Annual Spring Meeting of the American Ethnological Society* (Seattle, 1961), p. 29, and *passim.*

mentions forced trade. Malacca was typical in that its rise in the fifteenth century was due not to a policy of forcing merchants to call but to the strategic location of the port, its good harbor, fair treatment of visiting merchants, and possibly the conversion of its rulers to Islam.[32]

The third instance of compulsion, apart from the Portuguese, concerns the port of Div. A source of 1545 says that in the time of Sultan Bahadur (1526-37) "all the ships going to Cambay went first directly to Div and from there afterwards to where they wished."[33] An official writing in the 1590s also mentions this, but expands considerably to say that Div was established specifically to be such a trade center, and was maintained as such by the rulers of Gujarat.[34] The earlier source is more likely to be accurate, as it was written only eight years after Bahadur's death. Div rose to be a great trade center for Gujarat because of its location, because of the dangers of the Gulf of Cambay for large ships, and because of the able administration of Malik Ayaz. An attempt to *compel* all ships to call there was presumably made by Bahadur only after he won close control of the port in 1528. Another Portuguese source implies that Bahadur's warships were used to protect Gujarati traders from the Portuguese rather than to force their ships to call at Div,[35] and this indeed seems the most likely reason why "all the ships going to Cambay went first directly to Div . . ." If, however, this was really forced trade, the idea was presumably copied from the Portuguese, and was a response to their claims. In any case, none of these three instances where forced trade may have existed invalidates what I have said about the situation when the Portuguese arrived in India.

This being the case, where did Asian trade fit on a general progression? European expansion in Asia went through four stages: itinerant trade on a basis of equality with other merchants in a foreign town; the establishment of a factory, which was often fortified; the seizure or acquisition of a port, and erection of a fort in it; the conquest of extensive land areas. In the fifteenth century Asian trade was in the first

---

[32]M. A. P. Meilink Roelofsz, *Asian Trade and European Influence* (The Hague, 1962), pp. 33-35, and pp. 36-59 for the organization of trade in fifteenth-century Malacca, where there is no mention of any compulsion.

[33]Gavetas, I, 776.

[34]Francisco Paes, "O Tombo de Diu, 1592" *O Oriente Português*, n. s. no. 4 (October 1932): 41.

[35]Francisco de Andrade, *Chrónica do muyto alto e muyto poderoso Rey destes Reinos de Portugal, Dom João o III deste Nome*, 4 vols. (Coimbra, 1796), II, 193-94.

of these stages. It was not organized or controlled on the basis of the state to which a merchant belonged, so there was no Arab or Gujarati factory in Calicut or Malacca. The Europeans, organized on state or quasi-state lines, moved straight to stage two, and often soon after to stage three. Stage four was not reached, except in Ceylon, the Philippines, and Java, until the late eighteenth century, when the British began their conquests in India.

What exactly was the position of a foreign merchant in the great trade centers of Malacca, Calicut, Cambay, Hurmuz, and Aden? With the exception of Cambay, the immediate hinterlands of these bustling cosmopolitan cities produced little; the list is virtually complete with pepper and ginger from Calicut and pearls from Hurmuz. All five, even Cambay, were economically dependent on foreign trade, so that the interests of the foreign merchants were safeguarded by the rulers.[36] The influence of the foreign merchants, however, was much less in Cambay than in the other four, for Cambay was part of a large and powerful sultanate. Aden, Hurmuz, Calicut, and Malacca were in practice small independent states, despite their nominal subordination to more powerful inland states.

In each of these five towns the resident foreign merchants tended to live in defined areas with their fellows, and to enjoy a large measure of autonomy. In Calicut, one hears of the heads of the Turkish merchants, of those from Cairo and the Red Sea, and of the local Muslim merchants.[37] There was also a head of all the foreign merchants in Calicut, who "governs and punishes them without the Zamorin having anything to do with this, except what the governor tells him."[38] The situation in Malacca was similar.[39] These heads or governors acted as intermediaries between the local ruler and the merchants they represented. The rulers had little contact with the merchants who made them rich. They provided the essential elements required by the merchants—among them freedom from arbitrary injustice, reasonable taxes, and religious tolerance—and otherwise left them alone. This semi-autonomous status for foreign merchants no doubt had to be conceded, for they could have left if a ruler had tried to impose

---

[36] As, for example, Bragança Pereira, *op. cit.*, p. 140.
[37] Castanheda, I, xxxvi; Júlio Gonçalves, *Os Portugueses e o Mar das Indias* (Lisbon, 1947), p. 415.
[38] Descrição, f. 36v; see also Ibn Batuta, *op. cit.*, pp. 189, 193.
[39] Correa, II, 253; *The Commentaries of Afonso Albuquerque*, III, 87-88; Pires, *op. cit.*, II, 264-65; Barros, II, vi, 3.

more direct irksome rule, but in any case such a status was conceded in most South and Southeast Asian ports at this time. It was enjoyed by the Dutch, English, and French in seventeenth-century Mughal India, and was later the basis of their claim to extra-territorial rights in many ports of Southeast and East Asia.

This brief survey is a summary of the major elements of the seaborne trade of Asia around 1500. This trade was carried on under conditions of considerable freedom, for those participating in it owed nothing to land governments except customs duties. Nor was there any forcible attempt to control trade on the part of those who lived by it, or by inland governments. Such sanctions as the merchants used were purely commercial. The ships were adequate for sailing before the monsoons, and as large as those used in Europe at the time. The European traders during their first 150 years in Asian waters did not open up trade in any important new product, or develop any new route, except that via the Cape of Good Hope to Europe, which was, after all, only an alternative to the existing Red Sea route.

Asian traders were open to new ideas. This is shown by the rise of Malacca, and later Div, in the fifteenth century. Indeed, perhaps the dominating characteristic, especially in regard to Gujarati traders, was flexibility and readiness to adapt. Thus, as Malacca developed in the fifteenth century, the Gujaratis almost ceased to trade past there to Indonesia, preferring to let Chinese and Indonesian goods be brought to them in Malacca.[40] The payment of customs duties in Malacca exhibits a similar flexibility. These were usually about 6 percent, plus presents, and were assessed by the captain, or *shahbandar*, of the group to which the merchant in question belonged. If he needed more money for political purposes at court, he would, with the consent of the merchant concerned, collect duties at a higher rate. If the *shahbandar's* group stood high at the time, he would take less in duties.[41] This willingness to compromise, to pay more if this was necessary to secure their trade, was to stand Gujarat's merchants in good stead in the sixteenth century.

The Economy of Gujarat

Having sketched the role of Gujarat's merchants in Asian-wide trade around 1500, it is now necessary to focus more closely on sultanate

---

[40]Pires, I, 45-46.

[41]Pires, II, 273. For *shahbandars*, see W. H. Moreland, "The Shahbandar in the Eastern Seas," *Journal of the Royal Asiatic Society* (October 1920).

Gujarat. What area was ruled by the sultan of Gujarat? This question is impossible to answer with any finality, as the area expanded under aggressive sultans, notably under Mahmud I (1458-1511) and Bahadur (1526-37), and contracted under others. Further, frontiers were not usually demarcated in sixteenth-century India; particularly on the edges there was considerable flexibility. Gujarat's westernmost boundary was somewhere on the Gulf of Kutch, or perhaps a little east of this.[42] Beyond was the kingdom of Sind. In the south the border with the sultanate of Ahmadnagar was usually Bombay.[43]

Gujarat's inland boundaries were also flexible, and thus not easy to define. The Portuguese chroniclers sometimes speak of Cambay and Gujarat interchangeably, but in fact the more careful of them were aware that Cambay was the heartland around the Gulf of Cambay, while Gujarat referred to the whole area subordinate to the sultans.[44] This heartland was essentially the ten *sarkars* which, after the Mughal conquest of 1572, in theory paid revenue; the other six *sarkars* continued to be governed by *zamindars*, usually Rajputs, and sometimes paid tribute.[45] Cambay's limits were approximately the fifty-meter contour line, except in the west where the Little Rann of Kutch must be excluded, and in the south where the limit of Cambay was the Tapti River. Areas outside this were excluded: the less fertile area south of the Tapti,[46] Kathiawar and Kutch, and the area north and east of the low-lying lands around the Gulf of Cambay, where Gujarat shaded off into Malwa and Rajputana.

For my purposes, Gujarat in fact usually means Cambay, for

---

[42]Castanheda, III, cxxx; VIII, cvii, has Mangrol in 1514, and "Variune," presumably Vavania, for 1535. Eredia has Cutch (DUP, III, 136), Couto has Dwarka (VIII, iii, 13).

[43]ANTTSL, VI, 31; Eredia, *loc. cit.*; but Castanheda has Gujarat in 1514 extending nearly to Chaul (III, cxxx). *The Cambridge History of India* (Cambridge, 1928), III, 310, basing itself on Arabic History, I, 28-29, attempts to define Gujarat's boundaries when they were widest after Mahmud I had conquered Champanir in 1484. The attempt is both confused and confusing, but clearly Gujarat at this time, and before and after this, included considerable areas which today are not part of Gujarat State in the Indian Union, but are included in Maharashtra, Madhya Pradesh, or Rajasthan.

[44]See a reference in 1619 to the viceroy "of Cambay and the other lands of Gujarat" (Assentos, I, 24), and Couto's mention of Humayon in 1535 conquering "all the kingdoms of Cambay" (IV, x, 3). In 1572 Couto spoke of Bassein and Daman as being part of the "Gujarati kingdom" — not the sultanate of Cambay, for these ports were outside the heartland (IX, cap. 13).

[45]Mirat, supplement, pp. 189-90.

[46]One may note that a Persian chronicle refers to Daman as a *"muzafat,"* an appendage, of the sultanate (Sikandar, p. 426). See also chapter III, f.n. 85.

economically these areas on the outskirts were of less importance. Kathiawar and Kutch produced horses, and timber and provisions came from the minor southern ports of Bassein and Daman.[47] Sawrath had been a wealthy area before it was conquered by Mahmud I; apparently its prosperity then declined due to unsettled political conditions,[48] although its ports of Porbandar, Mangrol, and Somnath continued to export some cotton cloths.

Within the heartland, the area known as Cambay, the greatest product was cotton cloths in an enormous variety of styles, qualities, colors, and patterns. For quality and durability it was considered to be the best in Asia. The great manufacturing centers were Ahmadabad, Pattan, Baroda, Broach, and Surat.[49] Silk weaving, using raw silk from Bengal, was a second great textile concern, especially in Ahmadabad, Surat, and Cambay.[50] Next to textiles ranked indigo, "the blue stone color," which was produced in Sarkhej, near Ahmadabad, but apparently refined at Cambay.[51] The sultanate also produced a great variety of drugs and medicinal products, especially opium, but also spikenard, carnelians, arrowroot, lac, borax, and Indian wormwood.[52] Other products were legion; there was a strong handicraft industry making weapons, furniture, and jewelry.[53]

[47]F. Mendes da Luz, ed., "Livro das Cidades e Fortalezas que a Coroa de Portugal tem nas Partes da India, 1582," *Studia* 6 (1960): 23, 26; Correa, III, 450.

[48]Sikandar, pp. 115-16.

[49]Barreto de Rezende, I, 64; W. H. Moreland, *India at the Death of Akbar,* pp. 167-71. For an excellent study of Gujarati textiles in the seventeenth century, especially strong on technical matters, see John Irwin in John Irwin and P. R. Schwartz, *Studies in Indo-European Textile History* (Ahmadabad, 1966), pp. 8-27. Coromandel and Bengal textiles are described in *ibid.,* pp. 28-56, while pp. 57-72 contain a very valuable and detailed glossary. For an account of textile manufacturing processes in northern India, see H. K. Naqvi, *Urban Centres and Industries in Upper India, 1556-1803* (London, n.d.), pp. 148-75, and for descriptions of fifty types of cotton cloths, *ibid.,* pp. 176-88.

[50]Duarte Barbosa, *The Book of Duarte Barbosa,* 2 vols. (London, 1918-21), I, 154; W. H. Moreland, *India at the Death of Akbar,* pp. 160-63; M. S. Commissariat, *History of Gujarat,* 2 vols. (Bombay, 1938-57), II, 296-97.

[51]Nikitin's account in R. H. Major, ed., *India in the Fifteenth Century,* p. 19; Duarte Barbosa, I, 154; A. Botelho da Costa Veiga, ed., *Relação das plantas e descrições de todas as fortalezas* (Lisbon, 1936), p. 21; Abu'l Fazl Allami, *The Ain-i Akbari,* 3 vols. (Calcutta, 1939-40), II, 248. See Eredia, in DUP, III, 138, for a description of the indigo plant, and also Jean Baptiste Tavernier, *Travels in India,* 2 vols. (London, 1925), II, 7-9. For Bayana indigo, see W. H. Moreland and P. Geyl, eds., *Jahangir's India* (Delhi, 1972), pp. 10-18.

[52]Duarte Barbosa, *op. cit.,* I, 154; Eredia, DUP, III, 138; *The Itinerary of Ludovico di Varthema,* pp. 44-45; Costa Veiga, *op. cit.,* p. 21.

[53]Barros, IV, v, 1.

THE SETTING   21

There is no record concerning methods of production in sultanate Gujarat. From early seventeenth-century Dutch and English records, however, one may get a picture of the methods used at this time, and there is little reason to suspect that they had changed radically around 1600. It can be assumed that production was done by artisans working at home with their families. They were advanced money by capitalists (usually working through a broker) so that they could buy their raw materials and support themselves while they worked. This indigenous putting-out system was later adopted by the Dutch and English in Gujarat. Although the form of the finished product was not as closely supervised by the capitalists as would have been the case had wage labor been used, some control over form was attained.[54]

The capitalists were called "shroffs" by the English, a corruption of the Arabic word *sarraf,* a banker. These people were apparently few in number, but played a pivotal role in the economy both under the sultans and later. They issued *hundis,* which could be used either as letters of credit to distant places or as short-term capital. They lent money on longer terms to officials and others. They financed the production on which Gujarat's prosperity was based, and its petty traders.[55] They changed money; and this raises the question of the degree of monetization of the economy of sultanate Gujarat.

It seems clear that rural Gujarat was not monetized until the seventeenth century, if then. Those areas which depended solely on producing cash crops presumably still paid their revenue in kind. In the great ports of Gujarat, however, money was widely used, along with barter methods, the sixteenth-century Portuguese accounts being full of lists of the rates of conversions of Gujarati and other coins into

[54]M. S. Commissariat, *op. cit.,* II, 302; W. H. Moreland, *India at the Death of Akbar,* pp. 175-76; W. H. Moreland, *From Akbar to Aurangzeb* (London, 1923), p. 192; Irfan Habib, "Usury in Medieval India," *Comparative Studies in Society and History* VI (July 1964): 395; Tapan Raychaudhuri, in B. N. Ganguli, ed., *Readings in Indian Economic History* (Bombay, 1964), pp. 71-73. We use the term capitalist in the strict sense of the term: a person controlling capital. Obviously, their economic role was quite different from that of a capitalist in a "free enterprise" economy.

[55]W. H. Moreland, *India at the Death of Akbar,* pp. 231-32; Irfan Habib, "Usury in Medieval India," pp. 400, 406; Irfan Habib, "Banking in Mughal India," *Contributions to Indian Economic History* I (New Delhi, 1964), pp. 2-3; Irfan Habib, "The System of Bills of Exchange *(Hundis)* in the Mughal Empire," *Proceedings of the 33rd Indian History Congress* (Muzaffarpur, 1972), pp. 290-303; D. R. Gadgil, *Origins of the Modern Indian Business Class* (New York, 1959), pp. 32-33; for the role of wealthy bankers in sultanate Gujarat and the availability of credit, see Sikandar, p. 404. For *shroffs* and *hundis* there is some interesting information in the Walker of

those of Goa.[56] It is possible that Gujarat was more monetized than Malacca at this time, for Barros claims that the merchants trading from there to India wanted nothing to do with gold; they made only 25 percent profit when they took gold to India, while on goods they made much more.[57] From the Red Sea Gujarat's main import was bullion and coin, which must also point to considerable monetization.[58]

"The pivot of the Delhi Sultanate is wheat and barley, and the pivot of the Sultanate of Gujarat is coral and pearl, because it has eighty-four ports under its control."[59] Thus reads an aphorism of Sultan Sikandar of Delhi in the early sixteenth century. Was overseas trade really a vital part of the total economy of Gujarat, or was it merely icing on the cake, froth on the beer? One can only present the evidence and some tentative conclusions. It should first be said that no impression can be formed of the extent of Gujarat's "international" inland trade in the sixteenth century. It was probably not large, for a glance at a relief map of western India makes clear the rugged nature of the areas surrounding Gujarat. None of Gujarat's rivers were navigable very far.[60] Further, even in the seventeenth century, when Gujarat was part of and surrounded by the Mughal Empire, land trade was liable to extortion by local *zamindars,* and to robbery by disaffected Kolis and Rajputs. Yet it seems clear that this seventeenth-century insecurity was less than it had been when Gujarat was independent, divided internally, surrounded by frequently hostile neighbors, and infested by unsubdued bandits. This is not to say

---

Bowland Papers in the National Library of Scotland, 184 c 7, pp. 235-36; 183 c 2, pp. 87-90; 184 c 11, pp. 29-31. Sylvia L. Thrupp says that the London merchants had a class status in that they had a distinctive economic position, referring to the conduct of wholesale trade, and a distinctive political position, that of controlling municipal government: S. L. Thrupp, *The Merchant Class of Medieval London, 1300-1500* (Chicago, 1948), p. xv. Gujarat's merchants, despite their ethnic and religious differences, seem to have had at least common occupational identification. They did not do manual work, but lived by employing their capital in trade and loans of various kinds. Their wealth did not make them distinctive, for some officials also were wealthy, but the fact that they employed their wealth in the way they did was distinctive. Officials also traded and loaned money, but they used most of their available capital for display and military and political purposes. Merchants did not.

[56]For example, R. J. de Lima Felner, ed., *Subsídios para a história da India Portugueza* (Lisbon, 1868), pp. 40-56, 61 *et seq*; APOCR, V, 324-25; "Provisões, Alvarás e Regimentos," HAG, II, 94-97.

[57]Barros, I, viii, 1.

[58]Duarte Barbosa, *op. cit.*, I, 154; Pires, I, 43.

[59]Sikandar, pp. 309-10.

[60]For an interesting, although not exhaustive, bibliographical study of roads and routes in Mughal India, see Jean Deloche, *Recherches sur les routes de l'Inde au temps des Mogols* (*Étude critique des sources*) (Paris, 1968).

that sea trade was secure, but it probably was more so than that by land.

It is possible to estimate the value of Gujarat's sea trade (that is, the value of goods passing through Gujarat's ports) from the available figures for customs receipts, and then compare them with other revenue figures and so get some idea of the role of overseas trade in the total economy. This attempt is worth making, even though margins of error are rather large.[61]

In 1571 the customs revenue of twenty-two ports in Gujarat, excluding Cambay, was Rs. 34,00,000, Rs. 20,00,000 of this coming from Broach, Surat, Gogha, Gandhar, and Rander, and the rest from seventeen ports in Saurashtra.[62] In 1572 the revenue of Cambay port was estimated as Rs. 6,00,000.[63] This gives a total customs payment of Rs. 40,00,000 in sultanate Gujarat, and a total value of sea trade, assuming duties of 5 percent, of Rs. 8,00,00,000. This figure is supported by one for Surat in 1644. The usual revenue of the port of Surat at this time was Rs. 2,50,000,[64] and with the Mughal duties of 2½ percent, this makes a total trade value of Rs. 1,00,00,000. As Surat by 1644 was the greatest port in Gujarat (and India), a value of trade in Surat equal to about one-tenth the value of all Gujarati sea trade seems about right.[65] (This assumes a rise in the value of all Gujarati sea trade in these seventy years.)

If these figures are correct, it is clear that sea trade played a very large role in the Gujarati economy, for the *jama,* or standard assessment, of Gujarat's land revenue in 1595-99, in the *Ain-i Akbari,* was just under Rs. 1,10,00,000.[66] With a rate of one-third under Akbar, the value of agricultural production in the part of Gujarat which paid

---

[61]Thus there is no way of knowing how uniformly duties were collected. Nor can one estimate how often a bribe enabled a merchant to avoid all or some duties. Most important of all, there is no way of estimating what proportion of goods passing through Gujarati ports came from, or were bound for, places outside Gujarat. There certainly was a sizable trade between Gujarat and Delhi, Agra, Malwa, and Rajasthan. Many of the exports from the Delhi-Agra area went through Gujarat, but probably more went via Bengal. My impression is that this overland trade was comparatively small, because of difficult terrain and unsettled conditions in the intervening areas.

[62]Mirat, p. 14.

[63]Couto, IX, cap. 13. In 1591 it was estimated at "much more" than Rs. 3,00,000, which points to a possible decline. (AHU, Codice 281, f. 139, also in APOCR, III, 293-95.)

[64]Mirat, p. 193.

[65]I note again that the average capital on English East India Company ships from 1601 to 1640 was only Rs. 2,00,000. (See f.n. 7 of the Introduction.)

[66]Irfan Habib, *The Agrarian System of Mughal India,* p. 406.

revenue at this time was Rs. 3,30,00,000. It should be noted that three-eighths of Gujarat paid tribute, so that the value of agricultural production in these usually infertile areas is not included in this Rs. 3,30,00,000. The total revenue of Gujarat in 1571 was claimed to be Rs. 5,75,50,000, but this includes revenue from land, taxes on sea and land trade, tribute from the non-revenue paying *sarkars*, and miscellaneous taxes.[67] It should also be noted that overseas trade in Gujarat was based on Gujarat's own products, unlike that centered on Goa, Malacca, Hurmuz, or Aden. In terms of the role of trade in the total economy this is important, as in Gujarat sea trade thus generated and stimulated production within the economy, which was not the case in the other places mentioned. Even given the scattered and unreliable nature of these statistics, one can say that sea trade was a very important element in the total economy of sultanate Gujarat. But sea trade was *not* directly important in the revenues of the rulers of Gujarat. The figures just quoted show that customs duties provided only 6 percent of the total revenue of Gujarat. This figure, as will be seen, has enormous implications. It is, however, impossible even to guess how much revenue sea trade produced. A figure here would include land revenue paid on crops destined to be exported, and inland duties paid on these goods, as well as customs duties.

It would be valuable to be able to compare these figures with those for the whole Mughal Empire, but unfortunately the much-used *Ain-i Akbari* is of little use here. Abu'l Fazl gives a figure of about Rs. 80,000 for the total port dues of Gujarat. He is clearly in error. The figures just quoted come from Portuguese and Persian sources. They confirm each other, and in all cases were written by men better informed on Gujarat than was Abu'l Fazl. Further, some Gujarati ships around 1600 carried cargoes worth Rs. 10,00,000 and more. At a Mughal rate of 2½ percent these ships would pay duties of Rs. 25,000—nearly one-third of Abu'l Fazl's total from one ship. But indirectly the *Ain* seems to show that Sultan Sikandar's aphorism was correct; sea trade was uniquely important in Gujarat. Abu'l Fazl gives no figures for the customs revenue of any province of Akbar's empire, except for the incorrect one for Gujarat. Clearly he did not consider it to be of much importance.[68]

[67] Mirat, pp. 12-13. Some of these minor taxes are listed in Mirat, supplement, pp. 154-57.

[68] Abu'l Fazl, *'Ain-i Akbari*, II, 257, and *passim*. For values of individual Gujarati ships, see p. 101.

THE SETTING   25

To complete the groundwork for later discussion, it is necessary to delineate more precisely who were the merchants of Gujarat in the sixteenth century, in terms of their ethnic and religious divisions. It has already been noted that merchants trading by sea from Gujarat were both Muslim and Hindu. There is evidence of a large and rich *vania* community resident in its own area of Calicut,[69] and Muslims from Gujarat also traded to there.[70] Gujaratis, both Hindu and Muslim, traded to Malacca and all the East African ports.[71] On the western Indian coast there were again many Gujarati Muslim merchants, but Albuquerque noted "the banyans of Cambay, who are the main Hindu merchants of these parts."[72] It is clear, however, that the crews of the ships, even those owned by Hindus, were Muslim.[73]

The great merchants at the ports of Gujarat were either Hindus, Jains, or Muslims originating from outside Gujarat but now resident there. The local Muslim converts were apparently of less importance, with the partial exception of the *bohrahs* and the *khojahs*. Most of these "foreign" Muslims were resident in Gujarat, with their own houses there,[74] and so were in fact subjects of Gujarat, whatever their country of birth, which could be Turkey, Egypt, Arabia, or Persia.[75] Some, however, were only itinerant, being domiciled in such places as Alexandria, Damascus, Persia, Syria, and Afghanistan.[76]

The heterogeneity of the Muslim population of Gujarat was not confined to merchants, for the sultans made a practice of tempting capable foreigners to Gujarat with handsome salaries, to serve in their armies.[77]

Among these great merchants living mostly by sea trade, it seems that Hindus and Jains outranked Muslims. The most capable early

[69] Descrição, ff. 55v-56; Bragança Pereira, *op. cit.*, p. 139.
[70] Ibn Batuta, *op. cit.*, p. 193.
[71] Castanheda, I, x; Descrição, ff. 1-3v.
[72] *Cartas de Affonso de Albuquerque*, I, 306-7; *The Itinerary of Ludovico di Varthema*, pp. 48-54.
[73] *Cartas de Affonso de Albuquerque*, I, 307. There is a list of the names of the masters of seventy-seven ships licensed by the Portuguese between 1618 and 1622. All of them, with two possible exceptions, appear to be Muslims. ("Consultas do Serviço de partes," HAG, III, 44-136v.)
[74] Ibn Batuta, *op. cit.*, p. 172; Varthema, *op. cit.*, p. 38.
[75] Duarte Barbosa, I, 119-20.
[76] Sikandar, pp. 144, 404; Correa, II, 636; Stephano's account in R. H. Major, ed., *op. cit.*, p. 9.
[77] As, for example, Malik Ayaz, Rumi Khan, and Khwaja Safar, for whom see chapter III.

sixteenth-century observer, Tome Pires, said of the non-Muslims that "There is no doubt that these people have the cream of the trade."[78] In the ports of Cambay and Surat were both Hindu and Muslim merchants,[79] but in Rander all the great merchants were Muslims, while the population of Div was most notable for the large number of Turkish merchants resident there.[80]

In the economy of Gujarat as a whole there is no doubt that the dominant group in all trade matters was the *vanias,* if only because of their numerical predominance. The Portuguese, and later Dutch and English sources, speak of "banyans," and variants such as "bunyan," "benjan," and "baneane," without any discrimination. In fact the *vanias* were a rather diverse group. They were by *varna vaisya,* and so traditionally were allowed to lend money. They were, and are, preeminently traders and merchants.[81] There were traditionally forty-one divisions among the group in Gujarat, but these divisions were usually not based on occupational characteristics as was the case with other *vaisyas.*[82] Many of these forty-one divisions in turn had Jain sections, some of the forty-one in fact being dominated by Jains. The Hindu sections were called *meshri;* during the period under discussion most of them became converted to the Vallabhacarya sect of *vaishnavism.* The Jain sections were called *shravak.*[83] Inter-dining between Hindu and Jain sections was common, but marriage was severely restricted even within the forty-one divisions.

It is clear that in the sixteenth century both Hindus and Jains of the *vania* group were important merchants. Early in the following century B. G. Gokhale finds Hindus dominant,[84] but there are records of rich Jains in Gujarat from the twelfth century at least.[85] The two greatest merchant princes of the first half of the seventeenth century—

[78]Pires, *op. cit.,* I, 41.
[79]Castanheda, III, cxxx; Descrição, ff. 15, 22v; Manuel de Faria e Sousa, *Asia Portuguesa,* 6 vols. (Lisbon, 1945-47), II, 193.
[80]Descrição, f. 22; Varthema, *op. cit.,* pp. 37-38.
[81]See Barbosa, *op. cit.,* I, 110-14; *The Voyage of John Huyghen van Linschoten to the East Indies,* 2 vols. (London, 1885), I, 252-56.
[82]I. Habib, "Usury in Medieval India," pp. 411-12; D. R. Gadgil, *op. cit.,* pp. 21-22; *Census of India,* 1911, vol. VII, part 1, p. 307.
[83]*Census of India, loc. cit.;* A. K. Forbes, *Ras Mala,* 2 vols. (London, 1924), II, 237.
[84]B. G. Gokhale, "Capital Accumulation in XVIIth Century Western India," *Journal of the Asiatic Society of Bombay* 39-40 (1966): 53-54.
[85]C. B. Sheth, *Jainism in Gujarat, A. D. 1100-1600* (Bombay, 1953), pp. 103, 154, 178; Sri Vidyavijay ji Muniraj, *Surishwar Aur Samrat. Akbar* (Agra, Vira Samvat 2405), p. 15.

THE SETTING 27

Virji Vorah and Shantidas Jawahari—were both Jains, and there were numerous Jain "millionaires" in the sixteenth century.[86] Jesuit sources of 1611 which speak of "another sort of baneane" are clearly referring to Jains. They are here said to be merchants and brokers and also handicraftsmen.[87]

Among local converts to Islam in Gujarat, the two most important commercially were the *khojahs* and the *bohrahs*. The former were an Ismaili shia sect, and today recognize the Agha Khan as their head. The latter split into two groups in the early sixteenth century, the larger part being sunni Muslims, most of whom were peasants, and the smaller Ismaili shias engaged in trade. In later centuries the shia part was split again several times by doctrinal and inheritance disputes. Their *dai*, or *imam*, moved to Gujarat in the 1560s, residing first in Ahmadabad and later in Surat. Both *khojahs* and *bohrahs* retained many Hindu characteristics in such matters as inheritance and even in religious matters; thus the most revered book of the *khojahs* dealt with the nine incarnations of Vishnu (who had been adopted by them as Adam) and with his tenth as Ali!

This less than complete conversion to Islam helped the commercial activities of these two sects. Under Muslim law the property of a deceased was greatly divided, with nine specific relatives, apart from the agnatic heirs, entitled to fixed shares.[88] It is clear that among Hindus the letter of the *sastras*, which also enjoined considerable division, was usually not observed in practice.[89] Linschoten claimed that "The Sonnes inherite all a father's goods,"[90] while among the *vanias* a woman's property all went not to her relatives but to her husband if she predeceased him. In the reverse case, wives of *vanias* could inherit a share of their husbands' property.[91] Thus by retaining Hindu succession practices, the *khojahs* and *bohrahs* avoided too great a division of property on death.

It seems clear that these two sects were also not hindered by the Islamic prohibition of usury. More orthodox Muslims usually did

[86] Muniraj, *op. cit.*, pp. 7, 27, 47.
[87] DUP, III, 137-38.
[88] N. J. Coulson, *A History of Islamic Law* (Edinburgh, 1964), pp. 16-17.
[89] J. D. M. Derrett, *Religion, Law and the State in India* (London, 1968), pp. 160, 190, 208.
[90] J. H. van Linschoten, *op. cit.*, p. 231.
[91] "Alvarás e Provisões de Sua Magestade," HAG, II, 16v, and generally ff. 16-20v, printed in APOCR, VI, 1267-73. See also AHU, Caixa 16, opinion of March 14, 1644, and Caixa 19, opinion of February 13, 1647.

observe this prohibition, but this gave the *khojahs* and *bohrahs* only a slight advantage, because stricter Muslims still had many ways in which they could make licit profits, as in the various types of partnerships and *commenda* arrangements used by many Muslims.⁹²

Such non-Islamic practices led to considerable persecution, especially during the sultanate period. The *Mirat-i-Sikandari* retails a gratuitous anecdote against the *bohrahs*, while a Turkish sunni visitor in 1538 said of the local Muslims that "when they have to give thanks to God at the hours of prayer they do nothing but beat gongs. Most of them are infidels and half-breeds."⁹³ In the seventeenth century, as now, the *bohrahs* were apparently more visible and wealthy than the *khojahs*.⁹⁴

It has already been noted how adaptable these Gujarati overseas traders were in their trade practices, especially in Malacca in the late fifteenth century. It is clear that this flexibility and receptivity to new ideas continued in the sixteenth century, and was manifested particularly in religious matters. It was mostly in the sixteenth century that the *vaisyas* were converted to the Vallabhacarya sect of *vaishnavism*. *Brahmans* and the few *kshatriyas* remained *saivite*. Among the Jains there were several important reform movements in this century, most notably that led by Hira Vijaya Suri. Early in the century the *bohrah* community split, with many becoming sunni Muslims, while the remaining shias split again into two rival sects in the 1590s. The head of the shia part arrived in Gujarat from the Yemen in the 1560s.⁹⁵ The

---

⁹²A. L. Udovitch in D. S. Richards, *Islam and the Trade of Asia*, pp. 42-50, 61-62.
⁹³Sikandar, p. 216; ANTTCC, 3-14-44.
⁹⁴M. S. Commissariat, *History of Gujarat*, II, 96; Factories, 1646-50, p. 157; Mirat, supplement, pp. 108-9; for these two groups in general, see S. T. Lokhandwalla, "Islamic Law and Ismaili Communities," *Indian Economic and Social History Review* IV (June 1967), and S. C. Misra, *Muslim Communities in Gujarat* (Bombay, 1964). Also see Ibn Batuta, *op. cit.*, appendix N by Mahdi Husain; R. E. Enthoven, *The Tribes and Castes of Bombay*, 3 vols. (Bombay, 1920-22), s. v.; Khan Bahadur Fazalullah Lutfullah, *Gujarat Musalmans* (n. p. , n. d.), pp. 24-57. Until the late seventeenth century the Parsis were not a wealthy community. See S. H. Hodivala, *Studies in Parsi History* (Bombay, 1920), p. 189, and P. S. S. Pissurlencar, *Portuguese Records on Rustamji Manockji*, 2 vols. (Nova Goa, 1933-36). John Fryer in 1675 found them to be "rather Husbandmen than Merchants." (John Fryer, *A New Account of East India and Persia*, 3 vols. [London, 1909-15], I, 295.) But earlier in the seventeenth century there were some Parsi traders in Div (LM, v. 28B, ff. 449-49v), and one described as a "principal merchant" in Broach in 1650 (Factories, 1646-50, p. 325).
⁹⁵*Census of India*, *loc cit.*; Muniraj, *op. cit.*, pp. 27, 47; S. T. Lokhandwalla, *op. cit.*, p. 171; S. C. Misra, *Muslim Communities in Gujarat*, pp. 19-30.

sixteenth century was a time of flux and change in Gujarati religious life. The population, including the merchants, was dynamic and open to new ideas, and this undoubtedly helped them to adjust to the contemporaneous demands of the Portuguese.

CHAPTER II

THE PORTUGUESE

The slow Portuguese progress down the west African coast in the fifteenth century, the rounding of the Cape of Good Hope by Dias, and da Gama's triumphant arrival near Calicut in 1498, were inspired by many motives, as with any great human enterprise; and during these decades of effort different motives predominated at different times. The desire of D. Manuel (1495-1521) and his predecessors to open a direct sea route to India was primarily economic, and secondarily religious, in origin. The latter provided a sacral coating for the former, more important, motivation. The two were, however, closely intertwined. Portugal was in some respects still a crusading nation, thrusting across into north Africa from 1415 in continuation of the effort which had freed her from the Muslims. D. Manuel expected that once Portugal found the way to the Arabian Sea the mythical, but hopefully Christian, Prester John would be discovered and made into an ally for a strike at the Muslim rear. Possibly other Christians would be found around the Cape, and if they were not found they should certainly be created. A strike at the Muslim rear would be a good and holy effort in itself, but more important it could very well combine profit with the laying up of eternal merit, for it was known that the spice trade to Europe was in Muslim hands up to Alexandria. D. Manuel himself put it neatly soon after da Gama's return, when he said: "for our ancestors the main basis of this enterprise was always the service of God our Lord and our own profit."[1]

By 1515 the Portuguese had established formal naval dominance in Indian seas, and seized several strategic ports. There were several stages in this considerable military achievement. In 1503 their first fort was built, at Cochin. (They thus wasted no time in moving to the third of the four stages describing European expansion in Asia.) In east Africa Sofala became a tributary of Portugal in 1505, and Mozam-

---

[1]ANTTSV, III, 513. Cipolla's verdict is that "religion provided the pretext and gold the motive." (Carlo M. Cipolla, *Guns and Sails in the early phase of European Expansion, 1400-1700* [London, 1965], p. 136.)

bique two years later. Soon after, Albuquerque foreshadowed his later aggressive policy by raids along the south Arabian coast as far as Hurmuz, which was also made tributary to Portugal. Muslim ships were freely attacked and sunk, in accordance with the king's orders to the second Portuguese expedition, in 1500, and thereafter.[2] A minor naval defeat at the hands of a Gujarati-Egyptian fleet off Chaul in 1508 was in fact more notable for the dramatic death of the viceroy's son than for any lasting significance. It was avenged in 1509 by the viceroy himself, D. Francisco d'Almeida, who defeated a combined Gujarati-Egyptian-Calicut fleet off Div. This was Portugal's greatest naval action in Asia in the sixteenth century; never again was there a formal naval engagement between a Portuguese and an Indian fleet. There were innumerable sieges on land and guerilla attacks at sea, but no Portuguese fleet was subsequently challenged by a hostile fleet in the Indian Ocean until the arrival of the Dutch and English.

The most important land conquests were made during Albuquerque's governorship, from 1509 to 1515. Goa was taken in 1510 from the sultan of Bijapur, and Malacca the next year from its sultan. A fort was built at Hurmuz in 1515 shortly before Albuquerque's death. Unsuccessful attempts were made to capture Aden and Div. Portuguese fleets roamed far and wide, attacking Muslim and other ships on sight. A flag-showing cruise was made in the Red Sea, and Albuquerque dreamed, not completely unseriously, of disposing of his Muslim enemies by diverting the Nile to the Red Sea, or alternatively by raiding Mecca and holding the Prophet's body to ransom. These were indeed glorious days. Much was conquered, even more was dreamt of, much booty was taken, many infidels were dispatched. Such heights were never achieved again. Yet many more conquests were made, so that by 1600 Portugal had some fifty forts or defended areas in Asia, stretching from Sofala to Macao. D. Manuel had anticipated all this in 1499 by adding to his titles that of "lord of the conquest, navigation, and commerce of Ethiopia, Arabia, Persia, and India."[3]

[2]*Annaes Marítimos e Coloniaes*, 6 vols. (Lisbon, 1840-46), V, 216.
[3]Cipolla has a good section on the reasons for these Portuguese successes: *op. cit.*, pp. 101-7. A late sixteenth-century account describes well the *brio* of the early Portuguese: "André Furtado de Mendonça was the last example of those first captains who founded the State of India—in pride and vanity *fidalgos* ["nobles"], in greed *vanias*, in prodigality nabobs, rough, fanatical, blood-thirsty warriors, heaping up [the bodies of] Muslims and gentiles like wild beasts, but ready for any task or danger, squandering their blood and their lives with the same delight with which

For the dour, close-fisted Manuel, this title was atypically grandiloquent, but it encapsulated Portugal's economic aims in Asia, which were to monopolize trade in some products and control and tax those people trading in all others. This policy varied only in details during the sixteenth century. It was dictated to the Portuguese by sheer economic necessity. Portugal itself was a small, poor country, with a population never over 1,500,000 in the sixteenth century. Any empire would have to support itself, and optimally return a profit to the home country. There was no question of Portugal's being able to maintain an empire simply for prestige, as was sometimes the case with other European empires in the late nineteenth century, and with large parts of Portugal's own empire in the twentieth century. The only way the Portuguese empire could sustain itself was through profits from trade and taxes on trade; an empire consisting of a string of forts on the Asian coastline derived little revenue from the land.

In Goa itself the revenue derived from customs duties as a percentage of the total revenue from the area from all sources was: 1545, 63 percent; 1586-87, 57 percent; around 1600, 56 percent; 1616-17, 44 percent. Over the whole Portuguese Asian empire in 1586-87, and around 1600, the only two times when there are statistics available, the percentage from trade was higher, for despite large sums from land taxes in Daman, Bassein, and Goa, over 65 percent of the total was from customs duties. These are no figures on the revenues from the customs payable on land trade between Portuguese and neighboring areas, but it is probable that if they were included the percentage would be close to seventy.[4] Further, some other items of revenue were also based on sea trade, especially the sales of the rights to trade to certain areas, which often yielded large sums: in 1602 a voyage from Goa to Macao and Japan raised about Rs. 55,000 for the crown.[5] There were also occasional windfalls from sea trade, especially when a ship trading outside the Portuguese system was captured. Such prizes could be worth Rs. 1,00,000 or more for the king, apart from the bounties for the crews of the Portuguese ships involved.[6]

---

they squandered gold and jewels." (F. R. Silveira, *Memórias de um soldado da India*, ed. A. de S. S. Costa Lobo[Lisbon, 1877], p. 90.)

[4]1545 from Gavetas, III, 213; 1586-87 from AHU, Codice 500, ff. 1-2v, and *passim*; 1600 from Luis de Figueiredo Falcão, *Livro em que se contém toda a Fazenda* (Lisbon, 1859), pp. 75-78; 1616-17 from AHU, Caixa 6, account of November 19, 1618. For 1545, see also Simão Botelho's *tombo* in R. J. de Lima Felner, ed., *Subsídios para a história da India Portuguesa* (Lisbon, 1868), p. 48.

[5]"Provisões dos vice-Reis," HAG, I, 96.

[6]For example, Correa, III, 419; Couto, VII, iii, 3.

Given this large state income from trade, it is not suprising that the governors of Portuguese India usually tried to foster trade and so increase the revenues of the crown. Albuquerque's conquests are described in detail in the literature, but his unobtrusive work to encourage local people to trade in Portuguese areas, and to reassure merchants that they were safe to come and live in Portuguese towns, goes largely unheralded. In Goa he quickly realized the importance of the trade in horses, and offered inducements as well as threats to encourage the merchants of Hurmuz to continue bringing their horses to Goa,[7] Similarly, D. João de Castro is well known as a conquistador, but he also took steps to foster the horse trade. A few weeks after he had bloodily beaten off the Gujarati forces besieging Div in 1546, he sent messages to towns nearby encouraging local merchants to return to trade and settle in Div.[8] This solicitude compares very directly with the policies of the rulers of Gujarat, as will be seen. The reason is obvious: Portuguese India got over 60 percent of its revenue from customs duties. Gujarat got only 6 percent.

The Portuguese System

To govern their far-flung empire the Portuguese set up a comparatively elaborate administrative hierarchy. At the top was the king in Portugal, and after 1580 in Madrid, assisted by his officials. The trade to the East, including the supply of ships, crews, and provisions, was organized by the *Casa da India* and the *Védoria* or *Conselho da Fazenda* at Lisbon, working conjointly if not always harmoniously, due to their interlocking and (at times) overlapping responsibilities. However, as a letter written in Goa received a reply at the earliest only after ten months had elapsed, the kings and their officials in Europe could lay down policy only in the most general terms. It was the authorities in Goa, and their subordinates elsewhere, who made the running.

The head of the Portuguese "State of India" was the viceroy or governor, resident at first in Cochin and after 1515 usually in Goa. A viceroy enjoyed a slightly higher status than did a governor, but their functions and powers were identical. They were undisputed heads of the civil and military government of the whole state, responsible only to the king, and to God.

---

[7] Correa, II, 74, 402; Castanheda, III, xcv.
[8] APOCR, V, 189; Couto, VI, iv, 5. For Nuno da Cunha's similar concern to reassure local merchants after the panic in Div following the death of Sultan Bahadur, see Barros, IV, vii, 8.

To assist him in Goa the governor[9] had at first a loosely organized council. These councils were not institutionalized; they were called into existence more or less at the whim of the governor, to give advice only on specific, usually military, matters. The members were always *fidalgos* (literally "son of a somebody," i.e., a "noble") but there was no fixed membership or procedure. In these councils the governor was often only first among equals. If he ignored the advice of the council, and, for example, proceeded with an attack, those disapproving of the action usually would not help him. In most cases, however, a concensus was reached and adhered to by all present.

During the sixteenth century this council evolved and became more institutionalized as the Council of State. Its members, as of 1604, were the governor (or viceroy) as president, the archbishop of Goa, two or three of the older *fidalgos* resident in Goa, the head of the High Court, the captain of the city of Goa, and the Vedor da Fazenda. This official was head of the smaller Conselho da Fazenda, which was dominated by officials and met regularly in the seventeenth century to decide economic and financial matters. The governor was also entitled to attend sittings of the High Court.[10]

Religious affairs were usually handled independently of the civil authority by the archbishop or by the heads of the several orders, though there were instances of God in his Goan incarnation trying to influence Mammon and vice versa. There was also the municipal council, elected by the Portuguese and Eurasian population and at times an influential force on the government.[11] Four areas of authority can thus be distinguished: in financial matters the Vedor, and later

---

[9] Here and later, when the reference is generic, "governor" means the head of the state, whether he was entitled viceroy or governor.

[10] Generally for all this section on the administration, see J. B. Harrison in the *New Cambridge Modern History*, III, 532-34; V. T. Gune, "An Outline of the Administrative Institutions of the Portuguese Territories in India and the Growth of their Central Archives at Goa—16th to 19th Century A.D.," *Studies in Indian History: Dr. A. G. Pawar Felicitation Volume* (Bombay, 1968); R. S. Whiteway, *The Rise of Portuguese Power in India, 1497-1550* (London, 1967), pp. 58-75; C. R. Boxer, *The Portuguese Seaborne Empire, 1415-1825* (London, 1969), pp. 296-99; J. B. Amancio Gracias, *Subsídios para a história Economico-Financiero da India Portugueza* (Nova Goa, 1909); F. P. Mendes da Luz, *O Conselho da India* (Lisbon, 1952); Eric Axelson, *The Portuguese in Southeast Africa, 1600-1700* (Johannesburg, 1960), pp. 1-2; *O Oriente Português*, I, 480-86; on the High Court, see "Livros Azul," HAG, I and II, published in J. I. Abranches Garcia, *Archivo da Relação de Goa*, 2 vols. (Nova Goa, 1872-74).

[11] See C. R. Boxer, *Portuguese Society in the Tropics* (Madison and Milwaukee, 1965), pp. 12-41, and *passim*.

the Conselho da Fazenda; in religious affairs the clerics; in legal the High Court; and in local government the municipal council. Only over the first did the governor exercise appreciable control. However, the governor, assisted by the Council of State, did control military matters and external relations, in a manner befitting the head of what was and in most respects remained a society dominated by the ethos of the conquistador.

The state government in Goa was a macrocosm of that of the other areas and forts. Each had a captain, usually assisted by a Vedor da Fazenda, other minor officials such as clerks, and more important the factor, who supervised the royal trade in the area. There were also various clerics, a judge, and in the larger areas a municipal council.

Apart from the officials, ranging from the lowliest clerk to the governor, and the clerics, there was in Portuguese India a sizable population of Portuguese not serving in any official capacity. Some of these "private" Portuguese, such as *fidalgos* resident in Goa while they angled for a new job, were ordinarily servants of the king and considered themselves as such, but many others had left official service and occupied themselves as artisans or traders. Most of these people had come to India as soldiers, and had left royal employment once their period of service was completed. A few had never worked for the king, but had come out as private subjects. Among these were a handful of large traders in Goa who were either self-employed or worked as agents for Lisbon financiers.

With this background, one can now consider Portugal's involvement in Asian trade. There were four strands: the trade in Portuguese ships, owned either by the crown or by people contracting with the crown, from western India to Portugal; voyages to specific areas within Asia, undertaken at first in royal ships and later in ships licensed by the crown; trade within Asia conducted privately by Portuguese; trade by local people all over Asia in their own ships but with passes from the Portuguese. The last involved more capital and ships than any of the others, and obviously concerns us most; however, before going on to delineate the methods and objects of this control, a little should be said about each of the first three strands.

The trade between India and Portugal was done in the celebrated *naos* or great ships. From a capacity of less than 500 tons in the early sixteenth century, they rose to as much as 2,000 tons by the seventeenth. Their passages were regulated by the monsoons. They left Portugal in February or March, reached India, usually Goa, toward the end of the year, and left again for Portugal as soon as possible in the new year. Figures quoted by C. R. Boxer show that between 1500 and 1635 an average of five-and-one-half ships reached India from Portugal each year, while three-and-one-half made the return voyage.[12]

From Portugal they brought men, money, and goods—men to reinforce Portugal's many garrisons and religious houses, money and goods to pay for the return cargoes.[13] Among the goods copper predominated, but other European products were also brought out to compete, often unsuccessfully, with identical goods coming via the Red Sea. The cargoes of these ships on their return voyages to Portugal consisted of spices (mainly pepper) for the crown, and a large volume of other goods owned by private merchants and officials in India. Among these goods Gujarati cloths predominated. In the later sixteenth century the capital involved in this private trade to Europe was, in Portuguese terms, considerable; apparently it amounted to about Rs. 40,00,000.[14] Customs receipts in Lisbon from this trade formed an important part of the royal revenues, being about 27 percent of the total customs received in Lisbon in 1593.[15] In addition, the king made profits from his own monopolistic trade in pepper. In the earlier sixteenth century this trade was usually handled by royal ships, although in an emergency private ships could be used.[16] From the 1580s private merchants often contracted with the state to send their ships to India, at their own risk but on behalf of the crown.[17]

The second area of involvement consisted of voyages to specified places within Asia on a monopolistic basis: only the designated ship could make a given voyage in a particular year. Cargo space on such ships thus sold at a premium. In the earlier sixteenth century voyages of this kind were done in royal ships, though a large part of the goods

[12]C. R. Boxer, *The Portuguese Seaborne Empire*, pp. 219, 379-80. These figures are for ships which reached their destination, not those which left from Lisbon and India respectively.

[13]V. Magalhães-Godinho, *L'Économie de l'Empire Portugais aux XVe et XVIe Siècles* (Paris, 1969), p. 317.

[14]Estimate based on Bocarro, Livro, part 1, p. 279, and customs duties paid at Lisbon in 1593 from F. Mendes da Luz, *Relação de todas as rendas da Coroa* (Coimbra, 1949), p. 58. This figure may be compared with my figure for Gujarat's total trade at about this same time of Rs. 8,00,00,000.

[15]F. Mendes da Luz, *op. cit.*, pp. 42, 58.

[16]C. R. Boxer, *The Portuguese Seaborne Empire*, p. 331; Couto, VII, i, 6; ANTTCC, 1-30-36.

[17]Couto, X, i, 9; X, iv, 5; X, vii, 6; X, x, 6.

carried belonged to private merchants.[18] Later it was decided that such a method meant that the king had too much of his own capital tied up in ships and incidental expenses, so individuals were licensed to undertake these voyages from at least the 1540s. The destinations included the Banda Islands, Sofala, the Coromandel coast, Siam, Bengal, China, and Japan. Such licenses, like appointments to official positions, were given out on several grounds. Sometimes they were bestowed as rewards for meritorious military service.[19] Others were given as dowries to the daughters of prominent but impoverished *fidalgos*, while some formed part of the perquisites of a particular post. The captain of Malacca had voyages to seventeen different places.[20] Most of the voyages, however, were sold to the highest bidder, either directly by the crown or by the person who had been granted the voyage for one of the above reasons. They could be extremely lucrative for the owner. The best of all was that from Goa to Japan via Macao. A captain on this route in the 1560s usually made a profit of about Rs. 70,000 after expenses. Later he made much more.[21]

Private trade in Asia conducted by Portuguese, whether officials, merchants, or clerics, was considerable. It has been noted that many captains owned certain monopolistic voyages during their tenure, and there is ample evidence of these and other officials trading extensively, sometimes illegally, within Asia. Concerning private Portuguese merchants there is less information, for they were usually deemed unworthy of notice by the chroniclers or by officials writing home to Portugal. They were evidently numerous. In 1523 it was reported that wood for shipbuilding was scarce in Cochin as it was all being bought by Portuguese who intended to settle in India, live by their own trade, and die there. They were trading to Malacca, Siam, Pacem, Bengal, Coromandel, the Bandas, Timor, Hurmuz, Chaul, and Cambay.[22] Private Portuguese were trading in Malacca in 1543,

---

[18] F. Mendes da Luz, "Livro das Cidades e Fortalezas que a Coroa de Portugal tem nas Partes da India, 1582," *Studia*, no. 6, ff. 77v-78. See "Livro de Leis de D. Manuel," ANTT, ff. 132-34, for the regulations for the factor on the Cochin-Hurmuz and return voyage of 1520.

[19] António Baião, ed., *História quinhentista (inedita) do segundo cerco do Dio* (Coimbra, 1927), pp. 296-333, for the rewards given by D. João de Castro after the second siege of Diu. See also ANTTCC, 1-67-12.

[20] E. Axelson, *op. cit.*, p. 2; F. Mendes da Luz, "Livro das Cidades," ff. 101-103v.

[21] *Ibid.*, f. 95; Luis de Figueiredo Falcão, *op. cit.*, pp. 125-26, for voyages and their values around 1600. For the voyage to China and Japan, see C. R. Boxer, *The Great Ship from Amacon* (Lisbon, 1959).

[22] ANTTCC, 1-30-36.

in Siam in 1525, in the Bandas in 1525, in the Hadramaut in 1522, 1529-30, and 1538, between Hurmuz and the Mughal Empire in 1546, in Coromandel and in Quilon in the 1550s.[23]

It will be remembered that the ships bound for Portugal carried large quantities of goods owned not by the state but by merchants or the crews of the ships. Larger Portuguese merchants found it profitable to have their agents in Goa to supervise their Indian trade.[24] In fact, it is clear there is little truth in the old canard about the Portuguese, which has every butcher's boy becoming a *fidalgo* as he rounded the Cape of Good Hope, and thereafter scorning to work, instead spending his time in profligacy in Goa and Cochin. On the contrary, their willingness to turn a quick penny was often such that they did not hesitate to trade with enemies of the state.[25]

The area most favored by private Portuguese traders for their operations was Gujarat, especially the town of Cambay, trade to which had started by at least 1509,[26] and continued thereafter. This trade was carried on despite discouragement from both church and state. The first Provincial Council, of 1567, disapproved of Portuguese settling outside areas in which there were priests, as such people would seldom have the chance to take the sacraments. The governors feared the Portuguese resident in Cambay could serve as hostages in the event of a war between Portugal and the sultanate, or, after 1572, the Mughal Empire; on the other hand, if the Goa-Gujarat trade was left to "baneanes," *they* could be hostages for Portugal in case of war.[27] The occasional prohibitions had little effect. When Akbar arrived at Cambay in 1572, during his first campaign in Gujarat, he found fifty or sixty Portuguese, and these, a remnant of the normal population, were only the ones who had been unwilling to leave the war zone because they had goods in the town.[28] In 1594 there were about 100 Portuguese families in Cambay; the number seems to have decreased

[23]Respectively, Manuel de Faria e Sousa, *Asia Portuguesa*, 6 vols. (Lisbon, 1945-47), III, 115; R. J. de Lima Felner, *op. cit.*, pp. 5-6, 9; Barros, IV, vii, 9; R. B. Serjeant, *The Portuguese off the South Arabian Coast* (Oxford, 1963), pp. 55, 61; Couto, V, v, 5; APOCR, V, 188, 193; ANTTSV, X, 128; DI, II, 130.

[24]*The Voyage of John Huyghen van Linschoten to the East Indies*, 2 vols. (London, 1885), II, 225-26; APOCR, III, 753-55; "Alvarás e Provisões de Sua Magestade," HAG, III, 73v-74v; Fazenda, VIII, 182, 208; IX, 71; X, 71.

[25]For example, R. J. de Lima Felner, ed., *op. cit.*, pp. 8-9; DI, II, 130.

[26]Couto, VII, iv, 9.

[27]Lima Felner, *op. cit.*, pp. 8-9; APOCR, IV, 52; III, 403-4, 588; "Senado de Goa—Cartas Régias," HAG, I, 28, 34-34v; "Livro Morato," HAG, ff. 126-27.

[28]Couto, IX, cap. 13.

in the seventeenth century.[29] Many of these Portuguese traders evidently settled permanently in Cambay and married local women, as a Jesuit who baptized 180 people in Bassein in 1573 noted that among them "were many Eurasian women and boys, children of Portuguese in Cambay . . ."[30] These Portuguese were apparently engaged in buying Gujarati goods to be sent to Goa, whence they were reexported to Europe and all over Asia on Portuguese ships. Some were presumably agents of large Portuguese merchants in Goa who preferred to buy their goods at the source rather than wait until they had been brought to Goa by Gujaratis.[31]

The detailed statistics which would enable one to rank by relative importance these three strands of trade, and the fourth which will be considered next, are lacking. However, it has been persuasively argued that in the course of the sixteenth century the rank of the first, the trade to Portugal, declined relative to the other three. This was a result partly of the great increase in the pepper trade conducted outside Portuguese control.[32] The change was also due to greater experience, and more detailed knowledge of conditions and markets in Asia, on the part of both Portuguese officials and private traders. The effect was that Portuguese India became increasingly self-supporting, financed almost wholly by profits on the monopolistic voyages licensed by the crown, and by customs duties derived from the trade of both Portuguese and locals.

Control of Asian Trade

In their private trade the Portuguese were involved in Asian trade on a basis of equality with other merchants in the area, as in Cambay. The fourth strand of involvement was different. In their attempts to control and tax Asian traders, the Portuguese tried to operate from a

---

[29] Father Felix, "Mughal Farmans, Parwanahs and Sanads issued in favor of the Jesuit Missionaries," *Journal of the Panjab Historical Society* V (1916): 8; Artur Viegas, ed., *Relação Anual das Coisas que Fizeram os Padres da Companhia de Jesus nas suas Missões*, by Fernão Guerreiro, 3 vols. (Lisbon, 1930-42), II, 393-94; P. S. S. Pissurlencar, *Agentes da Diplomacia Portuguesa na India (Hindus, Muçulmans, Judeus e Parsees)* (Bastorá, Goa, 1952), p. 99.

[30] DI, IX, 289.

[31] *The Voyage of François Pyrard de Laval*, 2 vols. (London, 1887-90), II, 246; *The Journal of John Jourdain* (London, 1905), p. 173.

[32] I. A. MacGregor in *New Cambridge Modern History*, II, 610-11; J. B. Harrison, in *ibid.*, III, 536-39.

position of dominance based on naval power. It was here, in their *cartaz*-armada-*cafila* system, that they produced their greatest impact on Asian trade.

Now it should be known, that after the Franks had established themselves in Cochin and Cannanore, and had settled in those towns, the inhabitants, with all their dependents, became subject to these foreigners, engaged in all the arts of navigation, and in maritime employments, making voyages of trade under the protection of passes from the Franks; every vessel, however small, being provided with a distinct pass, and this with a view to the general security of all. And upon each of these passes a certain fee was fixed, on the payment of which the pass was delivered to the master of the vessel, when about to proceed on his voyage. Now the Franks, in imposing this toll, caused it to appear that it would prove in its consequences a source of advantage to these people, thus to induce them to submit to it; whilst to enforce its payment, if they fell in with any vessel, in which this their letter of marque, or pass, was not to be found, they would invariably make a seizure both of the ship, its crew, and its cargo!

The passes thus described by a sixteenth-century Muslim author[33] were the main instrument used by the Portuguese in their attempt to control trade carried on by local people in Asian waters. These passes were something new for Asian merchants, but the Portuguese justified them, at least to themselves, with a legal underpinning.

In the fifteenth century, as was noted, there was no attempt to control sea trade; those states which profited from the presence of foreign and local merchants did so because they provided attractive conditions for these merchants. In juristic terminology the Indian Ocean was a *mare librum*, there being no concept of sovereignty over it except in some coastal areas and rivers.[34] The Portuguese justification for their attempt to control completely sea trade in Asia was given by the official chronicler, João de Barros. The Portuguese were in Asia lords of the sea, and made all other ships take a safe-conduct or *cartaz* from them. Ships trading to enemies of Portugal could be seized on sight. By common law the seas were open to all, but this applied only in Europe to Christians, who were governed essentially by the principles of Roman Law. Hindus and Muslims, on the contrary, were outside Roman Law as they were outside the law of Jesus Christ, which all men must keep to avoid the eternal fire. Further, Hindus and Muslims had no claim to right of passage in Asian waters,

[33]Sheikh Zeen-ud-Deen, *Tohfut-ul-Mujahideen* (London, 1833), pp. 89-91.
[34]C. H. Alexandrowicz, *An Introduction to the History of the Law of Nations in the East Indies* (Oxford, 1967), pp. 64-71.

because before the arrival of the Portuguese no one claimed the sea as hereditary or conquered property. There being no preceding title, there was no present or future right of passage.[35]

All ships trading in Asian waters were required to have a pass or *cartaz*. These were issued by the competent Portuguese authority, usually either the governor or the captain of a fort.[36] They were issued from at least 1502 onward.[37] The conditions set out in these *cartazes* varied little during the sixteenth century or later. They included a statement of who was the captain (*nakhoda*) of the ship, how big the ship was, and what crew it carried. The quantity of arms and munitions allowed was strictly limited. The ship was to trade only to a Portuguese fort, or at least had to call at a Portuguese fort to pay duties on its cargo before proceeding to its destination. A cash security had to be left at the fort where the *cartaz* was issued to guarantee that the ship would in fact return to pay duties there on its homeward voyage. At this time a certificate had to be produced if duties had been paid at another fort. Apart from munitions, both the cargo and passengers were restricted. Turks and Abyssinian Muslims, both regarded as enemies of the Portuguese, were not to be carried, and various goods were also forbidden—among them all spices and pepper, iron, copper, and wood, as this could be used to build enemy ships.[38]

Any ship without a *cartaz* was automatically confiscated as a fair prize if the Portuguese captured it, and its crew, if it escaped instant death, was liable to be sent to the galleys. Even a ship with a *cartaz* was confiscated if the terms were not kept. As the captain and crew of the Portuguese ship which made a fair prize received fixed shares of the value of the seized ship, they obviously checked very strictly. Thus in 1555 a Gujarati ship was confiscated because it had eight Turks on board. In 1540 another Gujarati ship was seized as its *cartaz* said it was bound for Kishm, but, judging by its position when the Portuguese checked it, it could not have been going there. Two other ships were seized in the same year, one for trading in Dobbah, with which the Portuguese were at war, and one for having a different

[35] Barros, I, vi, 1.
[36] From 1596 only the governor could issue a *cartaz* for a voyage beyond the coast of India. (AHU, Codice 281, f. 357.)
[37] Correa, I, 298; Marechal Gomes da Costa, *Descobrimentos e Conquistas*, 3 vols. (Lisbon, 1927-30), II, 110.
[38] "Consultas do Serviço de partes," HAG, III, *passim*; ANTTCC, 1-62-154; LM, III, 267-68; Correa, II, 50, 330; Bocarro, Decada, p. 56; APOCR, V, 264; Diogo do Couto, *Vida de D. Paulo de Lima Pereira* (Lisbon, 1903), p. 76.

captain from that named in the *cartaz*.³⁹ It may be noted that *cartazes* were required for the coastal trade in western India, whether done by Christians, Hindus, or Muslims, and even for trade from one Gujarati port to another.⁴⁰

The ultimate implications of such claims can best be seen in an incident of 1540. The governor of Surat, Khwaja Safar, had built a new fort to protect his port. The Portuguese viceroy wrote to the sultan of Gujarat asking him to make Khwaja Safar demolish this fort, "because it was bad to build a fort there when there was no need at all for it; because if he was a true friend of the king of Portugal he would not build forts on the edge of the sea, which belonged to the Portuguese, and because no one was ever going to attack him from the sea except the king of Portugal, who would only do so if he did not keep the peace which had been established between them."⁴¹

The arrival of the English and Dutch in western Indian waters in the early seventeenth century, and their attacks on the Portuguese until 1635 and 1663 respectively, made little difference as regards control of sea trade. The local merchants were now often required to take passes from the Dutch and English as well as from the Portuguese, but this was no hardship as these two European powers had no customs houses in western India; thus there was no obligation in their *cartazes* to pay duties.⁴² Meanwhile, despite their deteriorating mili-

---

³⁹ANTTCC, 1-67-47, 1-94-94. For other cases, see *Studia*, no. 3, pp. 81-82; ANTTCC, 1-106-135; LM, v. 28B, f. 379.

⁴⁰"Livro de Leis de D. Manuel," ANTT, f. 141; "Provisões dos Vice-Reis," HAG, II, 159; "Termo das Fiancas," HAG, I, *passim*; *Boletim do Conselho Ultramarino. Legislação Antiga* (Lisbon, 1867), I, 128; F. Paes, "O Tombo de Diu," *O Oriente Português*, n.s. V (1933): 47-48; ANTTSV, V, 155. This requirement, that all ships trading anywhere carry a Portuguese *cartaz*, and also the limitations on the cargoes, differentiate this whole system from modern parallels. Today a citizen of one country can travel and trade to another country subject only to the permission of these two countries. A third country has no jurisdiction over such travel. Thus the United States did not try to stop trade by others to "unfriendly" countries such as Cuba or China. Such control by a third country has been claimed occasionally in time of war, most notably recently by Great Britain in the Napoleonic and First and Second World Wars. The extent of the control over neutral shipping claimed in these cases was much less than that claimed by the Portuguese in sixteenth-century Asia, and even the prohibition on direct trade with an enemy was challenged by others. The British never claimed the right to direct all trade, and all cargoes carried, in the Atlantic.

⁴¹Correa, IV, 143.

⁴²Bal Krishna, *Shivaji the Great* (Bombay, 1932), I, 40; Factories, 1618-21, p. 2; 1622-23, pp. 215-16; *The Voyage of Thomas Best* (London, 1934), p. 108; *Diário do 3rd. Conde de Linhares*, 2 vols. (Lisbon, 1937-43), p. 255.

tary position in relation to the Dutch, the Portuguese continued throughout the seventeenth century to insist that *cartazes* be taken; and while there was increasing evasion, it is clear that by and large their claims were accepted. In the 1690s the Portuguese were still seizing ships in the Gulf of Cambay if they did not have *cartazes,* and Awrangzeb still took them for his ships.[43]

The fee charged for issuing the *cartaz* was negligible, a few rupees only,[44] but the *cartaz* did oblige the ship concerned to call at a Portuguese fort, both coming and going, to pay duties. This was the object of the whole exercise, the essence of the arrangement, for customs receipts were crucial to the finances of the Portuguese empire in Asia.

By comparison with those charged in sultanate or Mughal Gujarat, the rates were high. The most important customs house in western India was Goa, for the Portuguese attempted, with some success, to make it the focus for all trade between Gujarat and Malabar, and India and Europe. The rates varied according to the product involved, and were not levied on trade with Portugal, but until 1569 they were as they had been under Bijapur in the fifteenth century, 6 percent *ad valorem*. This was paid on both imports and exports, except that goods which had not changed hands in Goa paid no export duty. In 1569 a general meeting in Goa agreed to raise the rates by 1 percent to pay for warships.[45] During the seventeenth century the rates were increased several times to meet the cost of the struggle against the Dutch—to 8 percent by 1607, 9 percent by 1639, and 10 percent by 1659.[46] Further, a tax on food imports, known as the *collecta,*

---

[43]P.S.S. Pissurlencar, *op. cit.,* pp. 566-67; P.S.S. Pissurlencar, *Portuguese Records on Rustamji Manockji, the Parsi Broker of Surat,* 2 vols. (Nova Goa, 1933-36), II, 11, 33. See Alberto Iria, *Da Navegação Portuguesa no Indico no século XVII* (Lisbon, 1963), pp. 104-5, for evasion; and for a slightly modified version of the form of the *cartaz* agreed on in Surat in 1670, see *Boletim do governo do Estado da India,* October 10, 1873, pp. 367-68; Assentos, IV, 208-12.

[44]"Livro de Leis de D. Manuel," ANTT, f. 141; "Regimentos e Instruções," HAG, III, 122v, 124.

[45]"Provisões, Alvarás e Regimentos," HAG, I, 168-71; "Livro de termos e autos," HAG, ff. 182v-83v; R.J. de Lima Felner, ed., *Subsídios para a história da India Portuguesa,* pp. 47-48.

[46]Bocarro, Livro, part 1, pp. 279-80; APOCR, II, 213; "Termo das Fianças," HAG, II, 143-44; Fazenda, IX, 264v. In sixteenth-century Lisbon the usual duty was 20 percent, but many specified goods paid less. See *Boletim do Conselho Ultramarino. Legislação Antiga,* I, 157 *et seq*; F. Mendes da Luz, *Relação de todas as rendas,* (Coímbra, 1949), pp. 44-45, 59, 60.

was instituted in 1623. This was a sign of the desperate straits of Portuguese India at this time, for the free importation of food was one of Goa's oldest and most prized privileges.[47]

The rates at other customs houses were roughly similar to those in Goa. In Chaul, where duties were levied only from 1634, the rates were 8 percent for imports and 6 percent for exports.[48] In sixteenth-century Malacca, with some variations, they were 6 percent, and later 7 percent.[49] In Div the duties were only 3½ percent until the 1580s, when another ½ percent was added with the consent of the inhabitants to pay for the armada which protected the trade between Div and Cambay. Again the duties rose in the seventeenth century to meet the costs of defense.[50]

To avoid confusion in later discussion, it is as well here to mention another sort of *cartaz*, the free *cartaz*. These were given to local rulers for political reasons. Before 1571 the sultan of Bijapur had four a year, and by the peace treaty of this year he received two more.[51] The sultan of Ahmadnagar had seven a year, five for ships going to Hurmuz, one for the Red Sea, and one for Malacca.[52] Akbar was given one a year for a ship of his to go to the Red Sea. In all cases these free *cartazes* were sops to the rulers concerned, designed to prevent any attack by them on the Portuguese settlements on their coasts. The value of such *cartazes* lay in their exempting the ship carrying one from paying duties on the goods it carried. These ships were, however, still prohibited from carrying forbidden goods and people, and at least in the later seventeenth century they had to pay a small tax, the amount depending on the size of the ship.[53]

The Portuguese maintained several fleets of warships to check on *cartazes*, to impress local rulers, and to combat piracy. The first viceroy, D. Francisco d'Almeida, was instructed by D. Manuel to have two fleets cruising, one from the Red Sea to Cambay, and one from Cambay to Cape Comorin. After Goa was taken in 1510 regular

---

[47]See "Livro de contrato e concepção da colecta," HAG; "Alvarás e Provisões de Sua Magestade," HAG, III, 43-44v; "Provisões, Alvarás, e Regimentos," HAG, I, 28v-29.

[48]For its regulation, see LM, v. 19D, ff. 1196v-1203.

[49]R.J. de Lima Felner, ed., *op. cit.*, pp. 105-6; P.S.S. Pissurlencar, *Regimentos das Fortalezas da India* (Bastorá, Goa, 1951), pp. 256-60.

[50]F. Paes, "O Tombo de Diu," *O Oriente Português* IV (October 1932): 38-39; LMBP, III, 157; Fazenda, V, 197v-98v; LM, v. 19D, ff. 1198-1200; AHU, Caixa 10, account of September 30, 1634; Biblioteca da Ajuda, 51-VII-30, f. 97.

[51]APOCR, V, 828.

[52]"Consultas do Serviço de partes," HAG, III, 40v-41.

[53]*Boletim do Governo do Estado da India,* October 10, 1873, p. 368.

patrols were undertaken north and south of the town, the first going to Chaul or further north to Cambay, and the second to the Kanara and Malabar areas, and even across to the Maldive Islands.[54] As early as 1512 the Portuguese had a total of about fifty ships either operational or being built in India and Southeast Asia.[55] By the 1520s the total was around eighty, the exact figure depending on the source.[56] A list for the 1567-68 season gives a total in the nineties, while in 1620 there were sixty-five ships based on Goa alone.[57] For a special effort even larger numbers could be pressed into service. In 1539 the viceroy, D. Garcia de Noronha, commanded an armada of 121 ships, large and small.[58]

Apart from such special fleets, there were numerous regular cruises during the sixteenth century, regulated in their times of operation by the monsoons; thus no ship cruised between May and September on the western Indian coast. Off Malacca a small fleet cruised to force ships to call and pay duties.[59] Another fleet covered the Island of Manar, the pearl grounds of south India, and the Coromandel coast.[60] In the Persian Gulf patrolling seems to have been rather sporadic.[61] From Goa several patrols were sent out each season. One fleet was sent to cover the mouth of the Red Sea. The northern fleet cruised as far as the Gulf of Cambay, while others operated off Kanara and Malabar.

The duty of these armadas was to guard ships trading under Portuguese auspices—later in the century these mercantile ships sailed in convoys, accompanied by a small armada of warships—and to find and destroy pirates. Two small fleets based on Div patrolled respectively to the west, to make ships from west Gujarati ports call at Div, and to the Gulf of Cambay, to escort the small ships bound for Div from Cambay.[62]

Later in the sixteenth century the Portuguese were forced to

---

[54] Castanheda, II, i; APOCR, V, 26; Barros, III, i, 7; "Livro de Leis de D. Manuel," ANTT, f. 137v.
[55] *Cartas de Affonso de Albuquerque,* III, 350-51.
[56] R.J. de Lima Felner, ed., *op. cit.,* pp. 21-25; ANTTSV, XI, 12v-15v; ANTTCC, 1-30-36. By comparison, the home fleets in about 1550 operating off the coasts of Portugal totalled forty-three ships. (ANTTSV, III, 491.)
[57] Manuel de Faria e Sousa, *Asia Portuguesa,* IV, 27-28; LM, v. 22B, ff. 453-55.
[58] ANTTSL, IV, 247-50.
[59] ANTTCC, 1-30-36; Bocarro, Livro, part 2, p. 24.
[60] F. Mendes da Luz, "Livro das Cidades e Fortalezas," *Studia,* no. 6, f. 52v.
[61] ANTTCC, 1-35-52; ANTTSL, II, 203v-4; "Leis," ANTT, III, 113v.
[62] ANTTCC, 1-71-16; LMBP, V, 243; ANTTDR, XVIII, 54; XXIV, 57-57v; Couto, VII, iv, 3; Alberto Iria, *op. cit.,* p. 85.

institute a new form of trade control, the *cafila* or caravan of small merchant ships guarded by a Portuguese fleet. There are scattered references to merchant ships travelling in convoys for security earlier in the sixteenth century,[63] but by the 1560s it was the established practice for ships trading within the Portuguese system on the western Indian coast to sail together and be guarded by the Portuguese. In 1596 this was made compulsory: the viceroy decreed that all ships trading on the western Indian coast must travel in *cafilas*.[64] The reason for this compulsion, and for the earlier more or less voluntary system, was the threat of attacks by the pirates of Malabar on ships trading within the Portuguese system.[65] Apart from the regular Cambay-Div *cafila*, and a more spasmodic one centered on Hurmuz,[66] all the *cafilas* came to Goa.

To the north two or three *cafilas* left each year, stopping at Chaul, Bassein, Daman, and, in the seventeenth century, Surat, on the way to Cambay. It was this fleet of small ships which brought to Goa the vital private cargoes for the homeward bound fleet. Two hundred or more small ships could be included in the convoy. There are records of such *cafilas* from 1569, but they were not undertaken every year until late in the century, apparently after the 1596 decree made them compulsory. Before then they were used when the threat from pirates was great, but sometimes merchant ships simply came to Goa alone and unguarded.[67]

The *cafilas* to the Kanara area were equally crucial for Goa, for from there came food. Goa had a heavy rice deficit in the sixteenth century and later, so that each year a fleet of at least one hundred small boats made two, three, or four voyages to Barcellor, Mangalore, and Honavar and brought back food for the city.[68] This *cafila* was

[63]Marechal Gomes da Costa, *Descobrimentos e Conquistas*, II, 110, 199.
[64]APOCR, III, 36, 89; *O Oriente Português*, XVII, 70.
[65]DI, IV, 299; VIII, 120-1, 321, 370; Zeen-ud-Deen, *op. cit.*, pp. 157-58.
[66]APOCR, III, 36, 89; *O Oriente Português*, XVII, 70.
[67]Couto, VIII, cap. 30; IX, cap. 18; X, i, 8; X, vii, 11; *The Voyage of Thomas Best*, p. 34; Samuel Purchas, *Hakluytus Posthumus, or Purchas his Pilgrimes*, 20 vols. (Glasgow, 1905), III, 176; William Foster, ed., *Early Travels in India, 1583-1619* (London, 1921); p. 76, *Letters Received by the East India Company from its Servants in the East*, 6 vols. (London, 1896-1902), VI, 83; *Travels of Pietro Della Valle*, 2 vols. (London, 1892), I, 116-53, for his experiences in 1623 of such a *cafila*. For the official instructions of the *cafilas* of 1636, 1638, and 1642, see "Regimentos e Instruções," HAG, III, 19-20, 102; IV, 56v-57v. For the instructions for 1616, see Bocarro, Decada, pp. 654-56.
[68]"Senado da Goa—Cartas Regias," HAG, II, n.p., published in APOCR, I, ii, 109-10; *Diário do 3rd. Conde de Linhares*, pp. 20, 124; Assentos, III, 217; *Travels of Fray*

operating from at least the 1560s, and apparently on a regular basis.[69]

The third *cafila* came from Cape Comorin, via Cochin and Cannanor, to Goa. It began in the 1550s, again as a result of the threat from local pirates. It included larger ships from Malacca, China, Siam, Bengal, and Coromandel, which were met by the guard fleet at Cape Comorin. In Cochin many smaller ships were picked up, and they all proceeded together to Goa. Frequently more than one *cafila* came from the Malabar area to Goa each year. They brought goods from Southeast Asia, China, and the Bay of Bengal for the ships bound for Portugal which were loading in Goa, and for the markets north of Goa.[70]

As with the *cartazes*, these *cafilas* in theory embodied two principles: profit for the Portuguese customs houses, and protection for the native traders. In fact, pirates sometimes did attack *cafilas* and loot ships in them, but it can be conceded that ships in *cafilas* were safer than those sailing alone. Nevertheless, it is clear that many native merchants would just as soon have taken their chance outside the *cafila* system, and certainly would have preferred not to have to call at Goa to pay duties. Thus the escort fleet had two functions: to guard the merchant ships from pirates, and to make sure none of these same merchant ships slipped away to trade outside the Portuguese system.[71] Further, ships in a *cafila* were at the mercy of the escorting fleet; if it was needed elsewhere the *cafila* simply had to wait until it returned. If the Portuguese were at war with a ruler on the western coast, the *cafila* was of course not allowed to call at his ports.[72]

Manrique, 2 vols. (London, 1926-27), II, 3. For Goa's rice imports, see "Acordãos e Assentos da Câmara de Goa," HAG, IV, 20v, and Fazenda, III, 4v, 95-97. From this last one finds Goa spending Rs. 1,00,000 on rice in November and December of 1629 alone, both in the north and in Kanara. For the regulations for a Kanara *cafila*, see "Regimentos e Instruções, " HAG, II, 10v-11v.

[69]Couto, VII, x, 2; VII, x, 19; APOCR, I, ii, 109-10; *Studia*, no. 3, p. 77.

[70]Couto, VII, i, 7; VIII, cap. 29; X, ii, 15; ANTTDR, XXVII, 222; AHU, Caixa 22, meeting of December 15, 1653; Bocarro, Decada, pp. 77-78; LM, v. 12, f. 170v.

[71]Della Valle, *op. cit.*, I, 385-86, 393-94; "Cartas e Ordens," HAG, I, 55; "Livro Azul," HAG, I, 39; "Assentos e Juramentos da Câmara de Goa," HAG, f. 231. In a similar fashion, tribute missions to the court of Imperial China were "accompanied by troops who combined protection with surveillance." J. K. Fairbank, *Trade and Diplomacy on the China Coast*, 2 vols. (Cambridge, 1953), I, 29.

[72]Bocarro, Decada, pp. 67, 77-78. It may be noted here that the *cafilas* to Cambay and Kanara continued to run throughout the seventeenth century (John Fryer, *A New Account of East India and Persia*, 3 vols. [London, 1909-15], II, 41; S. N. Sen, ed., *Indian Travels of Thevenot and Careri* [New Delhi, 1949], pp. 163, 166, 183.),

The System in Operation

Such were the mechanics of the system set up by the Portuguese to control and tax local Asian trade. Its basic elements were *cartazes*, *cafilas*, and armadas, each designed to force local traders to pay customs duties to the Portuguese, and secondarily to provide sufficient protection so that those traders survived to make this payment. These at least were the objectives, but how effective was the system, and what was its practical impact on local traders?

Despite all the armadas and forts, and the stringent conditions of the *cartazes*, it is clear enough that there was in fact in most areas considerable flexibility within the Portuguese system. Indeed, given the motherland's size, poverty, and distance from its empire, and the extended nature of the empire, this was inevitable. In the decrees and king's letters Portuguese claims appear hard and inflexible, but in practice in most of Asia theirs was a "soft," low-profile presence. Specifically, there were gaps within the system itself, there was a good deal of what can briefly be called corruption, and, during the century, a tacit reordering of Portugal's priorities increased the flexibility of the system.

The most serious gap resulted from the failure to capture Aden. Despite attempts in 1513 by Albuquerque and 1548 by Castro this strategic port was never taken. This was a crucial weakness in the Portuguese system, for by possessing Aden and Hurmuz they could have blocked nearly all trade to Europe by routes other than their own via the Cape of Good Hope. As it was, a fleet had to be sent each season from Goa to lie off the entrance to the Red Sea, usually cruising between Aden and the Bab al-Mandab, and returning to Hurmuz in April. The lack of a closer base created serious logistic difficulties and reduced the fleet's effectiveness. Reports of its operations often indicate a comedy of errors. The fleet of 1530 consisted of ten ships, and it spread itself across the entrance to the Red Sea "like a net," with each ship in the fleet nearly in sight of the next. But it took few prizes as most of those desiring to trade illegally had left early and were already within the Red Sea.[73] In 1562 the armada saw more than fifty ships slip past and into the Red Sea without being able to stop

---

but the one to Malabar of course ceased once the forts there were taken by the Dutch in the early 1660s.

[73]Barros, IV, ix, 11.

them.[74] We are told that the captain of the 1538 fleet cruised diligently until the middle of April without stopping anything, whereupon "it being time to return, off he went."[75] The logistic difficulties involved led to the discontinuance of this cruise in the 1570s, except for special occasions.[76] Evasion became so easy for those wanting to take illegal goods to the Red Sea that Aden declined, no longer a necessary haven for ships running the Portuguese blockade.[77]

Another gap resulted from Portuguese dependence on puppet rulers, as in Hurmuz, Cochin, and Cannanore. The Malabar rulers in particular did not always dance in step to the Portuguese tune. One of the raja of Cochin's privileges concerned customs duties at his port. In 1530 João III (1521-57) had allowed him to levy duties on goods coming from Southeast Asia and China to western India if they were owned by Portuguese residents of Cochin. They were to pay 6 percent on goods landed in Cochin, to the raja. Later the raja unilaterally lowered his rates to 3½ percent. As a consequence, traders all over western India tried, often successfully, to pass off their goods coming from the east as belonging to a resident of Cochin, and thereby entitled to a rate of 3½ percent rather than the usual 6 percent rate levied at Goa and Cochin. Evasion became so common that the raja in 1584, under pressure from the Portuguese authorities, agreed to a reform. The Portuguese residents of Cochin then revolted, and finally the Goa government was forced to concede the lower rate. Evasion continued, to the detriment of Portugal's revenues.[78]

A third gap in the system was the failure to establish customs houses in Chaul and Daman. The farther a trader had to go out of his way to pay duties to Portugal, the greater was the likelihood of evasion. In 1589 Philip II of Spain (since 1580 also Philip I of Portugal) decreed that a customs house be set up in Chaul, as the crown needed

[74]Couto, VII, x, 3.
[75]Couto, V, ii, 7. For more successful patrols, see ANTTCC, 1-33-3, 1-94-94. Couto apparently considered this patrol, despite its frequent failures, to be worth continuing. (Diogo do Couto, *Diálogo do Soldado Prático* [Lisbon, 1937], p. 170.) For the comparable Dutch difficulties off Goa in 1638, see I.O., I/3/22, CCCLVIII.
[76]Artur Viegas, ed., *op.cit.*, II, 390; Couto, X, vii, 7; António da Silva Rego, ed., *Documentação para a história das Missões do Padroado Português do Oriente. India*, 12 vols. to date (Lisbon, 1947-), IX, 513.
[77]C. F. Beckingham, "Dutch Travellers in the Seventeenth Century," *Journal of the Royal Asiatic Society* (1951): 79-81; Philip Baldaeus, *A Description of the East India Coasts of Malabar and Coromandel* (London, 1703), III, 575.
[78]Couto, X, iv, 13; X, vi, 2; "Provisões, Alvarás e Regimentos," HAG, I, 119v; Bocarro, Livro, part 1, pp. 347-48.

the extra revenue this would provide. As was to be expected, the local inhabitants resisted this proposal. Although it was decided in 1592 that a customs house had to be established, the local Portuguese continued to resist, and it was not until 1634 that the decision was implemented. More shrill complaints to the king followed, and by the 1670s the offending institution had been withdrawn.[79]

In Daman the local Portuguese citizens were eager to see the establishment of a customs house, as they hoped this would lead to their port becoming a great trade center. They dreamed of Daman rivalling and even superseding Cambay. Both king and viceroy shared this dream; the difficulty was that if Cambay was in fact superseded by Daman, a rude awakening was likely to follow as an outraged Mughal emperor invaded Daman's scattered and poorly defended territory. But extra fortifications took time to build—several decades in fact—and it was not until late in the seventeenth century that a customs house was established.[80]

I have dealt more fully with the matter of corruption elsewhere.[81] Here it is necessary only to note that Portuguese colonial officials were chosen on strictly personal grounds, rather than on any abstract criterion of suitability or training. Most offices were given as a reward for past meritorious service, or were bought at auction. The holders expected to make a profit during their tenure over and above their meager pay. These profits were derived from the official privileges attached to an office, such as the monopolistic trading voyages to specified places, and unofficial perquisites, which were customary and tacitly accepted. These included minor bribes and levies. Beyond these again were outright abuses and extortion, such as forcing a native merchant to sell goods at an unrealistically low price. In sixteenth-century terms only the last, the extortion, was "corruption." Such abuses were seen as undesirable, and did unnecessarily lessen the efficiency of the administration. The abuses to which some officials subjected native traders who were trying to conform to Portuguese requirements simply increased the amount of evasion. Their incidence

---

[79]LM, v. 19D, ff. 1195-96v; LM, v. 21A, f. 42; v. 12, f. 109; v. 15, f. 6; APOCR, III, 206, also two copies of the same in AHU, Codice 281, ff. 30-30v, 37-37v; "Livro de registo dos alvarás, cartas etc. de differentes feitorias," HAG, f. 16. For the Regimento of 1634 setting up this customs house, see LM, v. 19D, ff. 1196v-1203.

[80]APOCR, III, 293-95, 492-93; LMBP, III, 155-56.

[81]M. N. Pearson, "Corruption and Corsairs in Sixteenth-Century Western India: A Functional Analysis," Blair B. Kling and M. N. Pearson, eds., *The Age of Partnership: Europeans in Asia before Dominion.* (Essays in Honor of Holden Furber.) Forthcoming.

apparently grew as Portuguese power declined later in the sixteenth century.

The third factor which helped to make Portuguese control less rigid than may appear from a study of the royal decrees was the change in the relative importance of the four strands of Asian trade with which the Portuguese were concerned. It has already been noted that the value of the trade to Portugal declined during the century, thanks largely to the growth of the "illegal" pepper trade. Portuguese India became increasingly autonomous, financed by the royal monopoly country trade within Asia to specified areas, and by the customs duties derived from local and private Portuguese traders.[82] The corollary of this was less rigidity in the Portuguese system. It was more important that people trade, and pay duties, than that enemies be denied trade with ships owned or licensed by the Portuguese.

A clear case was trade to the Red Sea. In the early years the Portuguese tried to ban all such trade, this being a hostile Muslim area.[83] Throughout the century such prohibitions were backed by the clerics, notably in their Provincial Councils.[84] Their views were increasingly ignored by the governors. There are records of trade licensed by the Portuguese from the Red Sea to Div from 1537, to Hurmuz from 1539, to Cannanor from 1546, and to Goa itself from 1556.[85] Similarly, it appeared that the crown would make greater profits if the special voyages were sold off instead of being done directly by the state. Albuquerque had opposed all private Portuguese trade, for he thought all Portuguese in Asia should serve the king. Apart from the impossibility of enforcing such an idea, the customs receipts from these traders were too valuable for their trade to be discouraged.

The end result of these three constraints was that the system never functioned perfectly anywhere in Asia. There was considerable flexibility, and relatively safe possibilities of evasion. Thus in 1513 the king was informed that copper was worth its weight in gold in India, as, thanks to the Portuguese blockade, none was now coming through from the Red Sea. A year later copper was reported to be extremely plentiful and cheap in Div. Many ships laden with it had recently

---

[82]See references used in f.n. 32 of this chapter.
[83]Castanheda, III, cxxxiii; Marechal Gomes da Costa, *Descobrimentos e Conquistas*, III, 281.
[84]DI, III, 537; IV, 492; APOCR, IV, 26, 126.
[85]For Div and Cambay, *Studia*, no. 10, p. 184; ANTTCC, 1-77-36, 1-100-28; Couto, V, ii, 8. For Hurmuz, Correa, IV, 84. For Cannanor, ANTTSL, III, 160, 162, 180. For Goa, ANTTCC, 1-102-47; DI, III, 569, 651, 712; IV, 427; V, 263, 754.

arrived from the Red Sea, despite the fact that to the Portuguese this was illegal trade.[86] More generally, the fate of the Portuguese attempt to monopolize the pepper trade is instructive, for it was in this area that the Portuguese made their greatest effort. This can be seen as a major test for the effectiveness of their whole attempt to control Asian trade. Throughout the sixteenth century and later, a stream of decrees and instructions from Portugal and Goa insisted that all trade in spices was reserved entirely for the crown and its agents. If this monopoly could be enforced, the Muslim powers in India, the Red Sea, and Egypt would lose their most profitable trade, while the Portuguese would be able to buy cheap in Asia and sell dear in Europe. But the Portuguese failed even here. The trade via the Red Sea to Europe was affected only occasionally by their fleets, while over the distribution of spices within Asia the Portuguese had no control at all.[87]

Despite the seeming rigidity of the Portuguese claims, it is clear that in fact the effectiveness of their system was often small. This chapter can be closed by a consideration in general terms of the whole practicality of Portugal's basic aims in Asia.

Aims and Methods

Was it ever realistic to try to monopolize some products and control trade in all others? Both Portugal's kings and their governors in India frequently issued decrees to regulate various aspects of Asian trade which were clearly not enforceable. The kings, operating in the remoteness of Lisbon, and after 1580 Madrid, can be excused their lack of realism, but the governors should have known better. In the early years they tried to stop all trade between Gujarat and the Red Sea, clearly an impossible task at this time when Aden had not been taken and Portugal had no forts in Gujarat.[88] In 1520 D. Manuel decreed that all ships from the Kanara ports were to trade to Goa, and nowhere else.

[86]*Cartas de Affonso de Albuquerque*, III, 70, 99.
[87]Recent discussions of this important topic include: Jan Kieniewicz, "The Portuguese Factory and Trade in Pepper in Malabar during the 16th Century," *Indian Economic and Social History Review* VI (March 1969); Vitorino Magalhães-Godinho, *L'Économie de l'Empire Portugais aux XVe et XVIe Siècles* (Paris, 1969), pp. 537-828; C. R. Boxer, "Portuguese Reactions to the Revival of the Red Sea Spice Trade and the Rise of Atjeh, 1540-1600," *Journal of Southeast Asian History* X (December 1969); M. N. Pearson, "Commerce and Compulsion: Gujarati Merchants and the Portuguese System in Western India, 1500-1600," Ph.D. dissertation, University of Michigan, 1971, pp. 106-29.
[88]Correa, II, 372-73.

Further, only very small coastal craft were to be used out of the Kanara ports, presumably so that the local merchants would be physically unable to make longer voyages to Gujarat or the Red Sea.[89] In 1595 Philip II decreed that no non-Christian resident in western India could trade, either directly or through an intermediary, to places other than those on the western India coast.[90] Early in the seventeenth century an attempt was made to ban all trade between Mombasa and the Red Sea; as the Portuguese had no forts north of Mombasa, and the fleet to guard the entrance to the Red Sea had been discontinued, this clearly could not be enforced.[91]

Such unrealistic decrees we may treat with contempt, as indeed did the native traders who were meant to be regulated by them. Of more importance is a consideration first of whether there was any alternative to the basic Portuguese aim of a monopoly of the spice trade and control of other trade, and second of whether the Portuguese used the most suitable methods if one assumes there was no alternative.

Returning to the basic progression in the growth of European power in Asia presented in Chapter I, which it will be remembered went from trade in foreign towns to factory to fort to land conquest, one has to ask whether the Portuguese could have traded as equals, possibly with the establishment of factories, or not. In Div, as will be seen, Malik Ayaz at least professed a willingness to have the Portuguese come and share in the trade of his port. Certainly he was attacked by the Portuguese, and not vice versa. In Malacca the merchants of Gujarat strongly advised the sultan not to let the Portuguese trade there; a reasonable enough request, for the Portuguese had been seizing their ships for several years.

In Calicut also the Portuguese started the hostilities. Da Gama's whole manner had been overbearing in 1498, and the instructions for the second Portuguese voyage laid down that Muslim ships were to be attacked on sight, and an attempt made to get the Zamorin to expel the Muslims (presumably those from the Red Sea only) from Calicut. This second Portuguese fleet found it difficult to obtain a cargo in Calicut, due to the opposition of the Muslim merchants—an opposition using commercial, not military, sanctions. Finally the Portuguese

---

[89] "Livro de Leis de D. Manuel," ANTT, ff. 139v-40v.
[90] APOCR, III, 540-42.
[91] "Alvarás e Provisões de Sua Magestade," HAG, I, 160-60v. Other fatuous decrees in APOCR, III, 900, 902, 906-7; LM, v. 12, f. 215; Correa, IV, 219; "Senado de Goa—Cartas Régias," HAG, I, 54-54v.

lost their tempers, seized a Muslim ship, and took its cargo. In retaliation a mob burned down the Portuguese factory. The situation from then on deteriorated quickly. The Portuguese responded by bombarding the town and then sailing south to Cochin to trade. Later they established a fort there, although the raja of Cochin was at least in theory a vassal of the Zamorin. In 1502 da Gama returned to India and demanded that the Zamorin expel from Calicut all Muslims from Cairo and the Red Sea. The Zamorin refused "to expel more than 4,000 households of them who live in Calicut as natives, not as strangers, and from whom his kingdom had received much profit."[92]

It is probable that the Portuguese could have traded on a basis of equality in all three of these great ports. Certainly those then in control of the trade would have competed hard, but on past performance it seems that they would not have been the first to use force. As for the rulers, the Portuguese would have been welcomed as merely another group of foreign merchants come to trade and would so increase their customs receipts. Further, given the lower costs of the Portuguese around the Cape of Good Hope, as compared to the Red Sea route, they could probably have taken over a large part of the spice trade to Europe. But peaceful competition was never the Portuguese aim.[93]

For the Portuguese, peaceful trade alongside Muslims on a basis of equality was impossible, for the crusade element was inherent in their presence in the Indian Ocean. The aim of the fifteenth-century kings was, it will be remembered, not only their profit but also the service of God. God, or at least the God of the Portuguese, could be served by the forcible dispossession of Muslim merchants, especially those based on the center of the abomination, the city of Mecca. To see these "moors" deriving huge profits from their trade was to ignite a short fuse in the easily-combustible Portuguese. If the Muslims could be ousted from the spice trade, not only would God be served but the true believers would profit on earth, as well as later in heaven, by replacing them.

The battle was thus joined, and can be seen as inevitable from the time Dias rounded the Cape. Yet even once the Portuguese aim of

[92] Barros, I, vi, 5. For these events, see Barros, I, v, 6; Zeen-ud-Deen, *op. cit.*, p. 79; Júlio Gonçalves, *Os Portugueses e o Mar das Indias* (Lisbon, 1947), p. 415. This modern Portuguese writer considers the forcible seizure of the cargo to be "Dangerous and unjust violence to which the tolerant commerce of the Orient was not accustomed." Also see Castanheda, I, xix, xxxvi, xxxviii, xxxix, xl; for the instructions of 1500, see *Annaes Maritimos e Coloniaes*, 6 vols. (Lisbon, 1840-46), V. 216.

[93] For a lone cry in the wilderness of Portuguese atrocities, a letter of 1510 calling for at least a little less force, see Gavetas, III, 758-60.

dominance is accepted, did they go about things in the most practical way? In particular, were fifty forts and one hundred warships really necessary? This opens up the subject of the debate between d'Almeida, the first viceroy, and Albuquerque, the first governor, over the *modus operandi* to be followed in achieving their common aim of dominance. D'Almeida's much-quoted advice to D. Manuel was that "As long as you may be powerful at sea you will hold India as yours; and if you do not possess this power, little will avail you a fortress on shore." In accordance with this policy he refused the offer of Malik Ayaz to hand over Div to Portugal after the Portuguese naval victory before the town in 1509.[94]

Albuquerque on the other hand followed an opportunistic yet reasonably coherent policy of seizing strategic points as occasion offered. In the Indian Ocean he desired only Aden, Hurmuz, Div, and Goa.[95] Three of these four were acquired, but later in the century gaps kept appearing in the net, so more and more forts were built in a vain effort to seal them. For any later governor it was a crowning ambition to build a fort somewhere, or anywhere, and have his name carved for posterity above the entrance. For the same reasons of prestige, almost no governor was prepared to scrutinize the merits of the forts under his control, and abandon those which were obviously inessential to the main design, although several acute observers in the sixteenth century and later in effect backed up d'Almeida by telling the king how costly and useless many of his forts were, and how much better his money could be spent on the armadas.[96] Following the disasters of the first third of the seventeenth century in the wars with the Dutch, one of the viceroys was even looking enviously on the English position in India, for they had no forts at all.[97]

[94]Correa, I, 947-49; Barros, II, iii, 7. Almeida's letter is in "Livro de varios papeis manuscriptos," Biblioteca da Academia das Ciências, Lisbon, Mss. Azuis, A64, f. 300.

[95]*Commentaries of Afonso Albuquerque*, 4 vols. (London, (1875-84), IV, 24.

[96]For example, M. B. Amzalak, ed., "Alegación en favor de la Compañia de la India Oriental, y comercios ultramarinos, que de nueva se instituyo en el Reyno de Portugal," by Duarte Gomes Solis, *Anais do Instituto Superior de Ciências, Ecónomicas e Financeiras*, XXIII, tome 1, p. 181; ANTTSL, V, 116v; A. de S.S. Costa Lobo, ed., *Memorias de um soldado da India*, by F. R. Silveira (Lisbon, 1877), pp. 232-38; ANTTCC, 1-71-43; D. João de Castro in ANTTSL, V, 126; *Arquivo Português Oriental*, ed. A.B. de Bragança Pereira, tome IV, vol. I, part 1, pp. 537, 551; and more recently Alfredo Botelho de Sousa, *Subsídios para a história militar marítima da India*, 4 vols. (Lisbon, 1930-56), I, 444-45; José F. Ferreira Martins, *Crónica dos Vice-Reis e Governadores da India* vol. I (Nova Goa, 1919), p. 562.

[97]"Livro de Ordens Régias," HAG, I, 193.

On a cost-effectiveness basis it is clear that the Portuguese spread themselves too thin, and would have done much better to have settled for a few strong forts, one land area, perhaps Ceylon, as a base for supplies, and a stronger armada. By trying to save every minor fort as it came under attack, Portugal only succeeded in spending more and more money on military purposes, with a smaller and smaller return. As early as 1564 Portuguese India was running a deficit of about Rs. 1,25,000 a year,[98] while the sums spent in the early seventeenth century on naval expeditions and the defense of Ceylon were often many times this; the high seas armada of Nuno Alvaro Botelho cost more than Rs. 10,00,000 in a period of a little over one year.[99] One may conclude that Portugal could have shared in and probably dominated the spice trade without using force, but that this was not attempted, and that her use of military means was in fact badly planned and designed in view of the ends she wished to achieve. In Gujarat, however, Portugal came closer than in any other area to realizing her goals.

---

[98]"Regimentos e Instruções," HAG, I, 10-10v; see also B. Mus. Addl. 20892, f. 38v, where the king in 1563 agrees with the municipal council of Goa that it is very bad that the Portuguese state in India is not living on its income.

[99]Alfredo Botelho de Sousa, ed., *Nuno Alvares Botelho, Capitão-general da Armada de Alto Bordo e Governador da India* (Lisbon, 1940), p. 55. The fleet which viceroy Azevedo took to Surat in 1612 to drive out the English cost nearly Rs. 2,00,000. (LM, v. 15, ff. 210v-15.) For the costs of the northern and Kanara armadas in the 1630s, see Baretto de Rezende, II, 146v, 149. For the large expenses in Ceylon, see *Diário do 3rd. Conde de Linhares, Vice-Rei da India*, 2 vols. (Lisbon, 1937-43), p. 182; ANTTDR, XLI, 66; "Noticias dos Estados da India extrahidos de Varios Livros e Papeis Manuscriptos," Biblioteca da Academia das Ciências, Lisbon, Mss. Azuis, A58, f. 45; Bocarro, Livro, part 1, pp. 378-403.

CHAPTER III

THE STATE

One day in 1581 at Akbar's court, Muhammad Qulij Khan was in attendance when an official brought to the emperor the *cartazes* that Akbar had requested from the viceroy of Goa. They gave permission for his ship to sail to the Red Sea. At this time Qulij Khan was aged 49, and had been captain of Surat fort since its conquest by the Mughals in 1573. He was a proud man, a strict sunni Muslim, a Turk of the Jani Qurbani tribe, and a confidant of the Emperor. Aiming to impress Akbar, he boasted that he also was going to send a ship to the Red Sea, but the *cartaz* it was going to carry was the handle of the dagger he had in his belt. He instructed his brother in Surat to prepare a ship so strong that it need not worry about the Portuguese.

News of this projected defiance spread quickly in Surat and soon reached Goa. A fleet of eight small Portuguese warships sailed north to blockade the Tapti River. After its *cartaz* was inspected, a fine ship of Akbar's was allowed to sail, but the captain of Qulij Khan's ship was warned not to leave without a *cartaz*. His ship was strong and well armed; the prudent Portuguese summoned three more small warships from Goa. Then the long wait began, with the tedium broken only by occasional skirmishes on land. In these the Portuguese did badly, suffering a heavy defeat from the troops of Qulij Khan's brother at Rander. The blockade, however, remained in effect.

Finally Qulij Khan, still at court, was advised of the stalemate. His response was apparently a crafty one. Without saying anything to Akbar he got the captain of Broach to undertake a diversionary attack on Daman. The local Portuguese withdrew to the city, sent off their women and children to Bassein, and desperately summoned help from Chaul, Goa, Div, and Bassein. Further, the blockading fleet had to leave Surat and sail south to help in the defense. But no major attack was launched by the powerful Mughal army. The captain of Broach was interested only in forcing the Surat blockaders to leave, so he spent his time making feints toward the city, and pillaging and burning in the undefended area the Portuguese had deserted.

When the rains of 1582 came he packed up and left, his mission accomplished.

Surat was unguarded, but Qulij Khan's ship never sailed. The merchants refused to load any goods on it. They had had seventy years' experience of Portugal's power at sea, and knew that even if the ship was now able to leave, there would certainly be a Portuguese fleet waiting for it when it came back. No doubt Qulij Khan had been very clever, but they were not going to risk their lives and property. Thus Qulij Khan lost after all, and soon was in deep trouble, for Akbar was furious with him for arranging the attack on Daman without his permission.[1]

Worse still, the caution of the merchants was proved justified, for after the rains of 1582 the viceroy sent twenty light ships into the Gulf of Cambay. Their mission was to retaliate for the attack on Daman by seizing all ships returning from the Red Sea. One of Akbar's was captured in Gogha, but after pressure from the governor of Cambay the viceroy released it, "for good and weighty reasons," which here means fear of irritating so powerful a ruler. One other ship was sighted, in September, and hotly pursued. After some days the captain agreed to hand over the ship and its cargo if the lives of those on board were spared. This was done, but such peaceful conquests were not to the liking of the Portuguese soldiers and sailors. Their aim was to board a ship, shouting "Santiago" and waving their swords. In the resultant confusion all sorts of trifles, such as jewels and gold, often disappeared, and so never appeared in the official inventory. Such trifles were later discreetly sold in Goa. Disappointed in their hopes of an easy fight and a profitable sack, most of the Portuguese mutinied and set off in fourteen of the ships to Daman. Here they took over the town, terrorized the locals, and waited for their unsporting admiral to came back so that they could murder him. He evaded them, and found sanctuary in a monastery. After twenty-four hours of negotiations the mutiny was ended when the admiral agreed to give the soldiers and sailors some of the booty.[2]

Qulij Khan was not the man to accept such a failure. In 1585 he

---

[1] For Muhammad Qulij Khan, see Sikandar, p. 455; S. A. A. Rizvi, *Muslim Revivalist Movements in Northern India in the sixteenth and seventeenth centuries* (Agra, 1965), pp. 218, 236 f.n.; Samsam-ud-daula Shah Nawaz Khan, *Maathir-ul-Umara*, trans. Henry Beveridge, revised B. Prashad, 2 vols. (Calcutta, 1941-52), II, 534-37. These events from Couto, X, ii, 4-8.

[2] Couto, X, iii, 4-5.

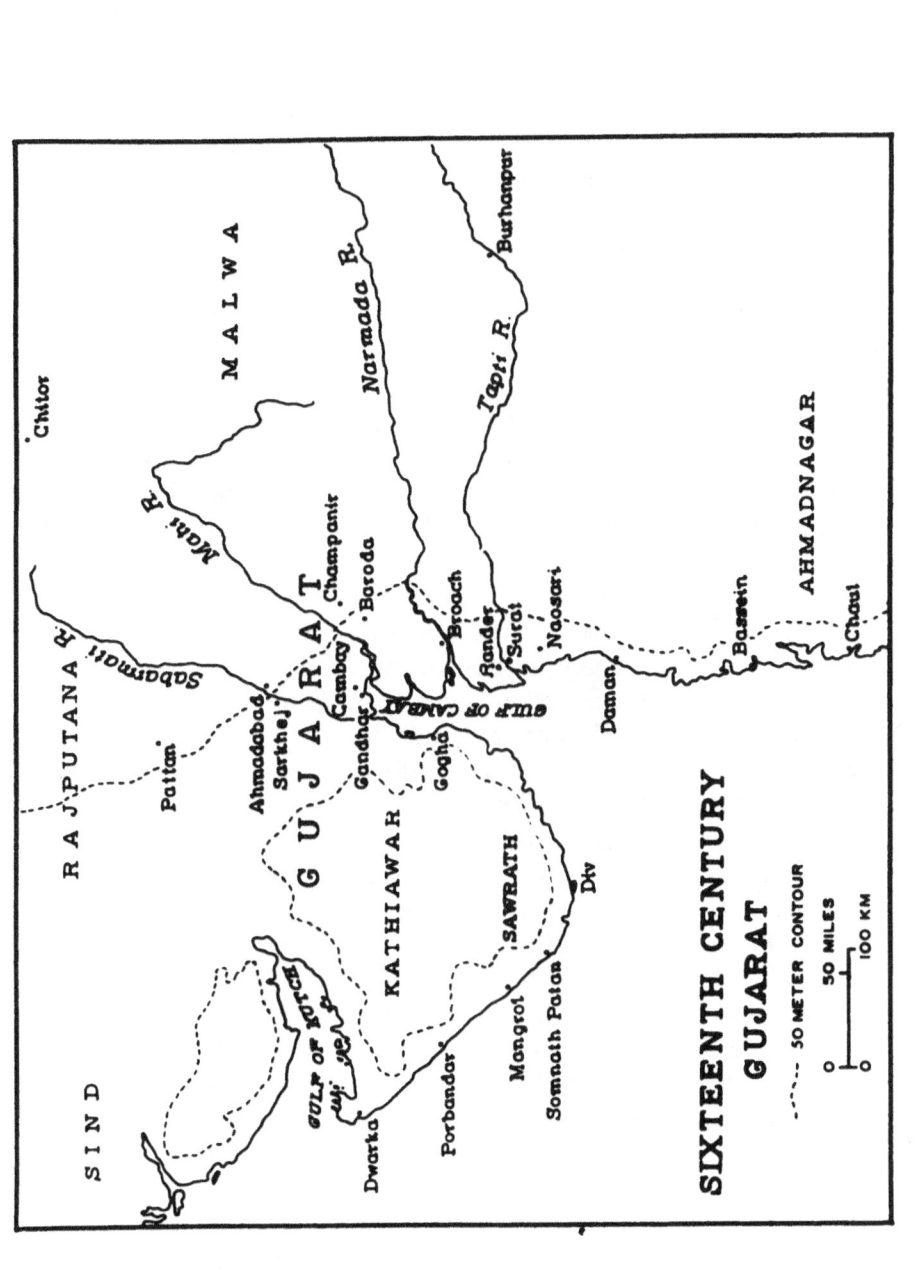

tried again. As usual the news travelled fast; a fleet of five ships was sent north from Goa. On the way they called at Daman, and were delayed by the local inhabitants, who complained strongly and demanded that the ships go no further. Daman's citizens knew that if anything happened to Qulij Khan's ship the lands of Daman would suffer as they had three years before. The admiral shrugged off these craven fears and proceeded to Surat, where he requested and got two more ships from Goa.

Again the cat and mouse game was played. The Portuguese admiral warned Qulij Khan not to dispatch his ship without a *cartaz*, and reminded the local merchants that they would do well to refuse to put their goods on the ship for the Portuguese intended to burn it if it left without permission. An attempt by the merchants to bribe the admiral into letting the ship sail failed. Finally they told Qulij Khan they were not going to risk their goods on his ship, which the annoyed *khan* then disarmed. The Portuguese, reassured, lifted the blockade.

This was another trick, for the ship left soon after, in April 1585, and without a *cartaz*. In Jiddah all the goods for the return voyage were off-loaded to ships with *cartazes*. Qulij Khan's ship was crammed with artillery and munitions and 200 chosen soldiers. In the midst of a storm it suddenly loomed up before the waiting Portuguese fleet in the Gulf of Cambay. Scorning their bombardment, it dashed right through their midst with cannon thundering from both sides. A narrow entrance north of Surat was missed, and Qulij Khan's ship ran aground. The Portuguese ranged up and for several days bombarded her at leisure. Anxious to save both his ship and his pride. Qulij Khan sent fourteen of his boats to aid the stranded vessel, coming in person with his cavalry. He told the Portuguese he had ordered troops south to invade Daman again, but the Portuguese staunchly held on and kept firing. Finally another storm arose. The ship broke up; Qulij Khan "lost both his ship, and, which disturbed him more, his reputation."[3]

What was the meaning of these alarms and excursions? Was Portugal often challenged at sea by Gujarat's rulers? Were merchants, both Portuguese and Gujarati, usually so circumspect?

This chapter will trace relations between the Portuguese and the Gujarati state. My aim is not to provide a detailed diplomatic survey, but rather to bring out the various constraints and perceptions among the rulers of Gujarat which dictated their response to the Portuguese.

---

[3] Couto, X, vii, 10; X, viii, 7.

This isolation of the upper political group, the administration, is not done arbitrarily, nor merely for organizational convenience. A full justification for treating the groups, state and merchants, separately will emerge later. Meanwhile, one may note that in sultanate Gujarat there were distinct links between various groups in the society; but to a large extent each group, including the upper, the military-political ruling elite, looked after itself and its interests and did not concern itself in detail with the affairs of other groups. In effect, I have sliced off horizontally the political elite. Other groups, and the vertical relations between them and the elite, will be elaborated later.

Sultans and Nobles in Gujarat

Two aspects of this upper political group in sixteenth-century Gujarat require elaboration. One needs to consider to what extent the sultans exercised effective control over the area known as Gujarat, and the relative weaknesses and strengths of the nobles vis à vis the sultans. For the purposes of this discussion, a noble is defined as a member of the court circle, entrusted by the sultan with some high-level governmental function. This excludes minor court functionaries, and also the hereditary Hindu nobility which controlled large areas of Gujarat, but as tribute payers were not members of the court circle.

The aim of any strong ruler of Gujarat was horizontal, territorial expansion rather than greater vertical penetration. The two most active rulers of sultanate Gujarat were Mahmud Bigarh (1458-1511) and Bahadur (1526-37). Both occupied themselves in conquests on their borders: Mahmud in Sawrath and to the east in Champanir, Bahadur to the south into Ahmadanagar, to the east into Malwa, and to the north into the Rajput states. Similarly, Akbar brought extensive areas, including Gujarat, into submission to his empire. By its conquest Akbar acquired additional revenue, and also power, for he now controlled more land. But he, and other conquerors, were also motivated by a desire for glory; a great king was one ruling a great area of land. Glory was not won by exercising closer control over one's subjects. Similarly, large areas were forced to tender allegiance to Gujarat at various times, but in considerable parts of the sultanate the Rajputs and Kolis, the pre-Muslim power figures in Gujarat, remained the effective rulers. These, and also local Muslim leaders, paid tribute only when they were forced to. When the center was weak they ran riot, but even under a strong sultan they were entitled to *banth*, or *chauth,* one-quarter of the land revenue, in their areas. Only one coherent attempt, and this one ultimately unsuccessful, was ever made to limit the power of these local figures.[4] Usually the sultans, and later the Mughals, contented themselves with trying to subdue only their top-level adversaries. In the three-eighths of Gujarat which, under the Mughals, were meant to pay tribute, the rulers were satisfied if tribute was paid occasionally. Precise sums, regularly paid, were never forthcoming. In the other five-eighths, where land revenue was collected, the ruler's control was greater but far from complete. In most of this area the payment of one-quarter due to the local power was accepted by the rulers. More important, many smaller divisions within these ten revenue-paying *sarkars* in fact did not pay revenue. Like the six tribute-paying *sarkars,* these smaller divisions were controlled by *zamindars* who paid tribute. Thus in a majority of the area of Gujarat there was in the sixteenth century no regular collection of land revenue, but only the payment of tribute, and this only "when it can be enforced."[5]

In effect then large, although unfortunately unquantifiable, areas of Gujarat were outside the direct control of the sultans or the emperors and their nobles. Even over the areas directly administered by one of his nobles a sultan was not always able to exercise complete control. Max Weber has elucidated the nature of tensions between a "patrimonial" ruler and his "notables,"[6] with the former trying to control closely the notables and the later endeavoring to expand their power, and ultimately become hereditary or even independent rulers. These tensions were clearly in existence in Muslim India in general, as evidenced in the rise of successor states when the centers of the Delhi Sultanate and later the Mughal Empire weakened. Sultanate Gujarat was not exempt from such tensions. Central authority was weak in the thirty-five years (1537-72) between the death of Bahadur and the conquest by Akbar; during these years Gujarat was in effect divided into several successor states which owed only nominal allegiance to the powerless sultans. In these fluctuating, and often mutually hostile, areas hereditary succession appears to have been the rule.[7]

---

[4] Sikandar, pp. 363-64; S. C. Misra, *The Rise of Muslim Power in Gujarat* (London, 1963), pp. 53, 66, 71, 284-85; Mirat, pp. 78, 149-50.

[5] Mirat, supplement, pp. 162, 164, 165, 173, 174, 181, 183, 189-200.

[6] Reinhard Bendix, *Max Weber: An Intellectual Portrait* (New York, 1962), pp. 341-60.

[7] For example, Couto, VII, ix, 8; VII, ix, 14. Generally for the situation in Gujarat in these years, see Couto, VI, x, 16; VII, ix, 8-9, 11-14; *Studia,* no. 3, p. 52; ANTTSL, III, ff. 296v-97; Sikandar, pp. 426-27, and 329-475 *passim.*

THE STATE   63

These tensions were muted, but not absent, in the years before Bahadur's death, when Gujarat's sultans were on the whole relatively capable. Indeed, the strongest of them all, Mahmud Bigarh, in effect encouraged his nobles to develop local bases of power, and continue their relatives in their possession, by his decrees. He laid down that when a *jagirdar* died, his son was to inherit his *jagir*. If he had no sons, his daughter was to be given half of it.[8] Many of his nobles built towns or villages, which points to their having a permanent base.[9] Thus Ahmadabad had 360 or 380 *puras* (suburbs; quarters), each of which was focused on the palace of the founding noble. Each *pura* had a mosque and was a city in itself, with all kinds of inhabitants there.[10] The sultans apparently seldom tried to move these nobles from one *jagir* to another. This could have restricted their ability to build up local power bases. Possibly the sultans simply never thought of such an idea, but more likely they usually lacked the power to be able to enforce such shifts, and so were dependent on other sanctions to restrain their nobles.

What in fact were the bases of power of the nobility and the sultans? Power consisted of control over resources, most notably land and people. A noble could attain this in two ways: through personal favor and influence with the sultan, assuming the latter was in relatively effective control, or through control of a specific area in Gujarat. In the latter case, distance from the sultan could be crucial, for if a noble's *jagir* was located far from the usual Ahmadabad-Champanir axis along which the sultans tended to move, his capacity to increase his power was enhanced. Conversely, a base in the environs of Ahmadabad would mean greater supervision from the sultan. Optimal power would be attained by a noble who could control a large distant local base while retaining influence at court.

This assumes, however, that a noble could in fact control his *jagir*. A sultan could pursue conquest on the cheap by assigning an area outside his control as a *jagir*. If the assignee could conquer the area, well and good; the area under the sultan's control thus increased. If the noble failed, the sultan still had lost nothing. In the fifteenth century one of Ahmad Shah's nobles was given a *jagir* of twenty-four villages in the wilds of Kathiawar, in an area infested by enemies and

[8]Sikandar, pp. 100, 131.
[9]Sikandar, pp. 162-67.
[10]Mirat, supplement, pp. 10-11. See also *ibid.*, pp. 11-17; James Burgess, *The Muhammadan Architecture of Ahmadabad*, part 1 (London, 1900), p. 55; M. S. Commissariat, *Studies in the History of Gujarat* (Bombay, 1935), p. 107.

robbers. He finally secured possession of ten villages. The narrator of this story remarked appropriately that "jagir" was best translated as "a place to be subjugated."[11] Such areas were usually far from the heartland. If control in such areas could be achieved by a noble, his power would be greater than that of a noble located nearer the sultan, but to achieve such control was not easy.

A sultan's task was essentially to maximize the degree of authority he had over his nobles, and extend the area of land ruled by himself through them. A strong sultan would thus seek to keep his nobles closely under his control, most typically by demanding frequent attendance at court for those controlling distant areas, and by extracting for himself as much as possible of the revenue collected by these nobles and by non-noble collectors. More obviously, control over greater amounts of resources could be achieved by conquests.

These observations need some qualification in detail:

1. The relative positions of sultan and nobles usually changed during the course of a reign. In the absence of any clear concept of primogeniture, a new sultan was usually dependent for support on his predecessor's officials. The story of nearly every reign is of the attempt of the sultan to reduce this initial dependance. Early in every reign rewards and favors were distributed by the new sultan to all who had supported him, and to all whose support he wanted. Later in the reign of a successful sultan rewards were given more often to men of his own creation, and established nobles were reduced at will.[12] The initiative was not solely with the nobility even early in a reign. In particular, the advantages to be derived from being one of the first supporters of an ultimately successful claimant to the throne were balanced by the dangers of overly precipitate support to a putative sultan who failed to make good his claim.

Three examples will illustrate these points. Mahmud III was aged eleven years when he became sultan, and for six years he was closely controlled by a noble called Darya Khan. In 1543 the sultan managed to exert his independence, mainly by taking advantage of the jealousy of the other nobles toward Darya Khan. A year later he was again relegated to puppet status as a result of an alliance of most of the powerful nobles against his favorite, a low-born bird-catcher whom

---

[11]*Selections from the Records of the Bombay Government*, n. s. no. XXXIX (Bombay, reprint of 1894), p. 29.

[12]Sikandar, pp. 173, 259-60, 263. For favors to nobles early in reigns, see *ibid.*, pp. 92, 93, 327-28. For the role of nobles in selecting a new sultan, Mirat, p. 74. For Mahmud Bigarh later in his reign, Sikandar, pp. 95-99, 113-14.

the sultan had elevated and who behaved arrogantly to the established nobility.[13] The general realignments of a new reign are illustrated by the career of Khan Jahan, who through four reigns retained his position, *jagirs,* and allowances, and was never removed or suspended. This was seen as extraordinary.[14]

The power of a relatively united nobility early in a reign, and their awareness that an established sultan could act freely, are demonstrated by the events following the accession of Sultan Daud in 1458. He at once began a very detailed inventory and checking of accounts, and started to elevate two low-born companions to positions held by established nobles. The nobles combined, and deposed the sultan, for, as they said, "If he performs such actions before he is firmly established, what will he refrain from doing when he is established?"[15]

2. In the matter of control over military resources the sultans were apparently at a disadvantage. Virtually the whole Gujarati army consisted of troops raised by the nobles. These troops were meant to be ultimately under the control of the sultan, yet in the event of a clash between sultan and noble they often stayed with their immediate superior, the noble. Apparently only Mahmud III tried to raise a body of troops directly under his own control and independent of his nobles, and this body consisted of a mere 1200 men.[16]

3. This apparent disadvantage was usually countered by another consideration, that of legitimacy. A sultan was, even when he was not of age or was ineffective, at least first among equals, and often first with no equals. Even a weak sultan was the fount of honors, titles and promotions for the nobles. As in the later Mughal Empire, so in Gujarat after 1537 the rulers retained this function to the end; and while an emperor or a sultan could be replaced, the institution remained even if it was shorn of all other sources of power except this one.

4. Influence with the sultan as a source of power for a noble was dependent on the effectiveness of the sultan. Thus, complete control of one of the later sultans bestowed less power than did moderate influence with, say, Mahmud Bigarh.

5. It is apparent that there was arable land to spare in Sultanate

---

[13]Sikandar, pp. 345-48.

[14]*Ibid.*, p. 218.

[15]*Ibid.*, pp. 92-93. The same thing happened to Sultan Sikandar, in 1526: Arabic History, I, 119.

[16]E. C. Bayley, *The Local Muhammadan Dynasties: Gujarat* (London, 1886), p. 449. The role of the army is elaborated in my chapter VI, pp. 151-52.

Gujarat. This acted as a check on the power of the nobles in their own areas. An unduly extortionate *jagirdar* could be checked by his peasants simply running away to live under a more moderate *jagirdar*, or in a tribute-paying area controlled by a Rajput or Koli. The harsh *jagirdar* would find his revenue decreasing as less and less of his land was utilized.[17]

6. The origins of the nobles were important. Sultanate Gujarat has not yet been subjected to the sort of treatment Athar Ali has given Awrangzeb's Mughal India,[18] and indeed it is probable that there is insufficient data in existence for such a study. It is, however, fairly clear that the situation in later seventeenth-century India, where 74.6 percent of *subahdars* were close relatives of previous or existing nobles,[19] was paralleled in sixteenth-century Gujarat. The son of a noble enjoyed a head start over an unknown in the battle for patronage. Further, a member of an older-established noble family had a more secure power base from which to operate; for it has been noted how frequently *jagirs* were hereditary, and how often nobles built towns and villages. Nevertheless, this was not a closed system. The new nobility included slaves, foreigners, and natives of lower origin.[20] These people could rise, but early in their careers they were necessarily much more dependent on the sultan's favor than were the older nobility. Some later managed to build power bases for themselves, as did Malik Ayaz in Div or Malik Gupi in Surat. A strong sultan, while taking care to conciliate the older-established nobles would prefer to rely mostly on new dependent nobles.[21] As a result of this, and also for reasons of status, there are examples of tension between old and new.[22]

7. This leads to a final and more important qualification. The

---

[17] For example, Sikandar, pp. 157-58.
[18] M. Athar Ali, *The Mughal Nobility under Aurangzeb* (New York, 1966).
[19] M. Athar Ali in *Medieval India: A Miscellany*, vol. I (Aligarh, 1969), p. 99.
[20] Malik Ayaz was a slave; two merchants of Rander helped Bahadur in 1526 in his rise to the throne, and were rewarded with incorporation in the nobility; and many of the nobles were foreign Muslims. An early sixteenth-century Portuguese account describes the nobility as speaking Arabic, Persian, and Gujarati, and coming not only from Gujarat but also from Turkey, Egypt, Arabia, Persia, Khorasan, and other parts of India. (Descrição, f. 17v.)
[21] From a noble's point of view, heredity combined with ability was the ideal. Thus in the late fifteenth century Jamal-ud-din, a grandson of Sultan Muzaffar, was made *fawjdar* of Ahmadabad. He succeeded brilliantly, and finally rose to be *vazir* of Gujarat (Sikandar, pp. 125-26), but perhaps he would never have become even a *fawjdar* if it were not for his ancestry.
[22] For example, Sikandar, pp. 162-65.

nobles were not a united or homogeneous group; a skillful sultan could balance one faction against another and so maintain or increase his control. There was a division between slave and free nobles, but there were also factions based on other criteria. The existence of such factions is clear, especially after the death of the last strong ruler, Bahadur,[23] when the struggle was over control of the sultan. The memberships of the factions of this time seem to have fluctuated considerably, and it is seldom possible to discern their bases. Undoubtedly private interest was important, but other considerations were also influential. Thus one noble, 'Imad-ul-mulk, was described in 1557 as the head of the foreigners,[24] and such a division, between foreign-born and Gujarati-born nobles, is an obvious one. Ten years earlier another noble, Mujahid Khan, was described as being supported by "all the Rajputs." The countries of origin of the nobles were clearly important, for in the 1550s there were Rumi (Turkish), Afghan, Habshi (Abyssinian), Persian and Mughal groups of nobles in Gujarat.[25] Other likely divisions, for which, however, evidence is lacking, would be based on kin networks, and on the basis of a particular noble's power. Those who controlled ports would presumably have different interests from those whose power was based on control of land; an exception was the celebrated quarrel in the 1510s, caused by the attempts of Malik Gupi, who controlled Surat, to foster his port at the expense of Malik Ayaz's Div.

Portuguese-Gujarati Relations

Until his death in 1522 the main adversary of the Portuguese in Gujarat was Malik Ayaz, the governor of Div. He combatted the demands of the Portuguese because acceptance of them would have been disastrous for him. He was successful because he had both military power and influence at court.

Malik Ayaz was born in Georgia. He had been enslaved and converted to Islam by the Turks, and finished up in the employ of Sultan Mahmud Bigarh (1458-1511) of Gujarat; he was thus one of the very large number of foreigners, usually Muslim, who served in military capacities in the sultanate.[26] According to the local legend, his rise

---

[23] Mirat, pp. 74, 80, 95, Arabic History, I, 318-19.
[24] ANTTCC, 1-102-47; Arabic History, I, 312.
[25] ANTTSL, III, 297; Arabic History, I, 312, 339, 407.
[26] For his death date, Sikandar, p. 213, has 929 AH (November 20, 1522-), Firishta 928 AH (December 1, 1521-)(John Briggs, *Rise of the Muhammadan*

to fame occurred after a bird defecated on the head of Sultan Mahmud. Malik Ayaz, who was in attendance at the time, brought the bird down with a well-aimed arrow, and as a reward was given the port of Div to govern. Despite his later wealth and power, he remained a slave of the sultans,[27] as indeed were so many important officials in other Muslim states. Under his rule Div prospered greatly from small beginnings, so that around 1500 it was starting to displace Cambay as the great transshipment center and mart of Gujarat; Malik Ayaz was second in power only to the sultan. In 1509 he was able to raise about Rs. 6,50,000 in a few days from his own resources and those of the merchants of his town.[28]

Unlike some of Gujarat's sultans and nobles, Malik Ayaz was not willing to accept Portuguese demands. True, he governed large areas in Sawrath apart from Div, and at different times also numbered Patan, Gogha, Surat, and Rander among his possessions.[29] Div, however, was his first and most crucial area. It was the basis of his power. The Portuguese estimated his total income from land revenue, customs duties, and other taxes in all his areas at Rs. 3,20,000 and half of this came from Div alone.[30] Apart from this, he was a very active trader on his own account. His ships sailed far and wide, and he bought up whole cargoes in Div and sold them inland.[31] He used his money to maintain a lavish proto-court, to fortify Div, to establish a strong fleet for its defense, and to maintain his influence at the sultan's court by heavy

---

Power in India, 4 vols. [Calcutta, 1908-10], IV, 95.) and M. S. Commissariat, 1522. (M. S. Commissariat, *History of Gujarat*, 2 vols. [Bombay, 1938-57], I, 279, 299.) Barros has him dead for more than eighteen months early in 1522 (III, vii, 8). His ancestry in Manuel de Faria e Sousa, *Asia Portuguesa*, 6 vols. (Lisbon, 1945-47), I, 255, and Barros, II, ii, 9. For foreigners in Gujarat, see Descricão, f. 17v; ANTTSV, XI, 108-8v; Arabic History, I, 27, 243, 439, 459-60. In 1546 Khwaja Safar, himself an Italian, had in his army men who had been in the siege of Rhodes. *Annaes Marítimos e Coloniaes*, 6 vols. (Lisbon, 1840-56), IV, 107.

[27]Sikandar, pp. 147, 162; "Dhamimah-i-Ma'athir-i-Mahmud Shahi," ff. 92, 107, 113: Faria e Sousa, I, 256; Nizam-ud-din Ahmad, *Tabaqat-i Akbari*, trans. B. De, 3 vols. (Calcutta, 1927-39), III, 282; Philip Baldaeus, *A Description of the East India Coasts of Malabar and Coromandal*, vol. III (London, 1703), p. 584.

[28]Marechal Gomes da Costa, *Descobrimentos e Conquistas*, 3 vols (Lisbon, 1927-30), II, 269-70. Assuming the same values as in appendix I, this is equal to $2,598,500 today.

[29]Castanheda, II, lxxv.

[30]Barros, II, ii, 9; R. J. de Lima Felner, ed., *Subsídios para a história da India Portugueza* (Lisbon, 1868), pp. 34-36.

[31]Castanheda, II, lxxv; Barros, II, ii, 9.

bribing and present-giving. The cornerstone of all these activities, and so of his very survival, was the possession of Div.

It is clear that Malik Ayaz would have preferred friendship and cooperation for mutual benefit with the Portuguese. He was more than willing to let them trade in his port; thus his customs revenues would increase, while the Portuguese, like all the other foreigners in Div, would benefit from the excellent facilities and location of the town. As the Portuguese chronicler recorded, Malik Ayaz was always pressing the viceroy to send to Div "two ships loaded with copper and spices so that he could trade with us. . . ."[32] Similarly, in 1513, after a surprise Portuguese attack on Div had failed, he nevertheless let the Portuguese establish a factory there.[33] This factory remained in operation for eight years, and other Portuguese, including agents of the king, traded in Cambay itself.[34] When Goa was besieged by a Bijapuri army in 1511, Malik Ayaz sent the defenders two shiploads of provisions and courtly letters.[35] Later he gave the Portuguese information on the activities of their enemies the Turks in the Red Sea; there is also extant a letter from him to the King of Portugal of 1519, consisting mostly of rhetorical flourishes and affirmations of friendship, but also offering D. Manuel a present.[36] I have already, however, demonstrated the nature of Portugal's demands in Asia. The choice for Malik Ayaz was between resistance and submission; cooperation was not offered.

To confront the Portuguese, he relied mostly on his formidable military strength. He had under his command a large army of both local and foreign soldiers, but the fortifications of Div and its navy were more important. The entrance to the port could be blocked by a large iron chain, and by three large hulks which were kept ready to be sunk when needed. There was also a stockade, and in the middle of the entrance a fort on an artificial island, surrounded by an artificial reef so that ships could not approach it. Other works and artillery were legion. His navy comprised at least 100 *fustas,* each one with twenty-five pairs of oars, one heavy cannon, and two lighter pieces. He also had a few larger war vessels, and many armed merchant

---

[32]Castanheda, II, lxxv.
[33]Faria e Sousa, I, 335-36, and generally Barros, II, viii, 5.
[34]*Cartas de Affonso de Albuquerque*, 7 vols. (Lisbon, 1884-1935), I, 138-39; "Cartas de Vice Reis," ANTT, no. 13; Castanheda, IV, xxxii; V, iii; Barros, III, iv, 7.
[35]Castanheda, III, lxxii.
[36]ANTTCC, 1-20-132; 1-25-95.

ships.³⁷ The Portuguese strategic position was weak, for with no base nearer than Goa or Hurmuz they were unable to lie off Div for the whole season when it was open to navigation.

The town was invulnerable to Portuguese attacks, but on the open sea Malik Ayaz's smaller craft were at a disadvantage. This was made apparent in 1508-9. The customs revenue of Mamluk Egypt had been seriously affected by Portuguese attacks on ships carrying spices from India to the Red Sea, so in 1508 a fleet under Amir Husain was sent south to drive out the Portuguese. Malik Ayaz joined thirty-four *fustas* of his own to this Egyptian fleet, and they sailed along the western Indian coast in search of D. Lourenço d'Almeida, the viceroy's son. Finding him in Chaul, the Egyptian fleet attacked at once, but Malik Ayaz waited until the outcome was clear, and then joined in to complete the rout of the Portuguese.³⁸ Despite their defeat; and the death of D. Lourenço, the Portuguese had fought well, and Malik Ayaz feared reprisals. To avert these, he tried to find D. Lourenço's body in order to give it an impressive burial. Failing, he hurried back to Div, where "on the one hand he wrote letters of condolence to the viceroy and on the other he fortified the city, as one who expected repayment for the help he had given Amir Husain, which repayment was not long delayed."³⁹

The viceroy, D. Francisco d'Almeida, arrived off Div early in 1509 with a large fleet, determined to avenge his son. He was successful. Although his own fleet suffered heavily, the Egyptian-Gujarati fleet, to which were joined ships from Calicut, was worsted in a long battle. Next day Malik Ayaz sent congratulations to D. Francisco, explaining that he had helped the Egyptians only because he had to, and offering to hand over Div to the Portuguese. It is unlikely that this offer was entirely sincere, for the town was as strong as ever, but to his surprise d'Almeida refused it anyway. His whole policy was opposed to the

---

³⁷Sikandar, pp. 162-65; Lima Felner, pp. 33-34; Barros, III, iv, 9; for his army, see Arabic History, I, 102-3.

³⁸Castanheda, II, lxxvii. My sole Persian source, the "Dhamimah-i-Ma'athir-i-Mahmud Shahi," claims that the Egyptian ships went first only as they were heavier and had artillery. (ff. 115-17.) In fact Malik Ayaz's ships also had cannon, and in any case this does not explain a delay of two days. For Sultan Mahmud's orders to Malik Ayaz to drive out the Portuguese, see "Dhamimah," ff. 106-7. For the battle and Sultan Mahmud's reception of the victors at Bassein, see Arabic History, I, 34-35.

³⁹Barros, II, ii, 9. See also Castanheda, II, xcvi, where one learns that he also treated the Portuguese captives he had taken at Chaul very lavishly, and got them to write D. Francisco praising his good treatment of them.

acquisition of land bases. Moreover, his own fleet had suffered in the battle, and he was sure he would not be able to hold Div if the sultan attacked from the land. Malik Ayaz had thus been able to test Portugal's naval strength at very little cost to himself, and he drew the obvious moral. The Portuguese *were* invincible at sea.[40]

In the remaining thirteen years of his life, Malik Ayaz concentrated on defending Div. As part of this defense, in the year before his death he tried to prevent the Portuguese from building a fort at Chaul, for this would give them a base much nearer Div and so increase the effectiveness of their patrolling. His small fleet was again worsted by the Portuguese, and the fort was built.[41]

During these last thirteen years Div survived easily two attacks by the Portuguese. In 1513 Governor Albuquerque, after narrowly failing to take Aden, decided to return to Goa via Div and see if he could surprise the port. Two of his ships arrived before the main fleet, so Malik Ayaz was forewarned. Ostensibly all was flowers and sunshine. He sent the Portuguese lavish presents and provisions, at the same time apologizing for his deficient hospitality, explaining that "he was nothing more than a customs collector for the king of Cambay."[42] Albuquerque asked to be allowed to establish a fort in Div, but Malik Ayaz regretfully explained that first he would have to get permission from the sultan. The conqueror of Goa, Malacca, and Hurmuz left in disgust, telling his captains that "he had never known a more suave courtier, nor a person more skilful in deception while at the same time leaving one feeling very satisfied."[43]

In 1520-21 the Portuguese tried again. After the rains of 1520 the governor, Diogo Lopes de Sequeira, sailed north. He had instructions from the king to take Div by force. To soften up the opposition he first cruised off South Arabia capturing ships coming from the Red Sea, and by this means caused considerable shortages in Div. Nevertheless, when he arrived to attack the city, he found it well prepared. Both sides dissimulated. Diogo Lopes pretended he had no hostile aims, while Malik Ayaz as usual was all friendship. Lavish provisions, secured with considerable effort, and presents were sent to the Portuguese ships, and he asked to be allowed to see a Portuguese woman,

[40]Barros, II, iii, 7; Correa, I, 947-48; Castanheda, II, ci; Gomes da Costa, II, 268; Faria e Sousa, I, 269-71.
[41]Barros, III, vi, 8-9.
[42]Castanheda, III, cxiv.
[43]Faria e Sousa, I, 335-36.

"as he wanted to see the women who could conquer [the hearts of] such gallant and noble men as were the Portuguese." Entering into the fun of it, Diogo Lopes produced a very beautiful Muslim woman, but "Malik Ayaz was so shrewd that he said 'Such a one as this could not conquer a Portuguese.'"[44] In a later reconnaissance Diogo Lopes was again deterred by Div's defenses, and was also tricked. Malik Ayaz's son told him that his father had gone to court to get permission for the Portuguese to have a fort in Div. Pleased with this good news, Diogo Lopes sailed happily away.[45]

Apart from the military attacks, Malik Ayaz had also to cover his rear by maintaining his influence at court and so preventing the sultan from granting Div to the Portuguese. True, even had the sultan done this, it is unlikely that Malik Ayaz would have tamely submitted. Div, however, would then have been vulnerable from the land. An attack by a Portuguese fleet backed by Portuguese soldiers operating on land, with or without help from the sultan's forces, would have posed a massive threat to Div. Malik Ayaz was thus concerned to block any rapprochement between the sultan and the Portuguese.

Such a rapprochement would almost certainly involve Div, for permission to build a fort there was the prime Portuguese demand, while to the sultans the port was not of crucial value. They received about Rs. 80,000 from the city,[46] much less than the Rs. 120,000 Malik Ayaz received. The port produced one-half of Malik Ayaz's official income, and a much greater proportion of his total income, as this included his trading profits from his operations based on Div. For the sultans Rs. 80,000 was a pittance. More generally, it will be remembered that customs duties in the whole state produced only 6 per cent of total government revenue.[47] They would probably be willing to let this or any other port go in the interest of a larger settlement.

Although he had told Albuquerque that he was "nothing more than a customs collector" for the sultan, and despite his status as a slave, Malik Ayaz was able in 1512-15 to counter a serious Portuguese attempt to get permission from the Gujarati court for them to build a fort in Div. Sultan Muzaffar Shah II (1511-26) had opened the negotiations by sending a messenger to Goa in 1512. The aim was to find

---

[44]Barros, III, ix, 7.

[45]There is some confusion in the sources on Diogo Lopes' visits; this seems to be the correct sequence. See Correa, II, 574, 606-8, 614-23; Castanheda, V, xlviii, li, lii; Barros, III, iv, 7; III, iv, 9; DUP, I, 376-82.

[46]R. J. de Lima Felner, op. cit., pp. 34-36.

[47]See also pp. 22-24.

some way of stopping Portuguese seizures of Gujarati ships, among them some belonging to Muzaffar himself. It seems clear that the court nobility were prepared to let the Portuguese have a fort in Div if in return their ships were allowed to trade freely. For most of the nobles their own sea trade was more important than whether or not Malik Ayaz kept Div, while one noble, a brahman called Malik Gupi who was governor of Surat, was actively in favor of a Portuguese fort in Div. This, he hoped, would eliminate Div as a rival to his own port.

In his opposition to such a fateful scheme, Malik Ayaz was helped by the intransigence of the Portuguese ambassador, who refused to allow free trade even if the fort was conceded; but his own efforts to win over his fellow nobles were more important. No doubt he argued strongly that such a fort would be equivalent to suspending a dagger over the heart of Gujarat's trade, and reminded Muzaffar of his loyal services to both himself and his father. Yet his main, and ultimately successful, weapon was perforce the lavish giving of bribes and presents to the nobles and the sultan. They could only be bought off, not convinced by what were in retrospect valid arguments, for only to Malik Ayaz was Div a crucial resource.[48]

The Malik died in 1522, and was succeeded by his oldest son, Malik Is-haq, as governor of Div.[49] Until the accession of Sultan Bahadur four years later, little changed. The Portuguese reestablished their factory, which had been withdrawn after the hostilities of 1521-22. Gujarati ships continued, as before, to trade under Portuguese auspices, with *cartazes*, and the Portuguese kept up their prohibition of trade to the Red Sea.[50]

Muzaffar Shah II had been a rather refined, ineffective figure, scholarly, pious, well-meaning, and indecisive. His third son, Bahadur, was different, as indeed he soon made apparent by his successful fight to gain the throne in 1526. His career provides a classic example of an expansionist ruler, both within and outside Gujarat. His armies expanded the sultanate's frontiers to the north, south, and east, at the

[48] For these dealings, see Barros, II, x, 1; Damião de Goes, *Crónica do Felicíssimo Rei D. Manuel*, 4 vols. (Coímbra, 1949-55), III, 243-44; Correa, II, 372-73; *Commentaries of Afonso Albuquerque*, 4 vols. (London, 1875-84), II, 210-17; III, 17, 245; IV, 59-61, 94-103; Castanheda, III, xcv, cxv, cxxcii, cxxxiii; for an excellent modern account, see Jean Aubin, "Albuquerque et les négociations de Cambaye," *Mare Luso-Indicum*, vol. I (Paris and Geneva, 1971).

[49] Sikandar, p. 203.

[50] Barros, III, ix, 3; IV, i, 5; IV, iv, 4; Castanheda, VII, viii; "Chancellaria de D. João III," ANTT, livro 36, f. 189; Couto, IV, i, 7; ANTTCC, 1-33-113, 2-166-56. The last shows that by early 1531 at least the factor had been withdrawn again.

expense of Ahmadnagar, Malwa and the Rajput states. Internally, Bahadur made concerted attempts to exercise a closer control over areas like Div which had been only loosely subject to his father's authority. He sought both horizontal and vertical expansion of his power, although in the latter area he penetrated only to the bottom of the upper level; he was concerned to reduce the independent power of some of his nobles, but he apparently made no attempt to exercise more than usual control below this.

Bahadur was given an easy excuse for an attack on Malik Is-haq, for the Malik had unwisely failed to climb aboard the bandwagon as Bahadur rode to the throne. Once firmly established, Bahadur used the traditional method of a Muslim Indian ruler to separate the loyal from the disloyal: he summoned Malik Is-haq to court to pay homage. The Malik prevaricated, saying he had to remain in Div to defend it from the Portuguese. Bahadur insisted on attendance.[51] Finally the Malik, despairing of his prospects in Gujarat, opened negotiations with the Portuguese. By handing over Div to them, he hoped to save his own skin and some of his treasure. Foiled by a subordinate loyal to Bahadur, he fled. Soon after, the sultan himself arrived and from then on exercised close control over the affairs of the port, a control manifested by his changing the governor of the town four times in the space of five years.[52]

Meanwhile, open war had broken out between Portugal and Gujarat. The immediate cause was a threat to the Portuguese fort at Chaul from Bahadur's forces, engaged in war with Ahmadnagar.[53] More important, however, was the bitter disappointment of the king of Portugal, D. João III, over the repeated failure of his governors to take Div, especially that of 1526 when Malik Is-haq had made his offer. The new governor, Nuno da Cunha, arrived in 1529 with instructions to take Div at all costs. He needed little urging, for it was clear that whoever could take Div would be richly rewarded by the king.

Hostilities opened in 1530 with a full-scale attack by a Portuguese armada on Surat — the first time a Portuguese armada had entered the Gulf of Cambay. The town was poorly defended, so its inhabitants

---

[51] Barros, IV, v, 6.

[52] F. de Andrade, *Chrónica do muyto alto e muyto poderoso Rey destes Reinos de Portugal, Dom João o III deste Nome*, 4 vols. (Coimbra, 1796), II, 193-94; Couto, IV, i, 7-8; IV, vii, 2; IV, vii, 4; IV, viii, 3; IV, ix, 1; Barros, IV, v, 6; IV, ii, 14-15; Sikandar, pp. 265, 274, 280; Castanheda, VII, vi-viii, xiii; ANTTCC, 1-35-37. (This letter refers to Malik Ayaz — the Portuguese used his name generically and applied it to his sons as well.)

[53] ANTTCC, 1-42-2.

with discretion had fled, taking all their valuables with them. The Portuguese landed unopposed and burned down the empty city. They then crossed the Tapti River to Rander, where light resistance was soon beaten off, and much booty taken. Rander was also burned, and indeed was never to regain its importance.[54] Early next year the governor himself sailed north to Div. He had with him 3,000 Portuguese soldiers and 5,000 Malabari and Kanarese auxiliaries, in a fleet of over 200 sail, the largest yet assembled by the Portuguese in India. A fortified island near Div was taken after a bloody resistance, but Div itself, bristling with defenses, was impregnable. To keep their spirits up, the Portuguese then returned to looting open cities, and in 1531-33 sacked and burned Gogha, Surat again, Mangrol, Somnath, Bassein and some other smaller ports.[55]

Even allowing for the hyperbole of the Portuguese chronicles, these attacks caused considerable destruction. Bahadur was unmoved, and indeed unconcerned. Gujarat's overseas traders were not closely controlled by their sultan in their commercial activities, but the reverse of the coin was that they were not protected by him either. It is true that Bahadur was more interested in sea trade and naval matters than perhaps any of his predecessors, with the possible exception of Mahmud Bigarh. He travelled frequently by sea, and pursued an active policy of building ships for both commercial and military purposes. These ships were admired by the Portuguese themselves, and were apparently as large in number of oars as contemporary Turkish vessels. Bahadur had a fleet of 160 sail at his death in 1537.[56] Yet all this was purely relative. While the Portuguese were raiding in the gulf, he was engaged on a more important matter, the conquest of territory.

It was only when he got into difficulties here that Bahadur remembered the Portuguese. In 1534 he found himself fighting against both the Rajput states of Chitor and Mandu, and the Mughal emperor Humayun, as well as the Portuguese. To free himself for the first two he liquidated the third. This was a clear indication of his priorities: eliminate the stings of the Portuguese and then get back to the really important matter of control over land.

[54]Castanheda, VIII, viii; Barros, IV, iv, 8.
[55]Barros, IV, iv, 12-15; IV, iv, 17; IV, iv, 22; IV, iv, 24; Castanheda, VIII, xxix, xxxi-v, xliii-v, l-liii; Couto, IV, vii, 2-5; Correa, III, 466-74.
[56]For travel by sea, see Sikandar, pp. 266-67; for ship-building, *ibid.*, p. 271; ANTTSV, XI, 97v; for the ships' sizes, ANTTSL, IV, 247-50; for Turkish sizes, ANTTSV, III, 306; for his fleet at his death, Barros, IV, vii, 7; for his attempts to prepare armadas of his own to guard Div's merchant ships, F. de Andrade, *op. cit.*, II, 193-94.

In December 1534 Bahadur signed a peace treaty with Governor Nuno da Cunha. The port of Bassein and its surrounding territories were ceded to the Portuguese. All Gujarati ships bound for the Red Sea had to call at Bassein to take a *cartaz*, and on the return voyage again go first to Bassein and pay duties. Ships trading to places other than the Red Sea were also to take *cartazes* but were not obliged to pay duties to the Portuguese, while coastal trade required no *cartaz* at all. Gujarat was to build no more warships, nor use those it already had. Other minor clauses concerned the restoration of Portuguese captives and the regulation of the horse trade.[57]

This treaty was in effect less than one year, and so had little practical importance. The provisions concerning *cartazes* and warships were potentially a considerable threat to Bahadur's independence, but only if they could be enforced. Bahadur in fact saw this treaty as a very temporary measure (as indeed it turned out to be). He ceded a less than crucial resource, the area of Bassein, to end what was to him a less than serious threat.[58] The cession of Bassein was the only tangible gain for the Portuguese, and this was not a great loss for Gujarat. Bassein was in the extreme south of the sultanate, and was only nominally subordinate to Bahadur at the best of times.[59]

His hopes were fruitless. By September 1535 he was in refuge in Div, a fugitive from the all-conquering Mughal armies. Humayun had won lightning successes, and Bahadur was desperate, ready to grasp at any faint hope. In the same month another, more fateful, treaty was signed with Nuno da Cunha. The Portuguese promised to help against Humayun. In return they were given permission to build a fort in Div. The cession of Bassein was confirmed, and ships trading to the Red Sea could now call at either Div or Bassein to get their *cartazes*. Other ships were still not obliged to pay duties to the Portuguese, but as before had to have *cartazes*.[60]

This treaty was in one respect a concession from the Portuguese,

---

[57]Couto, IV, vii, 8; IV, ix, 2; Barros, IV, iv, 27; B. Mus., Addl. 28433, ff. 174-75v; R. J. de Lima Felner, *op. cit.*, pp. 134-37; Castanheda, VIII, lxxxiv. Included in the ceded area was the small port, and fine harbour, of Bombay, which in the 1660s was ceded in turn to Charles II of England, and by him leased to the English East India Company.

[58]Castanheda, VIII, lxxxiv.

[59]José Wicki, "Duas Relaçoes sobre a situação da India portuguesa nos anos 1568 e 1569," *Studia* 8 (1961); 175-76.

[60]Couto, IV, ix, 7; Castanheda, VIII, c; Barros, IV, vi, 12; Lopo de Sousa Coutinho, *História de Cerco de Diu* (Lisbon, 1890), pp. 57-58; Arabic History, I, 214-15, 219-20.

for they had as yet no claim to any share of the customs duties paid at Div; thus ships trading to the Red Sea and calling at Div had only to take a *cartaz* from the Portuguese—they paid duties to Gujarat. The crucial clause, however, was the permission to build a fort, for this, the Portuguese hoped, would be only the opening wedge whereby they could later negotiate from a position of strength and acquire more rights in Div. In this they were successful, as will be seen, so this treaty was of fundamental importance in the achievement of their aims. In reality, the terms of the treaty made Div vulnerable to the Portuguese, and this was arrived at by chance, not military success. Their past attempts to take the port had all failed dismally.

Again one sees the importance of Bahadur's assessment of his resources. He also presumably could foresee that a fort would be only a first step for the Portuguese, but the *farangis* were so obviously anxious to have their fort, and their help against Humayun would be better than nothing. In any case, Div was not such a great prize to lose even if they did eventually take it all. The port was lost because Bahadur's interests were not those of Malik Ayaz; to the latter it was a vital resource, to the former it was not.

The stages by which the Portuguese acquired full control may now be quickly sketched. In a few months Bahadur bitterly regretted his concession, for Humayun, feckless as ever, decided to leave Gujarat with most of his army in order to deal with the emerging threat from Sher Khan in Bihar. Bahadur, with a very little help from the Portuguese, had no difficulty in retaking all of Gujarat. He had allowed the Portuguese to build their fort, but now had no need of their help. Early in 1537 he returned to Div, apparently interested in destroying the offending fort if this were at all possible. After a period of maneuvering, Bahadur was drowned after leaving a Portuguese ship to return to land. The Portuguese seized the chance to take over the whole island and, in an audacious attempt to interfere deeply in Gujarati politics, set up a previously obscure relation of Bahadur's as sultan. This man, Muhammad Zaman Mirza, gave the Portuguese "thousands and thousands and lakhs and crores [of money]" in return for their allowing his name to be included in the *khutbah* at Friday prayers in Div.[61] The Portuguese dictated to him a treaty making large concessions. But this puppet was soon deposed by the supporters of

---

[61] Mir Abu Turab Wali, *History of Gujarat* (Calcutta, 1909), p. 36. The inclusion of one's name in the *khutbah* was an important part of a struggle for a throne. It signalized, or constituted a bid for, support from the orthodox Muslim group.

Mahmud III (1537-54) and in 1538 their forces, helped by a Turkish fleet, reconquered the town of Div and laid siege to the fort.[62]

The successful defenses of Div in the two sieges of 1538 and 1546 are among the most renowned military exploits of the Portuguese. The Portuguese fort was built on the island of Div, but the island was easily accessible from the mainland. On the other hand, the fort was sited so that it could be provisioned from the sea. Thus the sieges took place during the rainy season (June to September) during which time navigation to Div was impossible or at least difficult. In both sieges the Portuguese garrisons were able to hold out, although only by the skin of their teeth, until the monsoon ended and help could come from Goa, Bassein and Chaul.

In the first siege the Gujarati forces were led by Khwaja Safar, an Italian who had been employed as treasurer to Mustafa Khan, a Turkish general who had besieged Aden and then come to Div in 1531 and entered Gujarati service. Mustafa Khan became Rumi Khan and served Bahadur until he deserted to Humayun in 1535. Khwaja Safar remained in Div. He was one of the only two people who accompanied Bahadur on his ill-fated visit to da Cunha's flagship and survived to tell the story. Subsequently, he cooperated with the Portuguese for a year, then left, was made captain of Surat, and returned soon after as leader of the Gujarati forces besieging Div by land.[63] In pressing the siege, however, the ships and artillery of the fleet provided by the Ottoman Turks were most effective. These Turks acted in a most overbearing manner toward their allies, while the Gujaratis were understandably concerned as to what exactly would be the price of the Turks once the Portuguese were defeated. Cooperation was minimal, and the Turkish fleet finally left in a huff. Its admiral later complained of the poor reception he had been given by the Gujaratis, and even cast aspersions on the quality of Islam in Gujarat.[64]

The Portuguese were thus able to hold out, and peace was establish-

---

[62] For these events, see Couto, V, i, 2; Lopo de Sousa Coutinho, pp. 80-84; Castanheda, VIII, clxvi; Barros, IV, viii, 6-10; R. J. de Lima Felner, *op. cit.*, p. 228; Arabic History, I, 222-23. The date of Bahadur's death was 943 AH and this was found in "Slain by the *farangi* dogs." (S. A. A. Tirmizi, ed., "Tarikh-i-Salatin-Gujarat," *Medieval India Quarterly* V [1963]: 71.) This dictated treaty of March 1537 gave the Portuguese the whole coastline between Mangrol and the Island of Bete, just east of Div, and between Daman and Bassein, extending five miles inland; see ANTTCC, 1-58-73.

[63] Faria e Sousa, III, 150-54; Correa, III, 784, 852-60; Castanheda, VIII, xv, xxvi, xxxiii, cii; Couto, V, i, 7-9; ANTTCC, 1-56-86; António Baião, ed., *História quinhentista (inedita) do segundo cerco do Dio* (Coímbra, 1927), pp. 5, 9.

[64] ANTTCC, 3-14-44. Also see Arabic History, I, 226-27.

ed in March 1539. Their large gains of 1537 were lost, but the wedge was driven in a little further. Their fort was to be separated from the city of Div by a wall, and all Portuguese were to return to the fort at night. All ships leaving Div were to pay customs duties at the customs house, after which they would be given a *cartaz* by the Portuguese captain, while ships sailing from other Gujarati ports were also required to obtain a *cartaz* at Div, but apparently not to pay duties there. These customs revenues were to be divided, with the Portuguese receiving one-third and Gujarat two-thirds of the total.[65] Late in the next year the proportions were changed to one-half each. The Gujarati nobles were at this time bitterly divided over who was to control the young Sultan Mahmud III, and their divisions enabled the Portuguese to obtain this concession after a little pressure had been applied.[66]

It was too much to expect Gujarat and Portugal to cooperate harmoniously in dividing up Div's revenues, and tension increased throughout the early 1540s, until its culmination in the second siege of 1546. On the Gujarati side there were numerous complaints, mostly justified, for the Portuguese consistently applied pressure on them and tried to extend their authority. In 1540-41 the Goa government complained to the sultan that Khwaja Safar was fortifying Surat, where he was still captain. The Portuguese rather arbitrarily considered this to be a hostile act, but they were sharply rebuffed by the sultan, who refused to acknowledge that they had any business in what was done in Surat.[67] Off Div Portuguese *fustas* patrolled, forcing all ships bound for Cambay to enter and pay duties in Div; while they were there, the Portuguese captain, D. João Mascarenhas, made these merchants sell him goods at low prices and in other ways abused his position.[68] Further, the Portuguese had destroyed the wall between the town and the fort, since they feared, probably with considerable justification, that it could be used for military purposes. Khwaja Safar complained of Gujarati ships being forced to take *cartazes* even when they were only going from one Gujarati port to another.[69] From the Portuguese side, there were complaints of cheating in the division of the customs revenues.

Tension increased as neither side was satisfied with the existing

---

[65] Couto, V, v, 8; Lima Felner, *op. cit.*, pp. 228-32.
[66] ANTTSL, V, 98; VI, 6v; Couto, V, vii, 1; Correa, IV, 215-16, 221, but he has his dates muddled.
[67] Correa, IV, 143, 159; *Studia*, no. 9, p. 233.
[68] Correa, IV, 454; Gavetas, V, 327.
[69] ANTTSL, V, 155; Couto, VI, i, 7.

situation. In October 1545 Mascarenhas advised the new governor, D. João de Castro; "If you don't have much on your hands there [in Goa] you should take a trip up here and capture this city for the king..."[70] Meanwhile, Khwaja Safar had either stopped asking for *cartazes* for his ships bound for the Red Sea or the Portuguese had refused to give them to him. His ships were now sailing well armed, and there were several clashes between them and Portuguese fleets early in 1546.[71] The sultan tried to secure support from Calicut, Ahmadnagar, and Bijapur for a joint attack on the Portuguese forts in western India. After the siege started these efforts were redoubled, and Castro in turn courted Sher Shah in Delhi. As it transpired, these attempts came to nothing and the second siege was undertaken by Gujaratis alone.[72]

The crucial point about these two sieges—crucial because it explains the Portuguese success and because of the light it casts on the interests of the Gujarati nobility—is that as far as Gujarat was concerned both were largely one man efforts. In the first Khwaja Safar was helped by the Turks, but not by the other nobles. In the second, Mahmud III undertook these diplomatic maneuvers, presumably at Khwaja Safar's instigation, but he did nothing else to help. Nor did any of the influential nobles at court. The besieging army was led by, and paid by, Khwaja Safar.[73] This Italian renegade had more reason than the other nobles to oppose the Portuguese. His ships, and those of merchants resident in his town of Surat, had been subjected to harassment and their crews to bad treatment in Div. Khwaja Safar's revenue was based on his possession of Surat, and thus ultimately on sea trade. It was a considerable revenue. In 1537 he was estimated to

[70] ANTTSL, V, 141v-42. See also ANTTCC, 1-77-36.
[71] Elaine Sanceau, ed., *Cartas de Dom João de Castro* (Lisbon, 1955), pp. 227-30.
[72] *Ibid.*, pp. 141-44, 242-43, 327-33; ANTTSL, III, 142-42v, 146v, 148, 150-50v, 152, 230v, 254; IV, 339; V, 235-38. On III, 150-50v is Mahmud III's letter to the Zamorin, in which he talks of his great captains who will attack the Portuguese and of how much money he is spending. Apparently this was all talk, solely designed to tempt the Zamorin into helping him by joining in attacking the Portuguese. These other rulers saw no reason to attack the Portuguese just because the sultan of Gujarat asked them to. But both before and after 1546, all three did challenge the Portuguese at times when their own interests were threatened.
[73] *Annaes Marítimos e Coloniaes*, IV, 107; ANTTSL, III, 53v, 60. The account in the Arabic History (pp. 231-41) is long and confused, but it is clear that Khwaja Safar was not helped by any of the important nobles of Gujarat, nor by the sultan, although the latter was annoyed at the failure of the siege. During the siege Afzal Khan and the sultan visited Khwaja Safar's camp for three days only, "by way of pleasure."

be worth Rs. 12,00,000 at least.⁷⁴ This vital trade was being hampered by the Portuguese in Diu. Apart from the economic loss here, he claimed it was "belittling" for Gujarati ships to have to take *cartazes* before they were allowed to sail on their own coast. He thus posed as the champion of Gujarat's traders, as well he might, for his wealth was dependent on their trade.⁷⁵

When Khwaja Safar built his fort on the Tapti River in Surat, the date of its completion was found in the chronogram "May this structure prove a load on the chest and life of the *farangis*."⁷⁶ Gujarat's other nobles did not feel nearly so bitter. Portugal's activities on the coast were of minor concern to them. They were at the time involved in an internecine struggle over control of Sultan Mahmud III. The really important prizes depended on the results of this struggle.

The siege of 1546 also failed, after another desperate defense by the Portuguese. During it Khwaja Safar, and later his son, were killed. The Portuguese reinforcements, headed by Castro's sons and later by the governor himself, drove the Gujaratis from the island; their fleets cruised in the gulf again, sacking and burning. Gujarati peace feelers in December 1546 and later⁷⁷ were turned down by Castro, and the destruction in the gulf continued. Gogha, Surat, Rander, Broach, and Daman were all taken, looted, and burned.⁷⁸ Castro's position, however, was weakening all the time. Bijapur attacked Goa, while various interests were hurt by the continuation of the war and the consequent cessation of trade between Portuguese areas and Gujarat. Such diverse people as the Raja of Cannanor, the citizens of Goa, and D. Francisco Lima, a prominent *fidalgo*, all advised the governor to make peace.⁷⁹ When this was done, in January 1549, the Portuguese were negotiating from a much weaker position than they had had late in 1546, for the war, especially as it involved great loss of customs revenues, was very expensive. This is reflected in the terms, which restored the complete *status quo ante*, neither side making any gains.⁸⁰

The Portuguese were only biding their time. In 1554-55 the Gujarati

⁷⁴*Studia*, no. 10, p. 191.
⁷⁵Couto, VI, i. 7.
⁷⁶*Maathir-ul-Umara*, II, 534. The addition of the numerical values conventionally assigned to the Persian letters of this sentence comes to 947, or the *hijrah* year corresponding to 1540.
⁷⁷ANTTSL, III, 296v-97; IV, 209.
⁷⁸DUP, I, 582; Faria e Sousa, *Asia Portuguesa*, III, 163-77.
⁷⁹ANTTCC, 1-81-104; ANTTSL, III, 185, 189, 480-81v.
⁸⁰Couto, VI, vii, 4.

nobility was even more divided than usual following the murder of Sultan Mahmud III. The Portuguese had been particularly worried in the early 1550s by the possibility of another Turkish-Gujarati attack on Div,[81] so they now seized the chance to take over the government of the whole island of Div, in 1554, and all its customs revenues in 1555. From this time, at least, they forced all ships trading to or from Gujarat to call at Div and pay duties to them.[82] The long conquest of Div was at last completed; fifty years after their first contacts with the port they had finally secured it completely for themselves. In their first year of full control the customs house yielded Rs. 2,40,000 for the king.[83] Div was not openly attacked from the land again until 1961 when India "liberated" the remains of Portugal's Indian empire.

The next target was Daman, for the possession of this port would provide another area in which Portuguese could be settled and given land as rewards. Further, a fleet patrolling from Div to Daman, a distance of about 120 miles, would be much more effective in guarding the entrance to the Gulf of Cambay than was one operating between Bassein and Div, a distance of 180 miles. Portuguese and Persian sources differ concerning the cession of this area to the Portuguese by a Gujarati noble. Sikandar has it being ceded in 1559 by Chengiz Khan, but two Portuguese sources have 1557 and 1558, with the noble responsible being Chengiz Khan's father 'Imad-ul-mulk.[84]

The most reliable of the three claims that the area was ceded by 'Imad-ul-mulk, at that time the most powerful noble in Gujarat, in return for peace with the Portuguese, as their attacks hindered the trade of his many ships. 'Imad-ul-mulk gained secure trade and lost nothing. Daman was effectively controlled by a party of Abyssinians. After its formal cession the Portuguese had to conquer it from these people. Like Bassein, Daman had apparently not been controlled by the center for some time. Thus, in 1540 after Bahadur had ceded Bassein, the governor of Daman attacked the Portuguese, claiming that part of the area given to the Portuguese was in fact his. The shadowy nature of Gujarat's control in this southern coastal strip is further shown in the way in which, as soon as the Portuguese took

[81]ANTTCC, 1-86-89; 1-86-120; 1-87-50. For divisions after Mahmud III's death, see Arabic History, I, 318-19.
[82]Couto, VI, x, 16; VI, x, 19; VII, i, 9; VII, ii, 3.
[83]Couto, VII, ii, 3.
[84]Sikandar, pp. 426-27; ANTTCC, 1-102-47; Couto, VII, iii, 1-2; VII, vi, 3; Arabic History, I, 350-52.

Daman, they started paying a tribute called *chauth,* later claimed by Sivaji, to another local raja. Further, the Persian source describes Daman as a *"muzafat,"* an appendage, of the sultanate, not as part of its *"mulk,"* or land.[85]

In the remaining thirteen years of its existence, the nobility of the sultanate became more and more factionalized, a situation which ultimately led to Akbar's easy conquest in 1572-73. The Portuguese apparently considered themselves at war with Gujarat, at least until 1561, but from when is not clear. In any case, this had little practical effect, and with one exception relations were in fact amicable enough. The exception was an attempt by the Portuguese to seize Surat in 1560-61 which in the event proved abortive.[86]

The change in the status of Gujarat in 1572-73 from an independent sultanate to a *subah* of Akbar's Mughal Empire made little difference to most of its inhabitants, nor did it to the Portuguese. During the conquest a gesture was made toward Daman, which Akbar pretended to believe was part of Gujarat. The attack was not pressed, and a treaty of peace, embodied in a *farman,* was signed in March 1573. The Portuguese were left with Daman, Akbar promised not to shelter the Malabar pirates, and he was given one free *cartaz,* on which no duties were payable, for a voyage to the Red Sea each year.[87]

By petitioning for, and receiving, the free *cartaz* Akbar tacitly recognized the Portuguese claim to be controllers of Gujarat's sea

---

[85] Couto, V, vi, 10; VII, vi, 6; Sikandar, p. 426. This Persian source uses several Persian words, apparently interchangeably, for "land" or "country": most often *vilāyat* (pp. 100, 101, 134, 144, 272), but also *bilād, mulk, 'arṣah,* and *aṭrāf* (pp. 272, 258, 99). The last of these can have the connotation of district, or environs. There does seem to be a distinction between words meaning "country," and *aṭrāf,* which implies an area of less than a total country, or *muẓāfat,* which implies a smaller area located on the edge of a *vilāyāt* such as Gujarat.

[86] Couto, VII, ix, 8-9; VII, ix, 11-14; the future chronicler, at this time aged 18, was a member of Portuguese forces which made this attempt. For the continuance of a state of war in 1557 and 1561 at least, see ANTTCC, 1-102-47; *Studia,* no. 3, p. 52.

[87] Couto, IX, cap. 13; the *Mirāt-i Ahmadi,* p. 100, has a story of the Portuguese being interested in picking up Surat during the confusion of the conquest, but seeing discretion as the better part of valor once they saw "the grandeur and power of his majesty." This is not mentioned in the Portuguese sources. See Couto, IX, caps. 19 and 28 for other negotiations in 1573-75 of little significance, and IX, cap. 32 for a minor crisis of 1575-76. A Portuguese ambassador to Akbar was imprisoned in Cambay as the governor of the town wanted to pressure the Portuguese captain of Div into giving him a very fine horse which the captain had just bought. The captain was forced to comply.

trade. Nothing so damaging to his dignity was ever openly admitted by a Mughal emperor, but throughout the seventeenth century they continued to ask for and receive their one free *cartaz* a year. Further, they occasionally would request variations in the usual form — perhaps an additional *cartaz,* or permission for the ship to leave from a port other than Surat. Akbar had as much pride as any ruler of India ever had. It is clear that he was prepared to do this because he, like most of the sultans and nobles before him, did not see this as a particular infringement on his sovereignty.

In any case, the situation was not wholly to the advantage of the Portuguese. They were well aware of Akbar's puissance, and of the vulnerability of several of their forts on the western Indian coast, especially Daman. Thus they took pains not to offend the Mughals, although at the same time insisting on their control of sea trade. There were occasions when a free *cartaz* ship was allowed to leave from Gogha instead of Surat, despite the loss this entailed to the customs revenues of Div, and an extra free *cartaz* was granted a few times.[88] In fact the whole business of the free *cartaz* was very irksome for the Portuguese. The merchants of Surat were no fools. In the Red Sea they would load all their most valuable goods onto Akbar's free ship, and these would go direct to Surat and not pay customs to the Portuguese. Their bulkier and less valuable goods were loaded on their own ships in the Red Sea, and paid duties in Div. The consequent loss to the Div customs revenue was variously estimated at Rs. 46,000 and Rs. 1,05,000.[89] Despite their grumbles, the Portuguese knew the price was cheap as it usually ensured neutrality from the Mughals.

Relations between the Mughals and the Portuguese were thus tranquil enough most of the time. Such minor clashes as did occur should be seen as aberrations, mistakes rather than attempts to change the *status quo*. The Portuguese felt that their crucial resources were being protected, while the Mughals felt that their interests were not being affected detrimentally, or, more likely, were not being affected at all. The clearest example is the episode narrated at the beginning of this chapter. It seems clear that Muhammad Qulij Khan was just a little

[88]Couto, IX, cap. 19; X, ii, 1; Bocarro, Decada, p. 396; APOCR, III, 198; A. Botelho de Costa Veiga, ed., *Relação das plantas e descrições do todas as fortalezas, cidades, e povoações que os Portugueses tem no Estado da India Oriental* (Lisbon, 1936), p. 21.

[89]Couto, IX, cap. 13; AHU, Caixa 3, no. 4; LMBP, III, 162-63; Artur Viegas, ed., *Relação Anual das Coisas que Fizeram os Padres da Companhia de Jesus nas suas missões,* by Padre Fernão Guerreiro, 3 vols. (Lisbon, 1930-42), II, 389-90.

slow to understand the system; it is also significant that he is described as being a devout sunni Muslim. Such a man would presumably feel less inclined to submit to the Christian Portuguese than would a Muslim who wore his religion more lightly. More important, perhaps, he was governor of Surat, and thus, like Khwaja Safar, Portuguese control was much more immediate to him than to most of his peers. Other Mughal officials apparently felt no need to emulate him. There was a half-hearted attempt to take Div by treachery in the 1590s, while the Portuguese remained interested in seizing Surat if this could be done on the cheap, which in fact was never possible.[90] Fairly minor clashes occurred in 1613-15, and 1630, which need not be detailed here, and there was great excitement once in Goa over the supposed conversion of a Mughal ambassador, Muqarrab Khan, who was a close friend of the emperor Jahangir.[91] The situation as regards *cartazes* hardly changed; they continued to be asked for and issued throughout the seventeenth century.

Analysis of the Response

The detail of this chapter deals with battles and sieges, defiance and retaliation, but it is clear that in fact Gujarati-Portuguese relations in the sixteenth century were on the whole fairly low key. The resistance or defiance of Malik Ayaz, Khwaja Safar and Qulij Khan should be seen as the actions of nobles with special interests. Bahadur was much more typical in that he abandoned Div in an attempt to safeguard what were to him and most of his nobles more important interests. Especially once the major Portuguese demand, the acquisition of Div, had been accepted relations were calm enough.

[90] APOCR, III, 201, 475-76; Couto, X. iv. 6-7: X, iv, 9; Faria e Sousa, *op. cit.*, V, 40-41: Artur Basilio de Sá, ed., *Documentação para a história das Missões do Padroado Português do Oriente. Insulíndia*. 5 vols. (Lisbon, 1954-), V, 153; B. Mus., Addl. 20861, ff. 109, 241v.

[91] For 1613-15, see Bocarro, Decada, pp. 221, 230, 259, 301-02, 308-14, 395-97; APOCR, VI, 986; AHU, Caixa 3, no. 37. The war started after a dispute over the Portuguese right to search ships with *cartazes* to make sure all their provisions were being observed. The Portuguese captain concerned was imprisoned and later fined for his over-zealous attention to duty. (LMBP, V, 112-13.) For the 1630 war, see LM, v. 14, ff. 319, 361-61v, 363-64; Assentos, I, 276. 531-35. For Muqarrab Khan's "conversion", see LM, v. 12, f. 23. "This embassy from the Mughal Empire, and the whole agreement, and the hopes people had from it, were all fabulous. As soon as the ambassador got home again he went on being a Muslim as before, with little respect to Christianity . . .". Thus the disillusioned viceroy.

Why was this? First, it must be stressed that there *was* an alternative. The sultans, let alone the Mughals, *could* have expelled the Portuguese from Gujarat. The two sieges of Diu failed, but in neither was the full force of the sultanate brought to bear, while Diu could never have held out against the expert artillery of the Mughals. Daman and Bassein, being larger and less well fortified, could easily have been overrun. The group of private Portuguese traders living in Cambay would of course have presented no military problem. Indeed, these people could be, and on occasion were, captured and used as pawns by the authorities in Gujarat in disputes with the Portuguese. Much more crucial to the Portuguese were the goods which went south from Cambay to Goa on the *cafilas* each year. This trade could easily have been stopped at its source, and this would have been disastrous for the Portuguese. It is true that a coordinated attack would have drawn retaliation in the Gulf of Cambay from the Portuguese, and they would have attempted to block all Gujarat's sea trade. But if Diu, Daman, and Bassein were taken, the Portuguese fleets, operating from Chaul and Hurmuz, could not have been effective enough to cause unacceptable damage to the sultans or the Mughals, while they in turn, especially by blocking the *cafilas*, could have hurt the Portuguese very badly. Such a coordinated attack thus could have succeeded, and been followed by negotiations in which perhaps the *cafilas* were allowed to start again in return for Gujarati ships not being obliged to take *cartazes*. It is fair to say that the whole Portuguese control of Gujarat's sea trade was based on a bluff. Why was it never called?

The answer is implicit throughout the previous discussion. The Portuguese *were* vulnerable, but only if most of the Gujarati upper political level felt threatened by their activities. Militarily they could have been challenged, but if the majority of the people in Gujarat who could have initiated such a challenge did not feel any urge to do this, then they were effectively invulnerable. They were able to operate their system, secure in the knowledge that the people who could have stopped them did not want to.

There were even many nobles in charge of Gujarati ports who did not oppose the Portuguese. These people are usually nameless in the historical records, but one can assume that they accepted the Portuguese system. Had they not, the Portuguese chronicles would mention them, if only as Moors who were defeated by the heroic Portuguese. Such people, the governors of Broach and Cambay for example, were only a small proportion of the total Gujarati nobility, yet their failure to challenge the Portuguese merits some consideration.

Part of the answer lies in economics. Ships sailing from their ports paid duties to the Portuguese in Diu, and sailed with *cartazes* under Portuguese control. Nevertheless, they still paid duties at their home ports. Thus neither the governors of these ports, nor the rulers of Gujarat, who derived revenue from their share of these duties, suffered economic loss. Malik Ayaz was not in this position, for the Portuguese wanted to capture Diu. Khwaja Safar was in between. The Portuguese did not stop him from collecting duties in Surat, but they did exercise their control in a very irksome way, attacking his ships and abusing the traders when they called at Diu.

These sorts of abuses were largely ended soon after the second siege of Diu. Complaints of ill treatment there continued, but over all it is clear that the Portuguese later in the century were concerned to encourage local trade under their control, both in Gujarat and elsewhere, for thus customs revenues increased. Portuguese India gradually became self-sustaining, its revenue based on the Portuguese country trade and on control of local trade rather than on the trade to Portugal. As the century wore on the Portuguese made it easier for these governors to accept their control.

It is indeed possible that the "corruption" of the Portuguese officials in Diu, as opposed to the straight abuses to which Khwaja Safar objected, made it easier for these few governors to accommodate. The evidence is skimpy, but it is reasonable to assume that Portuguese and Gujarati captains, both holding their offices as personal property rather than as public trusts, were at times able to reach agreements which resulted in mutual profit. There are some indications. The governor of Cambay town derived increased customs revenues from the new trade to Goa which the Portuguese helped to create. True, this trade represented only 5 percent of Gujarat's total trade, but it was at least something.[92] The private Portuguese living in Cambay also helped to increase the town's revenues.

Khwaja Safar himself used a Portuguese as his business agent in Diu and Goa. This gentleman, Ruy Freire, became so attached to his employer that he finally tried to betray the fort of Diu to him.[93] Khwaja Safar also at least once used a Portuguese as a source of capital, for on his death he owed an official in Bassein Rs. 12,000. This money had been lent to Khwaja Safar recently, presumably during the time when Khwaja Safar's ships were beating off Portuguese attacks near the Red

[92] Bocarro, Livro, part 1, pp. 279-88, and cf. pp. 22-24.
[93] Couto, VI, i, 6.

Sea. As soon as he heard of Khwaja Safar's death, the Portuguese official petitioned Governor Castro for repayment of his money from Khwaja Safar's estate.[94] Even as war loomed, and later raged, Khwaja Safar and the Portuguese official refused to have their commercial dealings interrupted. Similarly, Portuguese traders and their goods were welcomed in Khwaja Safar's port of Surat.[95] No doubt there were other arrangements reached—perhaps a small bribe would clear the way for a noble's ship to transport some pepper, or ease the granting of a *cartaz* for a "forbidden" area.

Nevertheless, too much should not be made of such accommodations. They seem to have been minor enough. Those few Gujarati nobles who were interested in sea trade accepted Portuguese control partly because they did not lose their own revenues by their acceptance, and partly because in the last resort they had no choice. The failures of Khwaja Safar showed clearly that the Portuguese could not be expelled by one noble, however powerful, yet the governor of Cambay, for example, must have known that there was no chance his fellow nobles would help him against the Portuguese.

What in fact were the main resources of Gujarat's nobles? Eric Wolf has noted that "There are political resources which are essential to the operation of the [political] system, and the system will try and remain in control of these. But there are also resources and organizations which it would be either too costly or too difficult to bring under direct control, and in these areas the system yields its sovereignty to competitive groups that are allowed to function in its entrails."[96] In the case of Gujarat, in terms of revenue, control over land was a crucial resource for both the sultans and the nobles, and the Mughal emperors later. Control of sea trade was much less crucial except for certain of the nobles. This, however, was not because sea trade was of little value, but because it was undertaxed. I have already attempted to assess the role of sea trade in the total economy of Sultanate Gujarat;[97] I found that it was of considerable importance. This trade was taxed at only 5 percent.

True, most export products were produced on the land, and so

---

[94] ANTTSL, III, f. 68.
[95] Correa, IV, 455.
[96] Eric R. Wolf, "Kinship, Friendship and Patron-Client Relations in Complex Societies," Michael Banton, ed., *The Social Anthropology of Complex Societies* (New York, 1966), p.1.
[97] Cf. pp. 22-24.

paid land revenue also. Further, there is no reason to suspect that customs officials in Gujarat were any more honest than their Portuguese counterparts; in effect, the bribes and perquisites which they undoubtedly took raised the rates a little. These extra levies can in fact be seen as part of the revenue of Gujarat; as customary perquisites they formed an accepted part of the salary of an official. Yet the official rates could have been raised, for the merchants were able to pay an extra duty to the Portuguese in Div without apparent hardship. In other countries rates were much higher: the usual rate in sixteenth-century Lisbon was 20 percent, while Mamluk Egypt took at least 30 percent from spices as they were transported from the Red Sea to Alexandria.[98]

The total revenue derived from customs duties at the end of the sultanate was only Rs. 40,00,000, while the five-eights of Gujarat's land area which paid revenue in the 1590s produced Rs. 1,10,00,000. It is impossible to express quantitatively the total contribution of sea trade to Gujarat's revenue,[99] but for my present purpose the point is that the loss of one or two ports would not be a fatal blow for the revenue of all of Gujarat. A noble actually in control of a port, however, naturally saw things differently. Obviously his port was crucial to him.

The same sort of mechanistic scrutiny needs to be applied to land areas. Here the distinction made in Chapter I between Cambay and Gujarat is important.[100] The loss of any part of Cambay would be disastrous, and would be resisted. The loss of any part of one of the "kingdoms of Cambay" would be less damaging. These areas, especially at the edges of the state, paid only tribute, and this only when they were forced to. They were not part of the heartland, and were at the best of times only very tenuously under the control of either the sultan or his nobles.

In the terms of Eric Wolf's already quoted analysis, control of sea trade was thus not a political resource essential to the operation of the Gujarati political system. In this area Gujarat yielded its sovereignty to the Portuguese, who were allowed to function in the entrails of the system. The only qualification to be made is that sovereignty was in fact not "yielded," for it has already been shown that the Portuguese

---

[98] *Boletim do Conselho Ultramarino. Legislação Antigo*, vol. I (Lisbon, 1867), p. 157 *et seq;* F. Mendes da Luz, *Relação de todas as rendas* (Coimbra, 1949), pp. 44-45, 59, 60; Castanheda, II, lxxv.
[99] Cf. p. 24.
[100] Cf. pp. 19-20.

introduced the concept of control over sea trade to Indian waters. They imported this innovative concept, and were allowed to act on its implications because virtually no one in Gujarat saw any point in trying to wrest control for themselves.

This in turn was a result of the whole ethos of the Muslim sultans of Gujarat and their nobles. It was, with few exceptions, intimately tied up with control over land and people, not over the sea. For these nobles, land was the crucial resource, for control over land gave control over men. In their terms, although not in those of a merchant, a wealthy man was a man with a large well-populated land area under his control.[101] Money as such was less important, for it was not very easy to translate money into control over land, and through land over men. Even within its own land area the premodern state of Gujarat controlled much less of its subjects' activities than does a modern state. It made no attempt to regulate what its subjects did outside Gujarat: this sort of control was inessential to the operation of the system. As a reflection of this ranking Gujarat maintained a large army but virtually no navy. Only Mahmud Bigarh and Bahadur seem to have been very interested in naval matters. They both had navies of some size and effectiveness, although they were not capable of standing up to a Portuguese fleet. Among the nobles only Malik Ayaz maintained a fleet of any significance.[102]

Some Muslim states, notably the Mamluk Empire, had large slave standing armies, and these were paid in cash or kind from the center.[103] The rulers who were the paymasters were thus interested in cash revenue from wherever it came. Sea trade in Egypt was extensive, and could carry heavy taxation, so that the rates were around 30 percent. The Gujarati army, however, was composed almost wholly of contingents raised by the nobles from the land they controlled.[104] The whole army was ordinarily paid in land grants, rather than in cash.

---

[101] Barrington Moore quotes R.H. Tawney on Tudor policy, "Which marks the transition from the mediaeval conception of land as the basis of political functions and obligations to the modern view of it as an income-yielding investment." Barrington Moore, *Social Origins of Dictatorship and Democracy* (Boston, 1966), p. 6.

[102] Malik Ayaz's fleet included some large ships. See "Livro de varios papeis," Biblioteca da Academia das Ciências, Lisbon, Mss. Azuis, A64, f. 292v.

[103] Ira M. Lapidus, *Muslim Cities in the Later Middle Ages* (Cambridge, 1967), pp. 16, 46, 51.

[104] V.A. Smith, *Akbar: The Great Mogul* (Delhi, 1966), pp. 261-62; William Irvine, *The Army of the Indian Moghuls* (London, 1903), pp. 57-58.

There thus seems to have been a fundamental difference between this territorially-oriented Gujarati regime, and such a one as Mamluk Egypt, where money rather than land was crucial.

Considerations of status were interrelated with this. For the nobles of Gujarat social honor was acquired from the size of one's contingent of cavalry. Glory was not won at sea; the whole military ethic of the Muslim rulers of Gujarat was bound up with land, and horses racing over the plains. As Bahadur said, "Wars by sea are merchants' affairs, and of no concern to the prestige of kings."[105] Similarly, Dr. John Fryer explained that Awrangzeb contented himself "in the enjoyment of the *Continent*, and styles the Christians Lions of the Sea; saying that God has allotted that Unstable Element for their Rule."[106]

This ranking of resources, together with the Portuguese failure to impinge decisively on the interests of most of the Gujarati nobility, provides an adequate explanation of their lack of hostility to the Portuguese. Other inhabitants of Gujarat were, however, much more affected by the Portuguese system. It is time to turn to the response of Gujarat's sea traders.

---

[105]Conde de Ficalho, *Garcia da Orta e o Seu Tempo* (Lisbon, 1886), p. 118.
[106]John Fryer, *A New Account of East India and Persia*, 3 vols. (London, 1909-15), I, 302.

CHAPTER IV

THE MERCHANTS

The initial reaction from Gujarati merchants to the presence of the Portuguese was friendly. In Calicut in 1500 a Gujarati Muslim had given his house to the Portuguese for their short-lived factory, and had taught the Portuguese the customs and trade of the area.[1] But once the Portuguese made attempts to stop the trade to the Red Sea, and to make all ships take *cartazes*, backing this up with armadas, the Gujaratis must have been suprised at such new and arbitrary claims. Soon they began to resist. In 1507 a Portuguese fleet attacked unsuccessfully a very powerful Gujarati ship, one of the many which were accustomed to loading in Gujarat, trading in the Bay of Bengal and Southeast Asia, then travelling direct to the Red Sea with spices. According to the Portuguese, "these ships are so powerful and well armed and have so many men that they dare to sail this route without fear of our ships, as this one did."[2]

Indeed, the Gujarati Muslims sometimes attacked, rather than simply acting in self-defense. Off South Arabia in 1517 a fleet of three Gujarati ships attacked unprovoked a Portuguese ship, and two years later the Portuguese factory in the Maldive Islands was sacked by Gujarati Muslims, and all eight Portuguese there were killed.[3] As late as 1538 a ship carrying the Portuguese admiral for the Malacca area was attacked by two Gujarati ships, and the admiral and thirty members of the crew were killed.[4] Reports of Portuguese attacks on Gujarati ships trading to the Red Sea, either from Div or South-

---

[1] A.B. de Bragança Pereira, ed., *Arquivo Português Oriental*, 10 vols. (Nova Goa, 1936-40), tome 1, vol. 1, part 1, p. 134.
[2] Correa, I, 787. Generally for trade to the Red Sea from Southeast Asia see C. R. Boxer, "A Note on Portuguese Reactions to the Revival of the Red Sea Spice Trade and the Rise of Atjeh, 1540-1600," *Journal of Southeast Asian History* X (Dec., 1969), and see also A.J.S. Reid, "Sixteenth Century Turkish Influence in Western Indonesia," in *ibid.*
[3] Barros, III, i, 10; Castanheda, V, ix.
[4] ANTTCC, 1-63-92.

east Asia, are legion until the 1530s; sometimes these attacks were beaten off by the well-armed Indian ships.[5]

In Malacca the leaders of the opposition to the Portuguese request to be allowed to trade were the Gujarati merchants resident there. Their influence with the sultan helped in 1509 to get the first Portuguese ships there attacked and the survivors imprisoned.[6] When Albuquerque arrived two years later, they redoubled their efforts, offering the sultan the help of 600 "white" (that is, non-Indian) men and forty cannons.[7] Such opposition is understandable, as the Portuguese were trying to stop the very valuable Gujarati trade from Malacca to the Red Sea via Gujarat; indeed, Albuquerque had taken five Gujarati ships engaged in this trade while he was on his way to Malacca in 1511.[8] Albuquerque was not to be denied: Malacca was stormed and taken.

Such open defiance from Gujarat's merchants, perhaps inspired if not aided by Malik Ayaz, virtually stopped in the 1530s. Some of the nobility still tried to avoid taking *cartazes*, but the merchants usually accepted Portugal's claims.[9] From this time on there seemed to be no alternative, most of the time and on most routes, to taking a Portuguese *cartaz* and paying duties at Div. The Muhammad Qulij Khan episode illustrates the situation perfectly. Here was a Mughal captain prepared to defy the Portuguese and send his ship to the Red Sea without a *cartaz*. Twice he was able to arrange for his ship to leave Surat unmolested by the Portuguese. What was the reaction of the merchants of Surat? Not joy at being able to escape the thralldom of the Portuguese, but a careful consideration of the chances of the ship returning safely, and finally nearly universal refusal to have anything to do with the "free" voyage.[10]

There is abundant other evidence of the way in which the Gujaratis accepted Portuguese control. The *cafilas* to Goa are one example. Several hundred small local ships went each year from the Gulf of

---

[5]Castanheda, III, xiv; Barros, III, ii, 3; Gavetas, IV, 128; ANTTCC, 2-145-115; Barros, IV, i, 5; IV, ii, 11; IV, iv, 20; Couto, IV, i, 7; IV, iv, 9.

[6]Tomé Pires, *The Suma Oriental of Tomé Pires*, 2 vols. (London, 1944), II, 255; Castanheda, II, cxiii.

[7]*Commentaries of Afonso Albuquerque*, 4 vols. (London, 1875-84), III, 69.

[8]Castanheda, III, li.

[9]Elaine Sanceau, ed., *Cartas de Dom João de Castro* (Lisbon, 1955), pp. 227-30. See Couto VI, vii, 6, for an isolated case in 1549 when three rich and well-armed ships beat off a Portuguese fleet near Surat.

[10]For this episode, see the opening of chapter III.

Cambay to Goa under the auspices of the Portuguese. Indeed, this trade had been established before the fort at Div was built in 1535; Gujarati traders were eager to sail this route *before* the Portuguese had established any sort of effective control over the trade of the gulf, although to do so they had to take *cartazes* and pay duties at Goa.[11]

Once Div was taken, it is clear that few ships traded from Gujarat to the Red Sea without a *cartaz*, and so without calling at Div to pay duties. As early as the season of late 1537, thirty-nine ships from the Arabian coast, Aden, and the Red Sea called at Div.[12] Late in 1545 there were more than twenty large ships from the Red Sea alone in Div. A Portuguese fleet in 1554 stopped twenty-one ships from Gujarat bound for the Red Sea. All of them carried *cartazes*.[13] Other examples of Gujarati ships being inspected by Portuguese ships and being found with the correct *cartaz* are numerous, much more so than are the very scattered references to Gujarati ships without them.[14]

This acceptance of Portuguese control became deeply ingrained. It continued in the seventeenth century, despite the precipitate decline in Portuguese fortunes under the attacks of the Dutch. *Cartazes* continued to be taken, with little modification in the strictness of their terms, throughout the century, but merchants now also took them from the Dutch and English. An example from 1640 is indicative. A Gujarati official asked for a *cartaz* so that one of his ships could sail to China. He had already obtained one from the Dutch for this voyage. The Portuguese agreed eagerly, for they themselves were unable to trade from Goa to Macao because of the Dutch blockade off the Goa bar. They sent a factor and numerous goods on the Gujarati ship. Their effective power would seem to have been small, yet no chances were being taken by the Gujaratis.[15] Div's revenues did decline in the seventeenth century,[16] for many merchants sent their goods on Dutch

[11]Francisco Paes, "O Tombo de Diu," *O Oriente Português*. n.s. 5 (1933): 48.
[12]*Studia*, no. 10, p. 184.
[13]ANTTCC, 1-77-36; 1-94-94.
[14]For example, Couto, V, ii, 8; VI, i, 7; ANTTCC. 1-62-154; 1-67-47; 1-100-28.
[15]Fazenda, V, 85v-87; "Regimentos e instruções," HAG, III, 200v-201. For Gujaratis taking Dutch and English passes, see *The Voyage of Thomas Best* (London, 1934), pp. 108, 118; Factories, 1622-23, pp. 215-16; for the continuance of *cartazes* in 1670, and a slight modification of their form, see *Boletim do Governo do Estado da India*, October 10, 1873, pp. 367-68; Assentos, IV, 208-12. For *cartazes* in 1696 and later, see Assentos, V, 14-15, 148, 244.
[16]Bocarro, Livro, part 1, pp. 113-14; Biblioteca da Ajuda, 51-VIII-30, f. 118v.

and English ships, thus avoiding the payment of duties to the Portuguese; many others, however, continued to take *cartazes*.

Gujarat's merchants buckled after their initial defiance and accepted Portuguese control partly through fear and partly because Portuguese control was not in fact so excessively irksome. There were advantages to be gained from cooperation with them. Officially the Portuguese used a stick to enforce compliance; unofficially there was also a carrot. For Gujarat's merchants there was sometimes something to gain, and always a lot to lose.

For logistic reasons the taking of Div was crucial in enforcing Portugal's claims. Once Bassein was acquired in 1534 and Div a year later, the Portuguese were able to patrol effectively along most of the Gujarati coastline. An even tighter grip was possible after the seizure of Daman in 1559. Evasion of Portuguese fleets was now very difficult for a ship leaving the Gulf of Cambay.

The 1530s were also decisive because it was then that the full force of Portugal's conquistador fury was first turned on Gujarat. The invincibility of her fleets, and the ruthlessness with which she retaliated when attacked, became very clear in the minds of Gujarat's merchants. Fear of being butchered was undoubtedly a potent weight on the side of acceptance.

Although the Portuguese had seized Gujarati ships from 1500 onwards when they were found trading to their enemies, or without *cartazes*, and her naval power was demonstrated clearly enough in the battle off Div in 1509,[17] it was not until 1529-30 that she first raided in the Gulf of Cambay. These raids followed Nuno da Cunha's thwarted large-scale attack on Div in 1529. His subsequent tactic was to force the cession of Div by inflicting unacceptable losses on Bahadur's coastal areas. These tactics failed, but the destruction of the raids of 1529-34 must have brought home to all sea traders how ruthless the Portuguese were. Every port of any consequence from Bassein around to Mangrol was raided, looted and burned, except for Cambay, which presumably was inaccessible to the Portuguese ships.[18]

The reprisals after the second siege of Div, in 1546-48, were even more effective, thanks to D. João de Castro's inspiring leadership.

---

[17]Correa, I, 226-27, 346-47; II, 508, 565; Barros, III, i, 7; *Commentaries of Afonso Albuquerque*, I, 112-15; II, 122; Castanheda, IV, xvi; Gavetas, IV, 387-88.
[18]Castanheda, VIII, viii, ix, xxix-xxxv, xliii-xlv, l, lii; Manuel de Faria e Sousa, *Asia Portuguesa*, 6 vols. (Lisbon, 1945-47), II, 193, 202-3; Barros, IV, iv, 8; IV, iv, 21-24; IV, iv, 27; Couto, IV, vii, 5.

He told his son that "it seems best to me, and so I order you, to cut the throats of as many Gujaratis and Moors as you capture, just as I am doing here."[19] Later he proudly told the king how he had sent on ahead of the main fleet "D. Manuel de Lima with twenty foists to cover all the gulf and burn and destroy the whole coast, in which he very well showed his diligence and gallantry, because he caused more destruction on the coast than was ever done before, or ever dreamt of, destroying every place from Daman up to Broach, so that there was no memory left of them [sic], and he butchered everyone he captured without showing mercy to a living thing. He burnt twenty large ships and 150 small ones... and the town squares were covered with bodies, which caused great astonishment and fear in all Gujarat."[20] After this the Portuguese seldom needed to repeat the lesson. The taking of Daman in 1559 no doubt helped to remind the traders of their power, as did their successful duel with Qulij Khan, but massacres like those of the 1530s and 1540s were never repeated for the Portuguese had made their point.

Ironically, these barbarities were really the dying gasp of the Portuguese conquistador. In the second half of the sixteenth century, the stick was seldom used; the carrot did more to keep the Gujaratis in line. On the official level, the Portuguese at least tacitly were more interested in seeing Gujarati trade flourish than in enforcing rigorous restrictions. Unofficially, there seemed to be evolving a network of mutual benefits from which most Portuguese and a few Gujaratis profited.

Response to the Official System

A contemporary plan of Div shows the city strictly divided between the Portuguese area and the Indian one.[21] This symbolizes the official divisions. Similarly, Portuguese restrictions on Gujarati trade remained on paper as stringent as ever. Thus, as late as 1595 the king decreed that no Gujarati was allowed to trade even through an intermediary to any place except western Indian ports.[22] It has, however, already been noted that during the sixteenth century the Portuguese

---

[19] ANTTSL, IV, 196.
[20] *Cartas de Dom João de Castro*, pp. 263-64. Other reports of these operations of 1546-48 in Faria e Sousa, III, 163-64, 168-70; DUP, I, 582; Couto, VI, iv, 3.
[21] B. Mus., Sloane MSS. 197, ff. 170v-71.
[22] APOCR, III, 540-42; cf. "Senado Régias," HAG, I, 54-54v.

empire in Asia became much more self-contained and self-supporting. Thanks to the growth of the "illegal" pepper trade, profits from the Goa-Lisbon route declined and the Portuguese became dependent on profits from their own trading voyages, both official and private, and on taxes on the trade of locals. Gujaratis were the most important of these.

The continuance and prosperity of Gujarat's trade was crucial to the finances of the Portuguese in two ways. First, the revenue from the customs house at Diu was second only to that of Goa as the single most important source of revenue in Portuguese India. In the palmy days of the sixteenth century, around Rs. 1,00,000 were left over after all the port's expenses had been met, and this profit was sent to Goa to help with the general expenses of the state.[23] Second, and more important, was the revenue both direct and indirect derived from the trade from Gujarat to Goa, and points south. From the time of Albuquerque it was realized that the revenue derived from Gujarat's trade to Goa, Cochin and Malacca was crucial to the revenues of Portuguese India; efforts were made to foster and encourage this trade, and to ensure good treatment for Gujarati ships and merchants.

When Portugal and Gujarat were at war, as in the late 1540s, Portuguese revenues suffered, and the revenue officials advised that peace be made on any terms; Portugal simply could not afford a long war with Gujarat.[24] Similarly, when the *cafilas* from Gujarat to Goa stopped during the 1613-15 war, the state revenues suffered badly; it was only by desperate measures that a cargo for the homeward bound ships was procured. Normally the private part of these cargoes consisted mostly of cloths and various other products from Gujarat, and the substitute cargo of 1615, inferior cloths from the Deccan, was far from satisfactory. Of twelve routes sailed from Goa around 1600, the greatest amount of capital was involved in that to Gujarat. All the others, except that to Portugal, were far behind.[25] In the seventeenth century Portuguese operations in East Africa depended to a great

[23] B. Mus., Addl. 28433, f. 116v; cf. LM, v. 19B, f. 517v.
[24] "Cartas Missivas," ANTT, maço 4, no. 208; *Cartas de Affonso de Albuquerque*, 7 vols. (Lisbon, 1884-1935), I, 51-52; "Provisões, Alvarás e Regimentos," HAG, I, 92v, printed in APOCR, V, 30; ANTTSL, III, 185, 189, 480-81v; ANTTCC, 1-81-104; Correa, IV, 614-15v.
[25] Barreto de Rezende, II, 125-26v, and cf. Bocarro, Livro, part 1, pp. 279-88. For the situation in 1613-15, see LMBP, III, 389; AHU, Caixa 3, no. 16; LM, v. 12, ff. 216-16v; *The Voyage of Nicholas Downton* (London, 1938), p. 113; Bocarro, Decada, p. 336. For the importance of Gujarati goods in the cargoes of ships bound

extent on having available cloths from Gujarat to exchange for gold, slaves, and ivory.[26]

Because of this dependence, the Portuguese did not do all that they could to stop Gujarati infringements of their official system, for this would have been to cut off their nose to spite their face. There continued to be numerous examples of the Gujaratis evading the Portuguese system, or failing to be influenced by Portuguese wishes. The best example of evasion concerned the lucrative pepper trade.

The Portuguese made a major effort to monopolize for themselves all trade in Asian spices. Recent research has shown how ineffective the Portuguese were. Most of the time, trade via the Red Sea to the Mediterranean was not seriously hampered by the Portuguese. More important, they never controlled the inter-Asian spice trade, which by volume was vastly more important then the trade to Europe.[27]

The area where the Portuguese got most of their pepper was Malabar. Here, however, they encountered fierce resistance from two sources. In the fifteenth century Calicut had been a wealthy city because of its role as the main entrepôt for Malabar pepper. Its rulers, the Zamorins, resisted the Portuguese during most of the sixteenth century. Local traders, who had made their living from the pepper trade and who had no alternative source of income, also continued to try to ignore Portuguese control. Often they were successful.

Gujarat's merchants, on the other hand, were happy to sit in their ports and let the Malabaris bring them pepper, if they could evade the Portuguese. There is no record of Gujarati ships going to Malabar to get pepper, but Gujarati ships, and others, did collect pepper in the Bay of Bengal and Indonesia, and from there take it direct to the Red Sea. Much of this pepper came overland from Malabar, but some came from the Malayan and Sumatran production areas. It was picked up by Gujarati and other traders in Siam, Sumatra, Bengal and Coromandel, and taken direct to the Red Sea. By sailing south

---

for Portugal from Goa, see AHU, Caixa 4, no. 98; LM, v. 13B, ff. 392-415v. It should be noted that some of the goods on the Goa-Cambay *cafila*, and some of the ships, were owned by Portuguese. That is, they sometimes bought goods to send to Portugal, or places within Asia, in Gujarat rather than waiting for the Gujaratis to bring them to Goa: François Pyrard de Laval, *Travels of François Pyrard de Laval*, 2 vols. (London, 1887-90), II, 246; *The Journal of John Jourdain, 1608-17* (Cambridge, 1905), p. 173.

[26]LMBP, V, 107; Bocarro, Livro, part 1, p. 10; "Alavarás e Provisões de Sua Magestade," HAG, I, 148.

[27]See f.n. 87 of chapter II.

of Ceylon, and stopping for water and provisions only in the Maldive Islands, they were able to avoid the Portuguese completely unless they were so unlucky as to be caught at the mouth of the Red Sea; the ineffectiveness of this Portuguese fleet has already been described.

These Gujaratis ostensibly traded innocently within the Portuguese system. They would take a *cartaz* before leaving Gujarat for a voyage to Southeast Asia, and indeed would often call at Malacca. From there until they got back to Gujarat the voyage was illegal, but rarely capable of being blocked by the Portuguese. There are records, or rather complaints, of this trade throughout the century, but it seems to have been particularly widespread in the early 1540s.[28] There is also evidence that some trade in pepper to the Red Sea from Gujarat itself continued, even after Div was taken, but this trade became increasingly dangerous and hence sporadic.[29]

Other examples of evasion were numerous. The free *cartaz* "ploy," by which a merchant's most valuable goods went on the emperor's ship and so avoided paying duties, has already been mentioned. This was extended in the seventeenth century. The free *cartaz* ship would set off, show the Portuguese its *cartaz*, and then send the document back to shore. Then another ship would leave, carrying the same *cartaz*, and thus also avoid the payment of duties.[30] Ships from the ports west of Div—Nagana, Cutch, Porbander and Mangrol—were meant to go to Div and pay duties before setting off for the Red Sea. Obviously they would not unless the Portuguese sent a ship or a fleet to make them, and it was not always possible to do this. In 1617 no fleet went, and thirty-one ships sailed direct to the Red Sea; the loss to the Div customs house was estimated at Rs. 80,000.[31] In the 1580s

---

[28] Barros, I, x, 5; *Alguns Documentos do Archivo nacional da Torre do Tombo* (Lisbon, 1892), p. 453; Descrição, f. 22; ANTTCC, 1-62-54; C. R. Boxer, *The Portuguese Seaborne Empire* (London, 1969), p. 59; in the official instructions from D. João III to the new governor, D. João de Castro, in 1545, the king said that after the ships for Portugal had their cargoes of pepper loaded, licenced private trade in this product to the Bay of Bengal should be allowed. But this was not put into effect as Castro collected a barrage of expert opinions in Goa saying that this would only make it easier for the Gujaratis, and others, to trade to the Red Sea with pepper. ("Cartas de Vice Reis," ANTT, nos. 75, 146; ANTTCC, 1-77-15 to 33; 1-77-42; 1-78-8; 2-240-53; 3-15-31; 3-16-21.)

[29] ANTTCC, 1-108-78; APOCR, III, 364; "Livro Vermelho," HAG, I, 271v-73.

[30] ANTTDR, XLVIII, 333v. It is not known how the Gujaratis got around the fact that each *cartaz* was meant to include the name of the ship's captain and its size.

[31] Fazenda, I, 80v-81; AHU, Caixa 6, account of January 17, 1619; ANTTDR, XXIV, 57-57v.

Muslim Chaul increased its trade greatly, as the Nizam Shahi ruler gave favorable conditions. Many merchants of Gujarat had agents there, and did as much trade as possible through this port rather than through Goa or Div, where they had to pay the high Portuguese duties.[32]

In the seventeenth century it was possible to load goods on English or Dutch ships and so avoid paying duties to the Portuguese, although presumably the freight rates charged took account of this. Some Gujarati ships sailed without *cartazes* but with the protection of English and Dutch ships.[33] The whole situation was summed up in a report to the king of 1597. He was advised to start sending a fleet to the mouth of the Red Sea again, to force the Gujarati traders to call at Div and pay duties. If the armada was not there to force them, they would abandon the surety they had left in Div as an earnest of their intention to call there on their return voyage to pay duties, and would recoup the loss of the surety by loading a bigger cargo in the Red Sea.[34]

Apart from such evasion, Gujarati merchants also were not usually influenced by wider Portuguese desires concerning the conduct of their trade. The Portuguese tried to encourage trade from Gujarat to Portugal's own possessions in Asia rather than to areas where they had no forts. In particular, they wanted Gujaratis to continue to trade to Malacca. Their trade to the Red Sea was discouraged, especially as Gujarat's imports from there competed with the goods the Portuguese brought from Europe. The reverse occurred. The trade to the Red Sea continued and flourished greatly in the sixteenth century, while trade from Gujarat to Malacca declined.

Throughout the century the trade to the Red Sea was the most important for Gujarat. In the 1570s, calculating on the basis of duties paid at Div, this trade employed 25 percent of all capital engaged in overseas trade in Gujarat. This figure is a little low, as it ignores the

---

[32] APOCR, III, 107; F. Mendes da Luz, "Livro das Cidades e Fortalezas," *Studia* no. 6 (1960): 18-20v; DUP, I, 262; F. Paes, *op. cit.*, pp. 49-52; *Studia*, no. 3, p. 55. Here the editor, J. Wicki, S.J., incorrectly identifies Chaul as Challé, in Malabar. It will be remembered that the Portuguese established a customs house in Chaul only in 1634. The Portuguese fort at Chaul was on the coast, but one-half league up the river from it was upper Chaul, part of the sultanate of Ahmadnagar, and a very large and busy trade center. (Couto, XI, cap. 32.)

[33] Biblioteca da Ajuda, 51-VII-30, f. 118v. In 1630 Gujarati merchants were reported to have over Rs. 10,00,000 invested in goods on Dutch and English ships: LM, v. 14, ff. 361-61v.

[34] APOCR, III, 680-83.

"illegal" trade from Gujarat to the Red Sea.³⁵ Some of the Gujarati ships sailing on the route were fabulously wealthy. According to its own "book," one of Akbar's vessels in 1582 came back from the Red Sea with gold and silver worth Rs. 12,00,000 ($4,788,000), among other goods.³⁶ A ship of Jahangir's returned to Surat from Mocha in 1622 with more than Rs. 2,50,000 in coin alone, most of which belonged to the merchants of Ahmadabad, Cambay, and Surat,³⁷ Another, of 1630, was again worth more than Rs. 10,00,000.³⁸ There are records of ships trading from the Arabian Sea to the Red Sea for two periods in 1612 and 1616, which show how dominant Gujarat was in this trade. In April of 1612 the total was fifteen, of which six were from Gujarati ports. During a short period in 1616 the total was forty-one, twenty-three of them from Gujarat.³⁹ The others were from places as various as Acheh, al-Shihr, Sind, Goa, and Calicut, and may well have included some more ships based on Gujarat.

In the fifteenth century Gujarat stretched out two arms: to Aden and the Red Sea, and to Malacca. In the sixteenth century the second arm extended its embrace over a wider area, including most of the Bay of Bengal and Indonesia. The dominance of Gujaratis in Malacca at the time of its capture by the Portuguese in 1511 is well attested. Thus, Albuquerque knew that "the Guzerates understand the navigation of those parts [of Malacca and vicinity] much more thoroughly than any other nations, on account of the great commerce they carry on in those places."⁴⁰ After the capture the Portuguese tried to encourage the Gujaratis to continue to trade to Malacca, and

---

³⁵See pp. 23-24, and Couto, IX, cap. 14. Here he speaks of twelve to fifteen ships going to the Red Sea each year, and the largest ones of them paying Rs. 36,000 in duties. This gives a total from this trade of about Rs. 3,00,000, and with duties of 3½ percent a total value of Rs. 85,00,000. Assuming an equal value for the return cargo, that totals Rs. 1,70,00,000. One must then add the value of the free *cartaz* ship, which was about Rs. 30,00,000 (see below, and remembering that these are all one-way values) which gives a total of Rs. 2,00,00,000 as against a total value of all sea trade of Rs. 8,00,00,000.

³⁶Couto, X, iii, 5.

³⁷*Recueil des voyages qui ont servi a l'établissement et aux progrez de la Compagnie des Indes Orientales formee dans les Provinces-Unies des Pais-Bas*, 12 vols. (Rouen, 1725), VII, 564-65.

³⁸Assentos, I, 291, 302, and taking a Veneziano at 1200 reis as in Bocarro, Livro, part 1, p. 124. See also Assentos II, 74; ANTTDR, XXXVIII, 23; LM, v. 14, ff. 215v-16, and C. F. Beckingham, "Dutch Travellers in the Seventeenth Century," *Journal of the Royal Asiatic Society* (1951): 171, for other values.

³⁹Samuel Purchas, *Hakluytus Posthumus, or Purchas his Pilgrimes*, 20 vols. (Glasgow, 1905), III, 190-93; *Recueil des voyages*, VII, 462.

⁴⁰*Commentaries of Afonso Albuquerque*, III, 58.

apparently, at least according to a letter of 1523, for a time they succeeded.⁴¹ As early as 1518, however, reports were made of the abuses to which the officials of Malacca subjected visiting merchants. A petition from the non-Christian merchants of Malacca of 1527 complained of their being forced to give loans to the officials, and not being repaid, and of not being paid for goods they delivered to the Portuguese factory.⁴² Malacca had made its fortune in the fifteenth century as a place where all the products of China and Southeast Asia were available. Now, this oppression discouraged merchants from calling there. Its status as a great trade mart declined.

In particular, reports of the late sixteenth century and after show that the Gujaratis had abandoned their trade to Malacca. The most noteworthy group of non-Portuguese merchants there in the seventeenth century was the Chinese.⁴³ The Gujaratis shifted their trade to a wider area—all around the Bay of Bengal, and in Indonesia to Acheh and Bantam. These two ports rose greatly in prosperity in the later sixteenth century thanks to the bad conduct of the Portuguese in Malacca, and Portuguese control in Southeast Asia in general was never effective enough to be able to force traders to come to Malacca. This change on the part of the Gujarati traders was, however, of little significance in their total trade organization. They had to disperse a little, and travel more, but the same Chinese and Southeast Asian goods were collected.⁴⁴

The Portuguese would also have preferred that Gujarati trade be handled by non-Muslims as much as possible. Here again they had little success. Chapter I described how Muslims, Hindus, and Jains

---

⁴¹ANTTCC, 1-30-36; Artur Basilio de Sá, ed., *Documentação para a historia das Missões do Padroado Portugues do Oriente, Insulíndia*, 5 vols. (Lisbon, 1954-   ), I, 50-51; *Cartas de Affonso de Albuquerque*, III, 221-22.

⁴²ANTTCC, 1-37-84; for 1518, see A. B. de Sa, *op. cit.*, I, 100, and for 1544, Correa, IV, 338.

⁴³P.S.S. Pissurlencar, *Regimentos das Fortalezas da India* (Bastorá, Goa, 1951), p. 260; Barreto de Rezende, II, 215 (in this copy of Barreto's work on f. 215 "Cambaia" is written, but clearly Camboja, i.e., Cambodia, is meant); P. A. Leupe, "The Siege and capture of Malacça from the Portuguese in 1640-41," *Journal of the Malayan Branch of the Royal Asiatic Society* XIV (1936): 102-5.

⁴⁴B. J. O. Schrieke, *Indonesian Sociological Studies*, part 1 (The Hague, 1955), p. 42; *The Voyage of Thomas Best* (London, 1934), p. 256; *The Travels of Peter Mundy in Europe and Asia*, 6 vols. (London, 1905-36), III, 135, 329; *Letters Received by the East India Company from its Servants in the East*, 6 vols. (London, 1896-1902), III, 126, 227; M.A.P. Meilink-Roelofsz, *Asian Trade and European Influence* (The Hague, 1964), p. 243. For Gujaratis trading in Sumatra in the fifteenth century, see Castanheda, II, cxi.

were all engaged in sea trade around 1500, and all three were active throughout the following century. Muslims certainly were, and continued to be, the actual sailors and captains of the trading ships, whoever the merchants travelling as passengers or as owners may have been.[45] In Surat in the early seventeenth century some of the richest merchants were Muslims, but by number Hindus and Jains were far superior.[46] In Div, judging by the signatures on petitions to the Portuguese, Hindus and Jains again considerably outnumbered Muslims, at least in the seventeenth century; this appears to mark a change, for in Malik Ayaz's day Div was known as "Div, the port of the Turks." Most of the foreign merchants coming to Div from the Red Sea or South Arabia were Muslims.[47] There is, however, strong evidence that in the later sixteenth century these foreign Muslims began to lose ground to Gujarati *vanias* in this trade. Around 1600 many Hindus and Jains were settled in the South Arabian ports and also inland.[48] Basically, however, Gujarat's overseas traders in 1600, as in 1500, were a heterogeneous group. They included, and continued to include, Hindus, Jains, and Muslims both foreign and local.

The Portuguese could have taken stronger measures than in fact they did to enforce their policies. For example, they well knew that the Gujaratis were trading in Southeast Asia without calling at Malacca, and that they were taking pepper to the Red Sea. Logistically it would have been possible to retaliate by more raids in the gulf and a blockade of its trade. The Portuguese, however, would in the long run have been the main losers. They did not like these evasions of their system, and the Gujarati failure to trade to their areas, but given their dependence on customs duties deriving from Gujarati trade, there was little they could do to stop them.

[45]*Cartas de Affonso de Albuquerque,* I, 307. A list of seventy-seven captains of ships issued with *cartazes* between 1618 and 1622 shows only two possible non-Muslims: "Consultas do Serviço de partes," HAG, III, 44-136v.
[46]Jean Baptiste Tavernier, *Travels in India,* 2 vols. (London, 1925), I, 6; W. H. Moreland, *From Akbar to Aurangzeb* (London, 1923), p. 85; J. N. Sarkar, *Shivaji* (Calcutta, 1920), pp. 102-3.
[47]APOCR, III, 681-82; ANTTDR, LI, 131-31v, 136-36v; AHU, Caixa 14, petition of September 10, 1642; Caixa 17, petition of August 20, 1644.
[48]Artus Viegas, ed., *Relação Annual das Coisas que Fizeram os Padres da Companhia de Jesus nas suas Missões,* by Fernão Guerreiro, 3 vols. (Lisbon, 1930-42), II, 389-90; I.O. I/3/40, DLXXIX; C. F. Beckingham, *op. cit.,* pp. 69, 78; R. B. Serjeant, *op. cit.,* pp. 32-33; *The Journal of John Jourdain* (London, 1905), pp. 95, 99, 104. In 1616 the Dutch factor van den Broeke found 3,000 "benjans" living in Mocha, occupied as merchants, goldsmiths, bankers, and artisans: *Recueil des voyages,* VII, 462.

Indeed, Gujarati merchants formed something of an elite economic group in Portuguese India, especially in Goa and Div. In 1646 it was estimated that there were 30,000 "baneanes" in Portuguese India.[49] In Div especially they were, despite being considered "gentiles," "niggers," and "cowards," in effect the dominant group in the town. They had their own captain and by concerted action could usually win a favorable response when they complained to the governor or the king about some abuse to which they were being subjected.

There is a case as early as 1545 in which the merchants of Div, by concerted action, forced the Portuguese captain to moderate the demands of one of his officials. In the 1590s the Portuguese king, in one of his recurrent phases of intolerance, decreed that all Hindu temples and Muslim mosques in Portuguese areas be destroyed, except in the puppet town of Hurmuz. The governor replied that these orders "cannot be put into effect in Div, because everyone would leave and then there would be no trade there."[50] In 1603 Div was given the title of city, with its own municipal council. Representation on this was restricted to Portuguese, and they used their new powers to oppress the Indian population. Following complaints from the latter, the title and council were withdrawn.[51]

The Portuguese were even prepared to complain to other Europeans on behalf of Div's merchants. In 1635 a ship of a Muslim merchant of Div was robbed by an English pirate. The governor complained on the merchant's behalf to the English president at Surat, and asked Philip IV of Spain to approach Charles I about this pirate.[52] There are many other cases in which the government in Goa showed its concern to protect the merchants of Div from the abuses of local officials and religious. The profits derived directly and indirectly from the trade of Div outweighed for the governors and kings the claims of patronage clients, and even the church.[53] According to one

---

[49] AHU, Caixa 18, letter of January 25, 1646.
[50] ANTTSL, V, 133; AHU, Codice 281, f. 260v.
[51] AHU, Codice 282, f. 126; AHU, Caixa 3, no. 4; ANTTDR, XXIV, 23v; B. Mus., Addl. 20863, f. 89v.
[52] Assentos, II, 74; ANTTDR, XXXVIII, 23.
[53] For petitions from Div merchants asking for, and usually getting, redress from either the governor or the king: APOCR, III, 840; LM, v. 16B, f. 299; v. 14, ff. 332-33v (part printed in APOCR, VI, 1250-51); v. 19A, f. 238; "Cartas e Ordens," HAG, III, 73, 80-80v, 84, 124v-25; ANTTDR, LI, 131-31v, 136-36v; LIV, 220; LV, 196; LM, v. 28B, f. 419; AHU, Caixa 3, decree of November 20, 1639; Caixa 14, petition of September 10, 1642; Caixa 16, opinion of February 18, 1644.

Jesuit, the Gujaratis in Div dominated the hapless clergy and were able to prevent anyone except themselves from trading to the Red Sea.[54] A disgruntled Portuguese told the king in 1545 that the "niggers" were given a free hand in Div by the Portuguese captain, as he was an eager trader and anxious to be friends with them, so that "it is better to be favored by the niggers than by the Portuguese...." But on most occasions the Gujaratis in Div looked after their own affairs. Thus in 1653 the Hindu and Muslim Gujaratis in Div petitioned through their captain, Goridas Parekh, to the governor in Goa. They complained that a Portuguese judge in Div had interfered in a case concerning debts and inheritance "that the Captain of the said people with four main men, his advisers, was judging." The Gujarati captain had had the guilty imprisoned, "as is the very ancient use and custom which his predecessors used," but the judge had released them.[55] By doing this, according to the Gujaratis, he had exceeded his authority.

In Goa itself the *vanias* were less dominant than in Div, but they still formed what was apparently the wealthiest Indian group in the town, with the possible exception of the Saraswat Brahmans. In 1659 the governor told the king how the Dutch blockade had ruined Goa's trade, leading especially to an exodus of the Gujarati merchants who had lived there. There were now only seven or eight rich ones left, and about forty agents for Cambay merchants, and "this group was always the most beneficial of all for the revenues of the customs house."[56] Despite this, in the same year the governor was able to raise a loan in a matter of days of perhaps Rs. 1,00,000 from the Gujarati merchants in Goa. It is significant that when money was needed urgently it was the Gujaratis to whom the Portuguese applied. If it suited them, these merchants were even able to get the Portuguese to delay the sailing of the *cafila* to the gulf. Their captain in Goa received various privileges from the Portuguese king, including freedom from imprisonment for any debt.[57]

The elite position of Gujarati merchants on the official, aboveboard, level was also extended to individuals. A Gujarati Muslim in

---

[54]APOCR, I, ii, 213; ANTTCC, 1-81-93; Artur Viegas, *op. cit.*, II, 390.

[55]Gavetas, III, 214; LM, v. 28B, ff. 422-26.

[56]LM, v. 26B, f. 408. See my article, "Indigenous Dominance in a Colonial Economy: The Goa *Rendas*, 1600-1670," *Mare Luso-Indicum*, vol. II (Paris and Geneva, 1973): 61-73 for the position of the Saraswat Brahmans in Goa.

[57]Fazenda, VI, 131v-32; IX, 247v-48v; X, 55; "Chancellaria, D. Affonso VI," ANTT, book 39, ff. 372-72v. For another loan from the Gujaratis in Goa when money was needed urgently, see the diary of Viceroy Sarzedas in "Noticias dos Estados da India," Biblioteca da Academia das Ciências, Lisbon, Mss. Azuis, A 58, f. 47v.

Bassein in the 1540s was greatly cossetted by the Portuguese, and given concessions in the customs houses and as many *cartazes* as he wanted for trade to the Red Sea. At the end of the century, a Jesuit was sent to Cambay to investigate the possibilities of his working there. He travelled from Div to Cambay on the ship of an important Brahman merchant of Cambay, whose agent in Div had written to him asking him to assist the priest.[58] He was well received in the town. In 1644 the governor wrote to the judge of Bassein that "Nagagissa, a merchant residing in this city, is going to Div to see about curing his sick wife, and as he is a person to whom I am obliged, I order you to give him all the help and favor that may be necessary."[59]

Acceptance of Portuguese control was thus not too irksome for the Gujaratis. The main disadvantages were the necessity to bribe appropriate officials in Div, and to pay duties there. Both these simply increased costs a little, and these were no doubt recouped later. The necessity of paying customs both at one's home Gujarati port, assuming one did not reside in Div, and at Div, was not particularly troublesome, for these two duties together never exceeded a rate of 10 percent in the sixteenth or seventeenth centuries.[60]

Indeed, there is clear evidence that the merchants of Gujarat not only accepted Portuguese control, but actually cooperated with them in the working of their system. There was a willingness to give and take a little on both sides in such matters as the issuing of *cartazes*, the organization of the *cafilas* to Div and Goa, and the collection of duties by the Portuguese. Around 1570, after considerable negotiation, Div merchants granted to the Portuguese a raise of 1 percent in the duties they would pay on indigo and a particular cloth, in return for a reduction from 5 percent to 3 percent on the duties for bullion.[61] Three times between the 1580s and 1634 Div's general customs rates were raised, by ½ percent each time, and each time this increase was

---

[58] R. J. de Lima Felner, ed., *Subsídios para a história da India Portugueza* (Lisbon, 1868), p. 2; Artur Viegas, ed., *op. cit.*, II, 393-94. "Brahman" here is almost certainly a mistake for *baneane, vania*.

[59] "Correspondencia de Baçaim," HAG, f. 88.

[60] In Div the rates were 3½ percent until about 1584. In this year, and again in 1605 and in 1634, increases of ½ percent were obtained, making a total of 5 percent. Allowing Gujarati duties of 5 percent under the sultans, and 2½ percent after 1572 under the early Mughals, the rates never exceeded 10 percent. This in fact even applies to the later seventeenth century, when the rates charged by Gujarat were raised by Aurangzeb. LMBP, III, 157; F. Mendes da Luz, *O Conselho da India*, p. 427; AHU, Caixa 10, account of September 30, 1634.

[61] B. Mus., Addl. 20861, f. 59v.

introduced only after the merchants of Div had been consulted and had agreed to the increase. Nor apparently were these agreements given only because the merchants felt they had no choice. They could have voted with their feet and left Div, as indeed at times they threatened to do. Rather, these agreements show the merchants prepared to cooperate with the Portuguese in the interests of all; the increases were at least partly for the good of the merchants, being designed to secure more money so that the Malabar "pirates" could be checked and Div defended against the Dutch.[62]

Another aspect of this cooperation was seen in the prodecure for paying duties in Div. The merchants of Cambay sent their cloths to Div on smaller ships, which were guarded by a Portuguese fleet. In Div duties were paid when the goods were transshipped to the larger vessels which took them to the Red Sea or elsewhere. With the fleet of small ships came lists of the contents of each of the bales of cloth, drawn up by the Gujarati merchants. These lists were used as the basis on which duties were paid in Div.[63]

Similarly, both sides were ready to compromise over the *cafila* from Cambay to Goa. In 1624 the *vanias* of Gujarat sent a message to the viceroy asking that he send the armada to accompany the *cafila* early, as they had already got their goods and ships prepared. It was neither easy nor convenient for the Portuguese to do this, but it was done anyway and the *cafila* reached Goa two months earlier than usual.[64] Seven years later the Mughal captain and merchants of Surat told the Portuguese they could not come to Daman to pay duties on those of their ships which usually paid there rather than in Div. They asked that the governor send an agent to Surat to collect the duties. After some discussion the Portuguese agreed to do this.[65] The point is that the merchants and the captain were not trying to avoid paying the duties, or to deny Portuguese control. They simply wanted a special change in the routine for this year, which the Portuguese agreed to make.

One other sign of the stabilization of the relationship, marking the end of any defiance from the Gujaratis, was seen in the 1560s. The

---

[62] LMBP, III, 157; Biblioteca da Ajuda, Lisbon, 51-VII-30, f. 97, printed in F. Mendes da Luz, *O Conselho da India*, p. 427; AHU, Caixa 10, account of September 30, 1634.

[63] ANTTDR, XVIII, 55. This method did apparently lead to considerable cheating.

[64] ANTTDR, XXII, 41v-42.

[65] Fazenda, III, 155.

Portuguese captain of Div had special grants from the crown to enable him to provide meals for the *fidalgos* and soldiers in Div, and to pay his own bodyguard. Such warriors were no longer needed or desired by the captains. They usually spent this money on paying people to go as their agents on trading expeditions to Bengal and Malacca.[66]

Unofficial Contacts

Restricting consideration of the Gujarati response to this official level of Portuguese activities, one has a picture of merchants giving in and adjusting partly through fear and partly because Portuguese control was in fact not too irksome. There was, however, an unofficial level of contact; individual Gujaratis and individual Portuguese in their private capacities, whether they were officials or not, engaged in mutual accommodations for mutual individual benefits. The evidence for this is not as full as could be desired, but there is no doubt that these sorts of "deals" existed, and that they helped to make Portuguese control easier to accept.

Unofficial contacts were based on the importance of Gujarat as a money market. To sixteenth-century European observers Gujarat was a fabulously wealthy country. An Italian in the 1560s said flatly that "In fine, the kingdom on Cambaia is a place of great trade, and hath much doing and traffique with all men..." At the same time a Portuguese claimed that "if in any land it can be said that gold and silver flow, it is Cambay." A Jesuit observer of 1600 described how Gujarat, then and for centuries past, received streams of gold from the Red Sea, the Persian Gulf, and China, and of silver from Portugal.[67] In 1537 as in 1646 Portuguese writers wondered at the wealth of the Gujarati merchants, some of whom had capital at their disposal of Rs. 2,00,000 ($798,000), and at the latter date even more.[68] The dependence of the trade from Goa to Portugal on Gujarati goods has already

---

[66] ANTTCC, 1-108-24. For negotiations in 1670 between Surat merchants and a Portuguese representative to work out a new form of *cartaz*, see *Boletim do governo do estado da India*, October 10, 1873, p. 367. Here both sides in effect cooperated to evolve a new form of subjection for Gujarat's merchants.

[67] Caesar Frederick in Richard Hakluyt, *The Principal Navigations, Voyages, Traffiques and Discoveries of the English Nation*, 12 vols. (Glasgow, 1903-5), V, 377; José Wicki, ed., "Duas Relações sobre a situação da India portuguesa nos anos 1568 e 1569," *Studia* no. 8 (1961): 177; Artur Viegas, ed., *op.cit.*, II, 389; Barreto de Rezende, I, 63v-64.

[68] *Studia*, nos. 13-14, p. 86; AHU, Caixa 18, letter of January 25, 1646.

been shown. The revenue of the customs house of Hurmuz was a similar case. In 1523 a new agreement was signed with the puppet sultan. He was to pay the Portuguese 60,000 *xerafins* a year, but if Gujarat was at war with the Portuguese only 25,000, for most of Hurmuz's revenue came from the Gujarati trade. This was a sensible reservation, for in 1547, as a result of the war following the second seige of Div, Hurmuz was "destroyed and no merchants came to it."[69] The customs revenue alone of Gujarat in the early 1570s was nearly three times the total revenue of the whole Portuguese empire in Asia in 1586-87, when it was at its height.[70]

This wealth was used mostly in trade and lending. Violet Barbour has shown how seventeenth-century Amsterdam's capital resources were built up partly because there was little land in Holland available as an outlet for surplus capital. Most of this capital was used in trade and associated activities, although some was invested in land outside Holland, and also in industry, in loans, in the expenses of public office, in display, and in other minor activities.[71]

The outlets for Gujarati merchants were even more restricted. They took no part in the upper level decision making of their state, and so had no ambitions, or expenses, here. Unlike medieval merchants in Amsterdam or London, they did not even participate in the formal government of their cities. A little was spent on secular display, but not too much, for an obviously wealthy man was increasingly a target for extortion. Rather more seems to have gone on religious display. There are records of Hindus and Jains endowing temples and other religious buildings. Around 1600 a very wealthy *vania* of Chaul (presumably a Jain) bequeathed Rs. 60 to each of the Christian confraternities of the city, and Rs. 8,000 to the bird hospital of Cambay.[72] It is not clear whether or not this conspicuously unequal distribution of patronage was made with malice aforethought.

Gujarati merchants did invest in city property[73] but apparently not

---

[69]Couto. V. ix, 1; ANTTSL, II, 69.

[70]See p. 23. and for the Portuguese figure AHU, Codice 500, *passim*.

[71]Violet Barbour, *Capitalism in Amsterdam in the Seventeenth Century* (Baltimore, 1951), pp. 28-29, 85.

[72]DUP, I, 253. A similar case in António da Silva Rego, ed., *Documentação para a história das Missões do Padroado Português do Oriente. India*, 12 vols. (Lisbon, 1947-   ), X, 76. For Jain endowments of temples, see M. S. Commissariat, *History of Gujarat*, 2 vols. (Bombay, 1938-57), II, 141, 244, 352.

[73]William Foster, "Sivaji's Raid upon Surat in 1664, part II," *Indian Antiquary* LI (January 1922); J. B. Tavernier, *Travels in India*, I, 6.

in rural land. Their wealth was not translated into control over men and land; they therefore did not compete with sultan or nobles for power in the elite sense. Nor was their capital used for investment as risk capital in proto-industrial ventures; it was lent only on short terms and for specific production.[74] As a Portuguese noted: "They [the *vanias*] aspire to nothing except to increase their profits, and to be allowed to dress freely and conduct themselves freely, which comes down to being allowed to use palanquins."[75]

There is no evidence that the Portuguese officials in Goa took advantage of this available capital, except for the seventeenth-century Goan instance already cited. On the contrary, the Portuguese complained that the bullion they brought to Goa from Japan and Europe was all vanishing into Gujarat's insatiable maw. Thanks to the flow from South America, silver in Europe was cheaper than in Gujarat. The Gujarat merchants trading on the Goa-Cambay *cafilas* thus took back from Goa little but this silver, and gold from China.[76] This was bad for the Portuguese, who wanted to sell their European goods rather than bullion; but from the Gujarati angle it was not such a great gain. The trade to Goa represented only 5 percent of their total trade. Most of the inflow came from the Red Sea.[77]

Private Portuguese were more willing to utilize Gujarati capital. The large number of Portuguese resident in Cambay, and living by trade, have already been mentioned. Many others visited the town regularly, while still others traded there from Goa. All these Portuguese used Gujarati brokers and their capital in Cambay. There seem to have been more Portuguese traders resident in Cambay than in any other Asian city, so one can assume that a considerable proportion of private Portuguese trade in Asia was financed with Gujarati capital.[78]

This implies a mutuality of interests between individual Gujaratis

---

[74]Tapan Raychaudhuri in B. N. Ganguli, ed., *Readings in Indian Economic History* (Bombay, 1964), pp. 64-77.

[75]AHU, Caixa 18, letter to king, January 25, 1646.

[76]APOCR, I, ii, 121; III, 348-50; Artur Viegas, ed., *op. cit.*, II, 389; K. N. Chaudhuri, *The English East India Company* (New York, 1965), pp. 117-22.

[77]See Aziza Hasan. "The Silver Currency Output of the Mughal Empire and Prices in India during the 16th and 17th Centuries," *Indian Economic and Social History Review* VI (March 1969): 93-95.

[78]François Pyrard de Laval, *Travels of François Pyrard de Laval*, 2 vols. (London, 1887-90), II, 246; *The Journal of John Jourdain*, p. 173; Caesar Frederick in Richard Hakluyt, *op. cit.*, V, 375-76.

and individual Portuguese. Other evidence describing the response in time of war reflects more clearly this point. On this level there was little hostility, especially from the merchants but also from individual officials and nobles. Rather, both sides tried to ignore the wars of their superiors. In 1539 peace was restored between Gujarat and Portugal following the bitter siege of Div in 1538 and some Portuguese raids in the Gulf of Cambay. The merchants appear not to have been particularly embittered by their losses, or if they were they were eager to recoup them as soon as possible. The peace was proclaimed, and the Portuguese ambassador told the merchants they could now return to Div. At this good news the merchants raised an "astonishing cry of joy" and 2,000 of them set off at once, delirious with delight.[79]

During the second siege, of 1546, the local *vanias* of Bassein continued to trade to Gujarat, and as soon as the besiegers were beaten off, and with the war still raging elsewhere, trade between Gujarat and the Portuguese in Div and Bassein was reopened. The viceroy, Castro, described in a letter to his son how his fleets were cruising in the Gulf of Cambay, looting and burning. But six days later, in another letter from Div, he said that "the land here is at peace and the trade caravans come and go."[80] While the war continued, a rich Muslim merchant of Cambay, Sidi Muhammad, came to Div with a present of fifteen cartloads of provisions. His aim was to persuade the Portuguese to ask the sultan for peace, or at least open negotiations with him, but in this he failed. He was apparently not acting on behalf of his sultan, but solely on his own initiative.[81]

In similar fashion, after the minor Portuguese-Mughal war in 1613-15 the usual *cafila* came to Goa in December 1615. As the *cafilas* had not run during the war, it was the largest for many years.[82] The fact that the emperor had not yet signed the peace treaty, or that the Portuguese had seized two ships belonging to the royal family and raided as usual in the Gulf of Cambay, was far from upsetting to the merchants of Gujarat. They wanted to get back to business as soon as possible. In fact, as an Englishman noted in the 1660s, "a merchant is free here to buy and sell in an enemy's camp unmolested."[83]

[79] Castanheda, IX, vi.
[80] ANTTSL, III, 53v-54; 94, IV, 209, 217.
[81] *Ibid.*, II, 3v, 7v-8, 444; III, 100.
[82] Bocarro, Decada, pp. 465-66; Manuel de Faria e Sousa, *Asia Portuguesa*, VI, 89.
[83] Factories, 1665-67, p. 5.

Mughal officials were usually no different. The Portuguese noted of one governor of Surat that he was always eager to avoid war because thus his ports were frequented by traders, no matter whether enemies or friends, and so his customs houses yielded more.[84] Most of the Portuguese were governed by similar desires. It will be remembered that the residents of Daman tried to stop Portuguese ships from going to blockade Qulij Khan's ship in Surat, as they feared the consequences for themselves. The rights and wrongs of the case were nothing compared to their own security. Similarly, in addition to the trade in "illegal" goods by Portuguese, such as in spices, other Portuguese traded with areas with which the state was at war—with Gujarat while the second siege of Div was in progress in 1546, and in 1614 during the war of 1613-15, and with the Dutch in 1633, 1638, and 1641.[85]

Doubtless Portuguese and Gujarati merchants cooperated in other areas also. Very likely some Portuguese invested in trade on Gujarati ships to areas where Portuguese were not allowed, most notably the Red Sea. The Portuguese resident in Cambay probably invested either their own or borrowed capital in the production of goods destined for the Goa *cafila* and ultimately Portugal. There is evidence of Gujaratis and Portuguese combining to cheat the Raja of Cochin. Indians had to pay higher customs duties to him than did Portuguese, and what could be more obvious than for a Portuguese to claim a *vania's* goods were his? The *vania* saved money on duties, and so sold his goods a little cheaper to the Portuguese.[86]

Another aspect of this cooperation lay in the city of Div. Granted that the Portuguese made Gujarati ships call there to buy *cartazes* and pay duties, yet this compulsion did preserve Div as a great trade center where goods from all over the world were available. Many Gujarati traders would no doubt have called there even if the Portuguese had not forced them to. This is confirmed by the large and

---

[84] ANTTDR, XLI, 29.
[85] ANTTSL, III, 227; APOCR, VI, 1025; AHU, Caixa 10, king to viceroy, February 5, 1633; "Livro de Segredo," HAG, ff. 17v, 45. See also DI, II, 130. Such perceptions of the nature of war were not restricted to Muslim India or to the Portuguese. In 1655 the Hindu inhabitants of the Kanara kingdom of Sivapa Naik showed a similar attitude. Portugal and Kanara were at war, but the local merchants either did not know or did not care. They continued to come to Goa with cargoes of rice. The Portuguese protested that such conduct was "much to be abominated" and "very damaging to the credit and reputation of the arms of his Majesty, whom God protect" but bought the rice anyway. Assentos, III, 395-98; Diary of Viceroy Sarzedas, in "Noticias dos Estados da India," Biblioteca da Academia das Ciências, Lisbon, Mss. Azuis, A58, f. 48.
[86] Fazenda, II, 25v-26.

wealthy resident Gujarati population of the town. They lived there of their own free will.[87] The prosperity of Div was not just preserved by the Portuguese; in fact it rose during the second half of the sixteenth century. The customs revenues derived from it by the Portuguese doubled between 1556, one year after the Portuguese took complete control, and the 1590s.[88]

Portuguese officials in Div also took advantage of the capital available in Gujarat. The captains of the fort had as one of their privileges the right to trade to various places, and this trade was often handled for them by *vania* agents. At least one *vania* resident in Div made his living from such activities. For thirty years he used his credit with his fellows to get capital for the captains. The latter used this to buy cargoes for their private trade, and to pay off old debts. One captain at the end of his tenure owed this *vania* Rs. 22,000.[89]

These Portuguese captains saw their posts as sources of profit rather than opportunities for service. Thus it is natural that they were ready to flout, or at least modify, standing orders in return for a bribe. This sort of cooperation was frequent enough in the area of granting *cartazes* which exempted a ship from calling at Div to pay duties.[90] In one particularly flagrant case a Portuguese sea captain used his fleet to protect such a transgressor not only from pirates but also from other more law-abiding Portuguese ships.[91]

In another area, it is clear that the head of the *vanias* in Div sometimes cooperated with the captain of the fort to the detriment of other *vanias* who presumably were out of favor with their captain. Div's captains had a monopolistic voyage from Div to East Africa. One of the main constituents of the return cargo was ivory. This the captain handed over to the head of the *vanias*, who in turn forced other merchants to buy it.[92]

Some of these activities are very close to being abuses rather than

---

[87] *Travels of François Pyrard de Laval*, II, 255; *The Voyage of John Huyghen van Linschoten to the East Indies*, 2 vols. (London, 1885), I, 58; Caesar Frederick in Richard Hakluyt, *op. cit.*, V, 374; F. Mendes da Luz, "Livro das Cidades e Fortalezas," *Studia* no. 6 (1960): 29v-30.

[88] ANTTCC, 1-102-47 for 1556. Couto, VII, ii, 3, has a higher figure for 1555, but admits this was exceptional. For the 1590s, LM, v. 14, f. 683, and another copy in AHU, Codice 281, f. 394. For the 1570s, see DI. X. 135; for 1586-87, AHU, Codice 500, f. 98; and for c. 1600, Luis de Figueiredo Falção. *Livro* (Lisbon, 1859), pp. 75-78.

[89] LM, v. 28B, f. 352; "Livro Morato," HAG, ff. 262-62v.

[90] For example, LMBP, III, 167-68; LM, v. 12, ff. 44v-45; LM, v. 28B, ff. 378-78v.

[91] Alberto Iria, *Da Navegação Portuguesa no Indico no século XVII* (Lisbon, 1963), p. 84.

[92] APOCR, VI, 1250-51; cf. ANTTSV, XXVI, ff. 93v-94v.

perquisites. There are numerous clear instances of straight abuses inflicted on local merchants by these captains. In these cases there was no cooperation; no one profited except the tyrannous captain. The most common practice was forced trade: a local merchant would be forced to buy a product he did not want, and at a high price, or sell to the captain or other officials at a low price. Other traders were forced to carry goods free on their ships, sometimes to places where they did not want to go. Forced "loans" were frequent, sometimes secured by means of arbitrary arrests.[93] Complaints of these abuses date from the 1540s, but they do seem to increase in frequency late in the century and into the seventeenth century. This is no doubt partly because the documentation for this period is much fuller than that for the earlier years, but it is to be expected that abuses would increase as Portuguese power declined. Div's revenues fell sharply in the seventeenth century, thanks to Dutch and English competition. The captains of Div were more and more driven to abuses to make up the sort of profits they felt they should gain from their position.

These activities were clearly dysfunctional from the official Portuguese viewpoint, and were recognized as such. They diverted part of Div's revenues into private hands, and increased the likelihood that Gujarati traders would avoid calling at Div if they could. The various perquisites, on the other hand, were functional, and part of the administrative system of Portuguese India. On balance, however, it is difficult to say much in favor of the whole Portuguese presence when one reverses the angle of vision.

In their defense, one can note that they opened a new trade route, to Europe, which employed perhaps 3 percent of the total Gujarati capital engaged in sea trade. They made some attempt to combat piracy in western Indian waters. Their own trade provided Gujarati capitalists with a new, but small, outlet. A very few Gujaratis profited directly, like leeches, from the services they provided Portuguese officials.

For the prosecution, one can leave aside such Portuguese activities as their own piracy in the Bay of Bengal (which increased as their power declined), forced conversions especially in Ceylon and Goa,

---

[93] J. Wicki in *Studia*, no. 8 (1961): 177-78; *Studia*, no. 3, pp. 75-76; "Provisões dos Vice Reis," HAG, II, 129-29v; ANTTCC, 1-97-26; APOCR, III, 105-6, 564-66; ANTTSV, XXVI, 93v-94v; Bocarro, Livro, part 1, p. 105; "Livro Morato," HAG, ff. 216v-17v; LMBP, II, 30; AHU, Caixa 14, petitions of September to December 1642; Gavetas, V, 327.

and the brutality so much in evidence all over the Indian Ocean throughout the century. The concern is with trade control, and here it can be claimed that the Portuguese directed Gujarati trade, and taxed it, but provided no service in return. Gujarati overseas trade had been rationally organized in the fifteenth century, and in areas not dominated by the Portuguese, notably Cambay, continued to be so organized. The Portuguese introduced an element of crude exploitation and arbitrary disorganization into the pattern. Accommodations existed, but were far outweighed by the abuses, so that a Portuguese writer could attribute the "universal hatred" in which his countrymen were held in India to the extortions of the captains of the forts.[94]

Before the Portuguese arrived, a ship could sail from Surat to wherever it liked, paying duties only in Surat and its destination. From the 1530s this was not allowed; extra duties were levied in Div. True, a bribe could obviate the necessity to call at Div, but in the fifteenth century no bribe was necessary. Portuguese control was essentially based on fear, not reciprocity or service, as was recognized by an early seventeenth-century traveller: "The merchants land there [at Div] willingly enough, as well for the good haven as for the cheapness of commodities; also because they fear to enter the Gulf, where contrary winds often prevent them coming out; but the chief cause is that the Portuguese constrain them to touch there, so as to reap the dues and customs, and thus to make the place more prosperous."[95]

If, however, the Portuguese demands are accepted as a given, a *fait accompli*, then one must agree that their presence was not as burdensome as it could have been. Their effective power was small in many areas of Asia, so they could be ignored. They could be bribed or manipulated so that even off Gujarat the king's commands were sometimes ignored. Their actions were crudely exploitative, but luckily not very efficient.

The merchants' compliance seemed, to the chroniclers of both Gujarat and the Portuguese, to be only what could be expected from the Gujaratis, and especially the non-Muslims, for it was notorious that they were cowards and weak effeminate people. D. João de Castro considered that "Gujaratis are such men that the women of all other nations are more formidable than them in dexterity, strength and

---

[94] F. R. Silveira, *Memórias de um soldado da India*, ed. A. de S. S. Costa Lobo (Lisbon, 1877), p. 159.
[95] *Travels of Francois Pyrard de Laval*, II, 255.

courage as well as in the art and practice of warfare and battles."⁹⁶ These strictures, and those of the chroniclers, reflected the ethic of the warrior, the *fidalgo* or *khan*. Perhaps the clearest illustration of this merchant attitude to wars, and of general acceptance of this attitude, occurred in 1451. Gujarat was being attacked by Malwa, and the sultan asked a friend, a grain dealer, what he should do. The merchant's advice was for the sultan to put all his treasure and women on board ship "and amuse himself fishing at sea." The sultan of Malwa would invade Gujarat, find nothing worth taking, and finally go home again in disgust. Sultan Muhammad was pleased with this advice, and actually began to prepare ships. Then a noble heard what was happening, and threatened the grain dealer with death for offering such pusillanimous, and influential, advice. The dealer replied, "Sir, you must understand that the sultan has avoided asking the advice of wise and brave men like you, and instead has asked me, a peaceful and timid grain dealer. Clearly the end product is not manly advice." The noble at once agreed with the dealer's analysis of the situation.⁹⁷

It was not the business of merchants to go around fighting and getting their ships sunk. Their job was to exchange goods and make a profit, and once the Portuguese had shown them that to continue to do this they would have to accept Portuguese control, they accepted it. There was no other way for them to carry on with their occupation. To a modern nationalist, this is clearly shocking behavior on the part of a wealthy and prominent group in the state, but the merchants were not thinking in these terms. From the viewpoint of their own interests, accommodation was the practical response; thus, and in modern nationalistic terms paradoxically, the group in Gujarat most affected by and most exploited by the Portuguese was the one most eager to acquiesce.

Faced with a given set of demands, which so far as they could see

---

⁹⁶Elaine Sanceau, ed., *Cartas de Dom João de Castro*, p. 142. In 1546 the Portuguese were at first incredulous that the effeminate Gujaratis had attacked Div without help from the Turks. (ANTTSL, II, 321; III, 495.) Similar opinions on the *vanias* in AHU, Caixa 18, letter of January 25, 1646; APOCR, III, 680-83. The chronicler Sikandar deplored the way in which the merchants had given in to Portuguese control. (Sikandar, p. 162.) For a similar early seventeenth-century English opinion, see *The Voyage of Thomas Best* (London, 1934), p. 230. In 1893 the *vanias* of South Africa told M. K. Gandhi that "Only *we* can live in a land like this, because, for making money, we do not mind pocketing insults. . . ." M. K. Gandhi, *Autobiography* (Ahmedabad, 1940), pp. 83-84.

⁹⁷Sikandar, pp. 66-67.

were enforceable, they accepted them and continued trading. This is both obvious and explicable. What at first sight is not explicable is how they could be allowed to do this, for today no merchant can act with regard only to his own commercial interests. Why were they able to respond in the way they did? How could the state let them reach an accommodation with the Portuguese, thus allowing its overseas trade to be controlled and taxed by infidel foreigners? The answer lies in the political position of these merchants within the state of Gujarat. Attention can now turn to an elucidation of this, for it is only when this position has been clarified that one can understand how and why Gujarat's merchants were able to respond as they did. Further, this elucidation will make specific the whole structure of relations, or lack of relations, between one group of subjects and the rulers of medieval Gujarat.

CHAPTER V

MERCHANTS AND THEIR STATE

Most Indian nationalist historians, when describing the response to the Portuguese in the sixteenth century, do not try to distinguish between different responses from different groups. But there were, as noted, different reactions. Thus the response to the Portuguese from Gujarat has not been considered as a whole, for there was no solid monolithic response. Rather, there were in Gujarat various responses — from those who had nothing to do with the Portuguese, those on whom the Portuguese impinged only slightly, and those affected directly by their claims. Merchants and rulers responded in very different ways. A few more examples will illustrate further the existence and functioning of these two groups in medieval Gujarati society.

A ship of the English East India Company first visited Gujarat in 1608, and four years later a factory was established in Surat. Trade expanded rapidly, but the legal position of the English in the Mughal Empire remained, in English eyes, rather insecure. The Company tried, notably by means of Sir Thomas Roe's embassy, to secure a firm legal basis for their trade in the empire, with such matters as customs duties, ownership of the property of their deceased, trial of English offenders, and their right to buy property and carry arms all clearly set out in a formal treaty. Jahangir did not make treaties in the European sense with anyone, certainly not with a small group of sea traders. The English, therefore, were forced to content themselves with *farmans* and orders from the emperor and his officials, which were not always observed and were revokable at the whim of the emperor. Friction was common during their early years in India, and it was usually provoked by the English, who had not yet comprehended their position within Mughal India. In 1619 they captured a Sindhi ship and confiscated its cargo because it had a Portuguese *cartaz*, and England was at war with Portugal. Some of the goods belonged to Indian merchants, who complained at court. The English refused to pay compensation, and finally their two factors in Agra were imprisoned and compensation for the lost goods taken from English possessions at Agra.[1]

There were other minor clashes in the early 1620s, and finally the English decided to use force to get a firm agreement laying down their rights and giving them redress for past grievances. In October 1623 three English ships arrived off Surat from the Red Sea, escorting eight Gujarati ships which they had seized. Most of the English factors then went on board the ships, and those remaining on land presented their demands. The important point about the ensuing negotiations is that for most of the time they were handled on the Gujarati side by the merchants, not by any official, although the English action was clearly an act of war against subjects of the Mughal emperor. Thus the final Gujarati reply to the English demands was given to them in a merchant's house, and by a group of chief merchants. Further, these merchants felt themselves competent to guarantee good treatment for the English from the officials. To the complaint of the necessity to bribe the customs officials to get their goods cleared, the merchants replied that "they will undertake for the future that our [the English] business shalbe done with more libertie and freedome, and if the contrary be offered by any of the officers here they will see us righted." Agreement was reached in November, and was signed by both Gujarati merchants and officials. The English then landed and were taken before Safi Khan, the *subahdar* of Gujarat. "The latter seemed to be glad to hear that an agreement had been reached, and questioned them as to the terms."

This was not the end of the affair. In January 1624 all the English ships left Surat, and the local merchants then used their influence at court to get the emperor, Jahangir, to pass a series of *farmans* against the English. The English were imprisoned, and their goods were confiscated. Negotiations recommenced, but while the English were actually in prison on the orders of the emperor, at least one Surat merchant still found it worthwhile to take a pass from them for his ship. A final agreement was reached in September, and was again signed by both officials and merchants. For our purposes, the grievances of the English and the terms of the agreements are not of immediate interest; what is important is the autonomous way in which the Gujarati merchants, operating through their recognized leaders,

[1] Factories, 1622-23, pp. xvi-xviii, 11, 57.

negotiated with the English. To the officials this was a merchants' quarrel, and thus of little concern to them.[2]

The arrival of the English, and especially the establishment of their factory in Surat in 1612, had upset the Portuguese considerably, for they foresaw that this would decrease the quantity of goods on the crucial Cambay-Goa *cafila*; in any case, England and Portugal were at war. Early in 1613 the Portuguese seized a Gujarati ship returning from the Red Sea, the aim being to force the Mughals to expel the English from Surat. In this case Jahangir himself was involved, as his mother had a large interest in the ship's cargo. A war, mostly notable for its sporadic nature, broke out between the Mughals and the Portuguese. Before it achieved any momentum, the Portuguese had regretted their rather rash action, and sent an emissary to Gujarat to invite the merchants to take no notice of the war, and to continue to trade to Goa.

At the end of 1614 the Gujarati merchants, who had suffered from the usual Portuguese raids in the Gulf of Cambay, acted independently to try to get peace. They offered to pay to Jahangir the value of the goods seized by the Portuguese, hoping that thus the dispute could be forgotten and they could resume trade. Peace was finally concluded in 1615, and was quickly ratified by the Portuguese viceroy. As far as the Gujarati merchants were concerned, this was enough. Jahangir in fact never ratified the treaty, but the merchants started trade at once, and with enthusiasm. If one were to seek a modern offer comparable to that of the Gujarati merchants in 1614, one might imagine American businessmen with Japanese trading interests offering to pay full compensation to the United States after Pearl Harbor so that war could be avoided. For Gujarati merchants war, no matter for what reason, was to be avoided or ignored if at all possible. They were quite prepared to offer full compensation to Jahangir for whatever losses he, their ruler, had suffered from the actions of the Portuguese, his enemies.[3]

There are other cases which show Gujarati merchants operating with similar independence in relations with their own rulers, and

---

[2]W. H. Moreland, ed., "Pieter van den Broeke at Surat, 1620-29," *Journal of Indian History* X, XI (1931-32): X, 2-6; Factories, 1622-23, pp. xvii-xix, 268-320; 1624-29, pp. v-viii, 27-30.

[3]Bocarro, Decada, pp. 189-92, 200-1, 221, 330-36, 398; *Letters Received by the East India Company from its Servants in the East*, 6 vols. (London, 1896-1902), II, 155.

handling for themselves negotiations over matters affecting their interests. It will be remembered that in 1546 Div was divided between the Portuguese fort and the town, which was ruled by Gujarat. When the merchants had a complaint against the Portuguese official in charge of valuing coinage in the customs house, they retaliated on their own, not by appealing to the appropriate Gujarati official but by organizing a boycott. The Portuguese backed down.[4] There was at this time considerable tension in Div between Gujarat and Portugal. On one occasion a minor Portuguese official was killed in the Gujarati town and war threatened, which disturbed the merchants. In this crisis they acted as mediators between the two sides, and finally the *status quo* was restored, with the merchants guaranteeing to the Portuguese the observance of the existing agreements between Gujarat and Portugal.[5] Their efforts were of course in vain, as the second siege of Div began soon after.

Two other cases, in the 1660s, again show the merchants operating through their recognized leaders, negotiating agreements between the officials of the country to which they were subject, and the Europeans, in Surat. In 1661 the English had a dispute with the governor of Surat, Mustafa Khan, over a debt, and finally were put under house arrest. They then attempted a reconciliation, and the agreement was negotiated by "the Shahbandar, and certain of the chief merchants . . . ." A year later the English, still feeling oppressed by Mustafa Khan, threatened to leave Surat altogether. The merchants complained bitterly to the governor, saying that his arbitrary actions were likely to lose them some of their best customers. The governor finally asked the merchants to come to some agreement with the English, which was done. The English got considerable concessions and guarantees of better behaviour in the future on the part of the governor, from *the merchants*.[6]

Finally, a case involving the Dutch may be noted. In 1649 they, like the English in 1623, had numerous complaints, the nature of which need not detain us here. In September they seized two ships belonging to the emperor Shah Jahan, took them to Surat, and demanded redress. The governor appointed several "deputies" to negotiate with the Dutch, these deputies apparently all being merchants. Agreement was quickly reached, probably because the

[4] ANTTSL, V, 133.
[5] ANTTCC, 1-77-36.
[6] Factories, 1661-64, pp. 12-15, 99-103.

merchants feared that once Shah Jahan heard his ships had been seized he would retaliate, and as usual the merchants would suffer. In this case, the merchants were negotiating to redress a grievance suffered not by themselves directly but by their own emperor.[7]

The merchants were also capable of operating autonomously in negotiations with their own government. In July 1616 the judge of the Surat customs house was dismissed, mainly because, to quote the contemporary English account, of

> some violence done by him to a chief bannyane, the whole multitude assembled shut up their shops and (as their custom), after a general complaint to the Governor, left the city, pretending to go to the Court for justice, but with much fair usage and fairer promise were brought back by Abram Chan [Ibrahim Khan, governor of Surat], who joining with them informed his master of many insolences committed by this peevish Customer [that is, the judge of the customs house], which, with your Lordships's [Sir Thomas Roe's] complaint, is generally observed to be the cause of his expulsion.[8]

Under Awrangzeb the generally tolerant religious policies of his predecessors were less and less in evidence. In Surat in the late 1660s there were several cases of forced conversion to Islam, and a particular *qazi* was acting toward the *vanias* in a very tyrannous way. Finally, in 1669, they struck back. All the heads of Surat's *vania* families, numbering some 8,000, left Surat en masse for Broach, and from there petitioned the emperor. They soon got a reassuring reply, and returned, to the pleasure of all.

> In the interim the people of Surat suffered great want, for, the Bannians having bound themselves under severe penalties not to open any of their shops without order from their Mahager or Generall Councill, there was not any provisions to bee got; the tanksell [mint] and customhouse shut; no money to bee procured, soe much as for house expences, much less for trade, which was wholy at a stand; and so it will continue till their returne.[9]

---

[7]Philip Baldaeus, *A Description of the East India Coasts of Malabar and Coromandel*, vol. III (London 1703), pp. 566-67, 569-72; Factories, 1646-50, pp. xvi-xxi; I.O., I/3/32, DXIV. For the buildup to this incident, see I.O., I/3/32, DIV-DX.

[8]*Letters Received*, IV, 320.

[9]Factories, 1668-69, pp. 190-92, 205. These instances point to the falseness of Sjoberg's characterization of the political role of non-elite members of a premodern society. He uses such terms as "inenviable," "cringe before their superiors," "harsh," and "inertia" to describe their position: Gideon Sjoberg, *The Preindustrial City: Past and Present* (New York, 1965), p. 223.

Clearly, here are two almost autonomous groups, responding in different ways to common demands from the outside, and negotiating with each other when necessary. There are two strands, which need to be carefully delineated: a large degree of autonomy for the merchants when the interests of the state are not involved; and the existence of connections between the two groups, which were used on the relatively few occasions when contact was necessary.

There were individual and unofficial monetary connections between merchants and rulers. Politically, the institutionalized link, when needed, was provided by the *mahajan*. More important, this body regulated that vast majority of merchant concerns in which the state took no interest.

Mahajan means different things in different parts of India; it can refer to an individual banker, a money-lender, a merchant, or an unspecified "great man." In Gujarat it usually meant a body representing a group of people engaged in the same commercial occupation, a governing council with an elected or occasionally hereditary headman. Sometimes *mahajan* meant simply a body governing all the *vania* merchants in a town, but it also applied more generally to "any assembled or collective body of merchants" regardless of creed or *jati*. Unless stated otherwise, the term is used in this wider sense in this monograph. The *mahajan* was ordinarily concerned solely with commercial matters, regulating such matters as prices, adjudicating disputes within the occupational group, and representing its members in disputes with other *mahajans*. Religious and social matters were outside its province, these being, as in other parts of India, handled by caste or *jati panchayats*.

Such *mahajans* existed only in large towns in Gujarat. In smaller towns and villages people of the same occupation tended to belong to the same *jati*, and thus the *jati panchayat* regulated commercial matters. Two other qualifications also need to be made. First, the regulatory body for artisans was often called a *panch*, the head being a *patel*, as opposed to the *mahajan*, whose head was the *sheth*; the *mahajan* usually functioned for higher economic strata, such as merchants of various sorts, and bankers. The membership of a *panch* was usually coterminous with a *jati* occupational subdivision. Second, at least in Ahmadabad there existed another sort of *mahajan*, headed by the *nagarsheth*. This was a city-wide body, on which sat representatives of all the occupational *mahajans* and sometimes some of the *patels* as well. It regulated general commercial activities in the city, such as rates of exchange and discount, and holidays.

The city-wide *mahajan* regulated commercial groups of all castes and also of all religions, while even the ordinary *mahajans* were not always coterminous with *jati*. This helps to explain why such *mahajans* were always stronger in Gujarat than in other parts of India. The commercial class in Gujarat was extremely heterogeneous, including both Hindus and Jains, both sunni and shia Muslims of local and foreign origin, and Parsis. In other areas one group tended to dominate, so that the communal organization could handle economic matters also, just as they did outside the main towns in Gujarat. Further, Gujarat had been an economically advanced area for three millenia, with an active, dynamic group of merchants. Cambay was a great trade center from the time of the Buddha at least, and Ahmadabad since its foundation early in the fifteenth century. Surat, similarly, was an important port for centuries.[10]

Such has been the general pattern of *mahajans* in Gujarat for at least the past two millenia. Their power and composition have varied from time to time, in accordance with the strength of the government, the religion of the rulers, and the creation of new merchant groups, most notably that of the several Muslim communities. The continuous existence of such bodies over this long period is clear, and their basic character seems to have changed little until the twentieth century.

[10] E. Washburn Hopkins, "Ancient and Modern Hindu Guilds," *India, Old and New* (New York, 1901), pp. 169-205; *Census of India*, 1911, vol. VII, part 1, pp. 308-9; vol. XVI, part 1, p. 469; D. R. Gadgil, *Origins of the Modern Indian Business Class* (New York, 1959), pp. 24-27; N. A. Thoothi, *The Vaishnavas of Gujerat* (London, 1935), pp. 122-34, 188-98; *Gazetteer of India: Bombay Presidency*, vol. IV (Ahmadabad, 1879), pp. 106-13; M. R. Majmudar, *The Cultural History of Gujarat* (Bombay, 1968), pp. 198-200; G. H. Desai, *Hindu Families in Gujarat* (Baroda, 1932), pp. 209-22; Walker of Bowland Papers, National Library of Scotland, 184 c 11, pp. 41-45; 184 c 2, pp. 435-36. The quotation on p. 123 is from 184 c 11, p. 45. For other commercial groupings, in Poona and earlier Gujarat, see D. R. Gadgil, "Immigrant Traders in Poona in the eighteenth century," *Artha Vijnana* I (March 1959); D. D. Kosambi, "Indian Feudal Trade Charters," *Journal of the Economic and Social History of the Orient* II (1959); for Tamil Nadu in medieval times, see Burton Stein, "Coromandel Trade in Medieval India," in John Parker, ed., *Merchants and Scholars* (Minneapolis, 1965); W. M. K. Wijetunga, "South Indian Corporate Commercial Organizations in South and South-East Asia," and S. Arasaratnam, "Aspects of the Role and Activities of South Indian Merchants, c. 1650-1750," both in *Proceedings of the First International Conference Seminar of Tamil Studies*, vol. I (Kuala Lumpur, 1968); Tapan Raychaudhuri, *Jan Company in Coromandel, 1605-1690* (The Hague, 1962).

There is ample evidence of their existence and functions in fifteenth-, sixteenth-, and seventeenth-century Gujarat. Thus, the great seventeenth-century Jain merchant Virji Vorah was the head of a *mahajan* in Surat, and also a religious leader. In Ahmadabad another rich Jain, Shantidas Jawahari, was the *nagarsheth* of the city-wide *mahajan*. I shall shortly examine the roles of these two men more closely. Sometimes one reads simply of "leading" or "chief" merchants, or the "most eminent" merchants, acting on behalf of others. These leaders were clearly *sheths,* or *patels,* most often the former.[11] In 1662, in order to solve a dispute between the governor of Surat and the English, "there was a councell called of all the cheife merchants and other the emanent persons in the towne...." In 1619 the merchants of Surat and Broach wanted to stop the English competing with them on the Red Sea route, so they forbade the sale to the English of any goods suitable for this trade. In Surat two merchants who disobeyed were imprisoned.[12] I have already quoted the case in 1669 when the "Mahager or Generall Councill" of the *vanias* of Surat shut down the whole town until their complaints over a missionizing *qazi* were settled.[13] In the 1650s the *mahajans* of Ahmadabad contributed Rs. 60,000 to repair the fort of the city.[14]

The roles of two individual merchants, Virji Vorah and Shantidas Jawahari, and of a particular official, the *shahbandar* of Surat, are worth examining in more detail. The two merchants are both described as being enormously wealthy. One Englishman said that Virji Vorah left an estate of Rs. 80,00,000 ($30,240,000 today) when he died in the 1670s. Both, as mentioned, were heads of *mahajans,* and also of particular Jain sects.[15] In their roles as heads of *mahajans* these

[11]*Letters Received,* I, 235; IV, 320; P. Baldaeus, *op. cit.,* III, 571; *Factories, 1622-23,* pp. 57, 276-77, 300-1; *1661-64,* pp. 12-15; Henry M. Elliot and John Dowson, eds. and trans., *The History of India as Told by its Own Historians,* 8 vols. (Allahabad, 1964), VII, 217; Barros, IV, vii, 6-8; IV, x, 6.
[12]*Factories, 1661-64,* p. 102; *1618-21,* pp. 56, 92.
[13]*Factories, 1668-69,* pp. 190-92.
[14]*Mirat,* p. 273. For *sheths, nagarsheths,* and *mahajans* in Surat, Ahmadabad, and Cambay in the first half of the eighteenth century, see *Mirat,* pp. 358-59, 363, 457, 576; M. R. Majmudar, *op. cit.,* p. 338.
[15]M. Escaliot, "The Plunder of Surat by Sivaji in 1664," *Indian Antiquary* VII (September 1879): 260; K. H. Kamdar, "Virji Vorah, Surat Millionaire Mahajan," in Gujarati *Journal of the Gujarat Research Society* XXX (October 1968): 277-79; M. S. Commissariat, "Imperial Mughal Farmans in Gujarat," *Journal. Bombay University* IX (July 1940); 17.

two men, and others like them, acted as the ultimate authorities within their groups (though normally by means of promoting a concensus rather than by dictate), and also on occasion as intermediaries between their *mahajan* and the government. They were called on by the officials to give advice to them on commercial matters, and to be informed of a government decision affecting the interests of their groups. At the same time, they interpreted such decisions to their groups, and passed on to the officials any grievances of the group subject to official action. They, and other *sheths*, were in their second, mediating, role "hinge" figures, standing between their *mahajans* and the officials and interpreting one to the other.[16]

In 1639 Virji Vorah was summoned to court by Shah Jahan to give an account of the grievances he and other merchants had against a governor of Surat. In 1650 the English were worried about which Malabari merchants they should give passes to, as sometimes they mistakenly gave them to people who turned out to be pirates. To avoid this, they got the governor of Surat to nominate to them for passes only those Malabaris known to Virji Vorah. In this commercial matter the governor was to use Virji Vorah as an intermediary, an interpreter for him of merchants' affairs.[17] Seven years later Shah Jahan fell ill, and his fourth son, Murad Bakhsh, who was *subahdar* of Gujarat, revolted and prepared to seize power. As sinews of war he got a loan of Rs. 5,00,000 from the merchants of Surat; this sum was advanced by Virji Vorah and another merchant on behalf of all Surat's merchants.[18] Again in 1664 he was acting with others as a representative of Surat's merchants. This was the year of Sivaji's first raid on Surat, and Sivaji presented his demands for ransom to the governor of the town and the three leading merchants of Surat,

---

[16]There is a problem of terminology here. Anton Blok has described four types of patronage ("Variations in Patronage," *Sociologische*, GIDS, 16th year, no. 6 [Nov-Dec, 1969.]), namely vassalage, brokerage, friendship and disguised patronage. His "brokers" are closest to the people we call "intermediaries," but are not identical. His brokers provide links in a segmented society between the urban central authority and the countryside. They do not settle disputes, for a world without conflict would need no brokers. They are frequently marginal men. None of these characteristics apply to our intermediaries. Nor is "mediator" an acceptable term, for Raymond Firth sees such men as external to the units immediately concerned in a dispute: R. Firth, "A Note on Mediators," *Ethnology* IV (1965): 386-88. He proposes either "intermediary" or "liaison agent" to describe "the more general roles of providing a link between sectors of a society. . ." I have chosen the former.

[17]Factories, 1637-41, pp. 108-9; 1646-50, p. 331.

[18]Jadunath Sarkar, *History of Aurangzeb*, 5 vols. (Calcutta, 1924-30), II, 298-99.

MERCHANTS AND THEIR STATE 127

one of whom was Virji Vorah.[19] Following the raid, there is a report that Virji Vorah and another merchant went to Awrangzeb to ask for better protection for the town.[20]

Shantidas, as the *nagarsheth* of Ahmadabad, was the chief merchant in the town, and also could act on his own as an intermediary between the whole merchant community of the city and the government. The clearest illustration of his position as a link between the two occurred during and after Murad Bakhsh's revolt of 1657. In addition to taking Rs. 5,00,000 from the merchants of Surat, he also extorted Rs. 50,00,000 from those of Ahmadabad. Of this, Rs. 5,50,000 was taken from the sons and brothers of Shantidas. Later in the war of succession, Shantidas travelled north to the combined camps of Murad Bakhsh and Awrangzeb, and received from Murad Bakhsh a *farman* guaranteeing repayment of this loan of Rs. 5,50,000. Four days later Awrangzeb showed his hand by arresting Murad Bakhsh and later having him killed. He did, however, accept responsibility for Murad Bakhsh's debts, and Shantidas was able to get a *farman* from Awrangzeb providing for repayment. More important, Awrangzeb used him as an intermediary to conciliate the people of Ahmadabad, and especially the wealthy business community. In a later *farman* he was permitted to leave Awrangzeb's camp and return home, and "after his arrival there, he should announce to all the business people, and to the Mahajans, and to all the inhabitants, our desire for just administration and our regard for our subjects, so that all may pursue with peace of mind and satisfaction of heart their respective occupations and professions."[21]

These two merchants both held recognized positions within their merchant communities, but neither held any official position within the Mughal administrative hierarchy. By contrast, the *shahbandar* of Surat was both a rich and influential merchant and an official. As such he was uniquely placed to act as a "hinge." The holder of this post between 1629 and 1669 was Haji Muhammad Zahid Beg. He was one of the richest men in Surat, a great trader and the owner of ships and several of the best houses in the town. He built there both a

---

[19] Factories, 1661-64, p. 299.
[20] K. H. Kamdar, *op. cit.*, p. 276.
[21] M. S. Commissariat, *op. cit.*, pp. 15-17; Mirat, pp. 210-11; generally for Shantidas, see M. S. Commissariat, *Studies in the History of Gujarat* (Bombay, 1935), pp. 53-76. The title of *nagarsheth* was made hereditary in his family. For the activities of his grandson in the office in the 1720s, see M. S. Commissariat, *History of Gujarat*, 2 vols. (Bombay, 1938-57), II, 420-21, and Mirat, pp. 442, 446-47, 487-89, 504-5, 516-18, 708.

sarai and a mosque.²² He seems to have been included in all the important negotiations between the government of Surat and merchants during his tenure of office. He was one of the three leading merchants who were summoned by Sivaji in 1664, he accompanied Virji Vorah on his reputed journey to court after the sack, and in 1657 was jointly responsible with him for lending the Rs. 5,00,000 to Murad Bakhsh. In 1630 he went with the governor of Surat to Balsar to negotiate peace with the Portuguese after the minor war of that year.²³ His predecessor, Khwaja Jala-ud-din Mahmud, and his successor, Hajima Ahmad Ali, also played important roles in similar negotiations affecting government and merchants.²⁴ Dutch records describe the *shahbandar* of 1615 as one of the main merchants in Surat. This man, Khwaja Hasan Ali, also played a role in official affairs, for in 1614 he asked the Dutch to come to Gujarat and attack the Portuguese.²⁵

Doubtless other links also existed. Thus Muslim merchants and rulers presumably had religious and even social ties. Of more importance, however, were financial connections between merchants and rulers. Capital and loans were available from Gujarat's merchants, and both sultans and nobles used these resources. As a result, there were clear links based on interest between the two levels and even some examples of merchants using their wealth to secure admission into the upper political level. Such mobility was usually restricted to Muslim merchants. Few Hindus of any caste became nobles, at least partly because of caste or *jati* restrictions on occupations, and the desire of most Muslim rulers to employ only Muslims, at least at high levels. For the same reasons, marriage ties between nobles and mer-

---

²²Jean Baptiste Tavernier, *Travels in India*, 2 vols. (London, 1925), I, 6; Factories, 1633-36, pp. 251, 255, 301; 1642-45, pp. 161, 247; 1646-50, p. 169; 1661-64, p. 297; M. Escaliot, *op. cit.*, p. 259.

²³Factories, 1630-33, p. 100.

²⁴Factories, 1622-23, pp. 269-70, 276-77; 1624-29, p. 30; *Boletim do Governo do Estado da India*, October 10, 1873, pp. 367-68. These cases seem to show that the *shahbandar* had a position as an official in Surat port, and Moreland and Foster agree that he was the harbormaster controlling the port and custom house: W. H. Moreland, "The Shahbandar in the Eastern Seas," *Journal of the Royal Asiatic society* (October 1920): 527; *The Voyage of Thomas Best* (London, 1934), p. 40, f. n. But Jadunath Sarkar calls Haji Muhammad Zahid Beg "the headman of the traders" (*op. cit.*, II, 299), and it is possible that the *shahbandar* in Surat was actually in a position analogous to that of the *nagarsheth* of Ahmadabad. In either case, his role as an intermediary was little affected, except that it would be facilitated a little if, as seems most likely, he was an official. It may also be noted that, if he was an official, he was clearly not subject to removal at regular intervals, as were most other officials.

²⁵I.O., I/3/4, LIII; I/3/6, LXXXVII.

chants were presumably limited to Muslim merchants. At a less formal level, however, where only loans, not potential equality, was at stake, Hindu merchants had as many links as Muslim ones with the nobles.

In 1526 Bahadur started his campaign for the throne in Surat and Rander. Here he had friends, two merchant brothers. They financed an army for him, and with their help he captured Rander, and later the whole sultanate. The brothers were rewarded with high administrative positions.[26] In the seventeenth century there are at least three cases of merchants, admittedly all Persian Muslims, acquiring places in the Mughal administration. Two, Danishmand Khan and Mir Jumla, rose to very high positions.[27] An inscription from Mangrol of 1396 points to a similar instance of upward mobility: "Thamim Malik Yakub, the son of Rai Multani, the pearl merchant, was carrying on the administration...."[28]

More generally, there are cases in the sixteenth and seventeenth centuries of the state, or individual officials, lending money to merchants, and merchants lending to the state or nobles. In seventeenth-century Mughal India this connection was especially strong because a *mansabdar* moving to a new position had to provide a security for the peformance of his duties; this was usually lent to him by a merchant. Many nobles, up to and including the sultan or emperor and their families, traded overseas in their own ships or in those of merchants. In the former case, merchants hired most of the cargo space.[29] Similarly, at least one noble in the 1560s used a *vania* as his "minister," the position entailing among other duties that of supervising his trading activities.[30] Malik Gupi, the brahman who governed Surat in the early sixteenth century, had a son called Mir Gupi, who was a considerable merchant;[31] in the early fifteenth century there is even a unique instance of two *vanias* becoming officials of the sultan.[32]

[26] Barros, IV, v, 5; ANTTSL, XI, 93.
[27] Mirat, p. 196; J. N. Sarkar, *Life of Mir Jumla* (Calcutta, 1951); François Bernier, *Travels in the Mogul Empire* (London, 1914), p. 4.
[28] M. S. Commissariat, *History of Gujarat*, I, 75.
[29] Irfan Habib, "Usury in Medieval India," *Comparative Studies in Society and History* VI (July 1964): 398, 407; M. Athar Ali, *The Mughal Nobility under Aurangzeb* (New York, 1966), p. 60; B.S. Cohn, "Recruitment of Elites in India under British Rule," in Leonard Plotnicov and Arthur Tuden, eds., *Essays in Comparative Social Stratification* (Pittsburgh, 1970); Satish Chandra, "Commercial Activities of the Mughal Emperors during the Seventeenth Century," *Bengal Past and Present* LXXVIII, no. 146 (July-December 1959): 93-97.
[30] Sikandar, p. 437.
[31] Correa, III, 543.
[32] A.K. Forbes, *Ras Mala*, 2 vols. (London, 1924), I, 318, 324.

A final, and fascinating, description of another merchant-state financial connection says that many *shroffs* in Gujarat were Nagar Brahmans. "During the Mogul Government they had charge of the Dufters or public accounts, and officiated as clerks, particularly in the department of the revenues. They bore an active share in all the Civil departments of Government," and had learned Persian to be able to do this.[33] This offers a tantalizing glimpse of a caste group in an enormously strong position, for some controlled large amounts of capital, and others controlled the finances of the government. All of these connections help to explain the generally benevolent attitude of most of the sultans toward the merchants, and the inclusion of them as one of the groups honored by a sultan on his accession.[34]

These financial connections between individuals no doubt played some part in political relations. The sources are silent here, presumably because the chroniclers saw it as unethical for a *khan* to be influenced by monetary obligations; but it would be extraordinary if a heavily indebted noble was not sometimes pressed to provide political advantages for his creditor. Bahadur's elevation of the men who financed him to the throne should be seen as an example of this, as also Awrangzeb's *farmans* to Shantidas. At least partly because he owed Shantidas money, Awrangzeb issued *farmans* favoring both him individually and the merchants of whom he was a leader. The merchants of Gujarat controlled an enormous money market, and this gave them, either together or as individuals, some political leverage.

The most important financial connection between the two also illustrates this. The main demand of a premodern state on its subjects in any sphere of activity was the demand for taxation revenue. Gujarat's merchants were in fact under-taxed, paying customs duties of only 2½-5 percent, minor inland taxes, and the usual bribes, while cultivators paid at least one-third. Nevertheless, customs revenues were to some individual nobles, those controlling ports, of crucial

---

[33] Walker of Bowland Papers, National Library of Scotland, 184 c 11, pp. 29-31.
[34] Sikandar, pp. 105, 137, 144, 245; Khwajah Nizam-ud-din Ahmad, *Tabaqat-i-Akbari*, 3 vols. (Calcutta, 1927-39), III, 189. The very important matter of merchant involvement in the collection of land revenue is at present rather obscure. An understanding of this and other urban-rural relations would shed new light on the whole nature of the state. An impressive start has, however, been made by B.R. Grover in a brilliant article which makes a fundamental contribution in this area: B.R. Grover, "An Integrated Pattern of Commercial Life in the Rural Society of North India during the seventeenth and eighteenth centuries," *Indian Historical Records Commission: Proceedings of the Thirty-Seventh Session* (Delhi, 1966), pp. 121-53.

importance. One example of the political significance of this was seen in the episode of 1669 when all the *vanias* shut up shop and left Surat in protest, having to be cajoled to come back.

The method of collecting taxes from the merchants is of considerable significance, for it illustrates again how weak the links between merchant and state were. Merchants obviously paid taxes routinely, in the form of customs duties, inland transit duties, and market taxes. On the face of it, this seems to establish a regular connection between them and the state. In fact, however, all these taxes were collected by chief merchants, and by them passed on to the government.[35] Thus, only these chiefs were linked routinely to the state. In this matter also all other merchants were in the same position as when the *sheth* negotiated on their behalf with the Europeans or the governor; they could be linked to the state, but only at one remove.

Despite these financial and political links, both official and individual, it must be stressed that the merchants were left strictly alone by the upper level in matters seen as affecting only themselves. In this premodern society, the scope of such matters was considerably greater than is the case today. In commercial matters the *mahajans* were completely autonomous. They regulated production standards, interest rates, holidays, and also their own membership. Unlike European guilds, the local governments exercised no control or restrictions over them.[36] Similarly, artisans and employees were left to negotiate on their own with the *mahajan* or individual merchants. If one accepts that there was considerable slack in the economy,[37] the former must have been in a weak position vis à vis the latter. The rulers limited themselves in economic matters to general expressions of goodwill, and very spasmodic assistance in times of acute distress. They collected taxes, but used the proceeds for things they saw as important, such as the Taj Mahal, the building of new towns such as Champanir, or the conquest of prestigious but relatively useless forts such as Qandahar.

Some of these commercial affairs are even today often not closely regulated by the state, but the merchant response to the Portuguese represents a considerable difference in degree, or even perhaps in kind. The state did not consider it to be of any concern to itself if Gujarat's merchants wanted to pay extra taxes to the Portuguese, and

[35] *Ibid.*, p. 126.
[36] Violet Barbour, *Capitalism in Amsterdam in the Seventeenth Century* (Baltimore, 1951), p. 71, for Amsterdam.
[37] Tapan Raychaudhuri, in B.N. Ganguli, ed., *Readings in Indian Economic History* (Bombay, 1964), p. 72.

sail under their direction. Autonomy in matters like this is unthinkable today.

This autonomy is why the state let the merchants respond to the Portuguese as they did, by accommodating and continuing to trade. Arrangements made between merchants and another power were outside the cognizance of the state, so long as its own interests were not detrimentally affected. In this case they were not; the interests of the state of Gujarat were relatively unaffected when its merchants chose discretion as their response to the Portuguese. In wider terms, nothing that happened at sea was going to worry most of Gujarat's nobles, for their pride, ethos, and concepts of power were intimately connected to the land. More important, the accepted perception of the position of these merchants in their state meant that they could be free to react as they did. Had their position been that of a modern citizen of a nation state, they could not have been allowed to do this. In sixteenth- and seventeenth-century Gujarat, the political authorities saw in their response no threat to the prerogatives or jurisdictions of the state. It was thus, at bottom, the perception of the position of a merchant in his state, of the relation between the two, which dictated that the state accept, or more often ignore, the response of its merchants to the Portuguese.

From the merchants' point of view, a commercial response was clearly best for their interests, once they had appreciated Portugal's strength and the small cost of compliance. This was *why* they submitted, and they were *able* to submit because the state made no attempt to stop them from doing so. Nor, clearly, did the merchants ask for help from their state against the Portuguese. First, they would not expect the state to concern itself in their affairs. Second, they would not want it to interfere. Their experience throughout the sixteenth century showed them that when the state (for its own ends, not for theirs) challenged the Portuguese, it was they, the merchants, who suffered. Thus, they usually tried either to ignore or to stop wars between the Portuguese and their rulers. This point is important, for it is sometimes claimed that the premodern state, although limited in its functions, did provide protection to its subjects in return for revenue. Here, however, the state did not provide protection, even though it could have; nor did its subjects, in this case the merchants, want to be protected. They wanted to be left alone to accommodate, and this they were able to do because of the nature of their relations with the state in which they lived.

CHAPTER VI

RULERS AND SUBJECTS

The semi-autonomy of the *mahajan*, and other merchant groups, and their relations with the state authority, were not unique in medieval Gujarat. There were many other groups in this society, all of which acted more or less independently most of the time, without reference to their rulers. It is true that there were links to the central authority available. These links provided Gujarati society with such vertical political integration as it had, for it was through them that social groups were connected to the ruling group. This occurred very infrequently; in terms of vertical political connection, this society was rather particularistic. It is important, however, to be clear on one point. There were other, horizontal, connections within medieval Gujarati society on two levels. As regards social groups such as merchants and many others, these links were frequently religious or economic. They were usually outside the cognizance of the rulers, for their activities did not impinge on the interests of the state. Yet it seems clear that these horizontal connections did more to integrate medieval Gujarati society than did the vertical ones to the rulers. The other horizontal links joined together the whole ruling group, and their effectiveness was limited to this group.

The ruler and his immediate subordinates, the people whose response to the Portuguese was described in chapter III, directed the rather limited number of activities with which the state concerned itself. At the center was, of course, the ruler, the sultan of Gujarat or the Mughal emperor. Radiating out from him were people directly connected to him, usually by patron-client ties.[1] The ruling group included all "nobles" as defined in chapter III, and in fact all officials

---

[1] Anton Blok defines patronage as "a structural principle which underlies asymmetric, personal transactions involving protection and loyalty between two persons or groups of persons. By definition, transactions refer to those sequences of interaction which are governed by reciprocity." "Variations in Patronage," *Sociologische,* GIDS, 16th year, no. 6 (November-December 1969): 365.

as set out in the standard books on the subject.[2] Some people not directly in the administration can also be considered as constituents here; all the people of the court, whether artists, singers, or employees of the *karkhanahs* (the state workshops), and in addition certain people with specialized military roles, such as the elephant corps, the artillery experts, and most notably the elite 7,000-strong body of *ahadis*, or proto-*mansabdars*.[3]

This ruling group exercised authority over the whole state, even though a nominal one in many places, but its members were not the bulk of the population. The vast mass of the inhabitants should be visualized as members of one or more semi-autonomous groups or sub-groups, rather than as "subjects" governed by the rulers. Each group had a head, whether elected, appointed, hereditary, or self-chosen. These heads had two distinct roles. First, and by far the more important because the more regular and frequent, they acted as the final authority within their groups, the supreme arbiters of disputes and the guides to correct action for members of their groups. The power of different heads varied greatly, but in most cases it was not arbitrary; they normally would simply discover and articulate the concensus of their group or of its more important members. The heads' second function was much less important. They could when needed act as the intermediary between their own group and the administration of the state,[4] and also as the representative of their group in contacts with other groups. Thus they transmitted orders, or requests, down from the administration to their members, and passed up complaints or requests from their members to the rulers.

The actual person with whom they dealt in the administration varied: some would have access to the emperor, some only to a *fawjdar*. These variations did not disguise the fact that when they fulfilled this second function all of them were hinge figures, facing both their own group and the ruling one—grounded in the group which they headed but having access to someone in the administra-

---

[2] See f.n. 1 of the introduction for examples.

[3] The distinction between the nobles of Chapter III and the administration, or ruling group, of this chapter should be made clear. The former were a small military-political elite, the latter included the nobles and others besides and should be seen as a social group, not all of whose members belonged to the elite. A good working definition of the term elite can be found in B.S. Cohn's "Recruitment of Elites in India under British Rule," in Leonard Plotnicov and Arthur Tuden, eds., *Essays in Comparative Social Stratification* (Pittsburgh, 1970), p. 121.

[4] See f.n. 16 of chapter V for the term "intermediary."

tion, and thus able to interpret one to the other. Most, in fact, were recognized, either tacitly or formally, by the administration.[5] But the key point about these people is that their most usual function was to act as head of their own group in matters affecting only their group. Their role as a horizontal intermediary with some other social group was less frequently played, and that of a vertical link to the rulers even less so.

Some examples in medieval Gujarati society may help to clarify the nature of these groups and the various roles of their heads. The merchants provide the best illustration: thanks to the large bulk of European documentation, more is known about them than about most other people in sixteenth- and seventeenth-century Gujarat. Shantidas Jawahari and Virji Vorah, and the *shahbandar*, were heads of groups who also acted as intermediaries between their merchants and different people at different times in the administration. Virji Vorah and Shantidas both went directly to the emperor on occasion, but normally they were connected at a lower level in the administration, perhaps to the *subahdar* of Gujarat or the captain of Surat. Further, a large group headed by such an important man as Virji Vorah can be seen as consisting of several sub-groups, such as all Jain merchants of a particular sect, or *jati*, or all the *sarrafs*, or all the *bohrahs*. The *mahajan* represented them all in a particular town, and its head, the *nagarsheth* or *sheth*, was their usual intermediary to the ruling group.

The members of a particular trade, with their governing body, the *jati panchayat*, and its head, the *patel*, formed another group. This was a less powerful one, so that the *patel* would connect much lower down on the ruling administrative network, for example to a *kotwal* or market superintendent. Clearly there were inter-group connections also, both between the various sub-groups beneath the *mahajan*, between them and *jati panchayats*, and between two or more *jati panchayats*. The head of the cloth merchants would have dealings on behalf of his group with the head of the cloth dyers' *panchayat*, and the dyers and the weavers would obviously have connections both between themselves, with the *nagarsheth*, and with the heads of merchant sub-groups.

Another example of a social group is provided by the sufis and their followers. Sufis were organized in *silsilahs* or orders and lived

[5] Abul Fazl, *Ain-i Akbari*, 3 vols. (Calcutta, 1939-49), II, 44.

in a *khanqah*, or hospice,⁶ under the guidance and headship of their *pir*. From the 1450s the most influential group of *pirs* in Gujarat was the Bukhari Sayyids. Of these, the most revered is Shah Alam, who died in 1475. One example of his function as an intermediary between his disciples and the administration may be quoted. A *qazi* of Broach, tiring of secular life, became a disciple of Shah Alam. Later Sultan Mahmud Bigarh wanted this man to become *qazi* of Ahmadabad. The former *qazi* wanted to remain a sufi, so the sultan approached Shah Alam, and finally got him to persuade his pupil to take the position. Shah Alam and his successors were lavishly patronized by the sultans of Gujarat. The sultans confirmed each new head of the Order.⁷ They frequently visited the *khanqahs* of the Bukhari Sayyids to get advice on both spiritual and secular matters, and in return supported by grants of land the *pir* and his disciples.⁸ Indeed, the influence of these *pirs* was even considered to linger on after their deaths. Sikandar retails several stories of these saints appearing in dreams to sultans, and giving them sage advice.⁹

There were other groups for which belief in a particular religious variant formed the solidarity tie. The Ismaili *bohrah* group, as shias, were regarded as heretical by the sunni rulers, and were not favored as were the sufis; but the *bohrahs* lived together, had their own heads, collected charitable taxes, and settled their own disputes. Their *dai*, or *mullah*, had the final decision in internal civil and religious disputes, and no appeal to the law courts or to government officials was allowed.¹⁰

⁶For the functioning of a *khanqah*, see K. A. Nizami, *Life and Times of Shaikh Farid-ud-din Ganj-i-Shakar* (Aligarh, 1955), pp. 46-55. On the political role of *dargahs* in seventeenth-century Bijapur, see Richard M. Eaton, "The Court and the Dargah in the Seventeenth Century Deccan," *Indian Economic and Social History Review* X (1973): 50-63.

⁷Mirat, supplement, p. 49; M.S. Commissariat, *History of Gujarat*, 2 vols. (Bombay, 1938-57), I, 428-29; K.A. Nizami, "The Suhrawardi Silsilah and its Influence on Medieval Indian Politics," *Medieval India Quarterly* III (1957): 144-49.

⁸Sikandar, pp. 60, 81, 218-19; Mirat, supplement, pp. 14-15, 27, 35, 49, 61, 66-67, 102. For the development of *silsilahs* in Islam, see S.A.A. Rizvi, *Muslim Revivalist Movements in Northern India in the sixteenth and seventeenth centuries* (Agra, 1965), pp. 6-7.

⁹Sikandar, pp. 229, 240, 298-99, 308.

¹⁰Mirat, p. 459; Mirat, supplement, pp. 13, 109; S.T. Lokhandwalla, "Islamic Law and Ismaili Communities," *Indian Economic and Social History Review* IV (June 1967): 171-72. Details on other Muslim sects and their organization in S.C. Misra, *Muslim Communities in Gujarat* (Bombay, 1964), and M.S. Commissariat, *Studies in the History of Gujarat* (Bombay, 1935), pp. 144-45.

Sayyid Muhammad of Jaunpur, the sixteenth-century Mahdi of Northern India, had a mass and devoted following. As compared with the Bukhari Sayyids, his relations with the state were however rather adversary than cooperative. Most nobles and rulers thought he was a heretic.[11] Similarly, the Imam Shahi sect was seen by most other Muslims as being heretical, but again its leader collected religious taxes and adjudicated disputes within the group.[12] The Imam Shahis thus formed a clear example of a group, with their *pir* as their head. But, like the *mahajans*, this group was itself sub-divided into several sub-groups. In this case the heads of these sub-groups were people called *kakas*, heads of Hindu caste groups converted to the Imam Shahi faith. These *kakas* provided some religious instruction, settled disputes, and most importantly acted as go-betweens between their groups and the *pir*.[13]

Some saints, though not heretical, considered close relations with a temporal power to be denigrating to and incompatible with a religious life. One gnostic *pir* was urged by his followers to approach Akbar and get grants and favors from the emperor. "'Darvishes,' remarked the Shaikh, 'should not be beholden to temporal rulers. The true King of Kings—God the Almighty—is enough for his creatures.'"[14] Such renunciation was atypical: most saints were eager enough to be patronized, although no doubt solely in order to increase the efficacy of their ministrations. In any case, whether a Muslim saint's relations with the state were close or remote, cooperative or adversary, his political position was similar to that of other saints, and to that of, say, a *sheth*. He acted as head of his group's own affairs; and indeed probably had more complete power here than did a merchant head, for a saint can be bolstered by divine sanctions. Again, in a similar fashion to other heads, a saint could act as intermediary for his group both to other groups and to the administration. The extent of this vertical role depended on how much favor and patronage a particular saint was able to, or wanted to, attract from the rulers. For the Bukhari Sayyids relations with the rulers were frequent and friendly; for the *bohrahs* the reverse was the case.

These saints were heads of groups distinct from the state authority,

---

[11] S.A.I. Tirmizi, *Some Aspects of Medieval Gujarat* (Delhi, 1968), pp. 114-15; S.A.A. Rizvi, *op. cit.*, pp. 68-134.
[12] W. Ivanow, "The Sect of Imam Shah in Gujarat," *Journal of the Bombay Branch of the Royal Asiatic Society* n.s. XII (1936): 43, 53-54.
[13] *Ibid.*, pp. 38-39.
[14] *Mirat*, supplement, p. 66.

but members of the *ulama* (s. *alim*) have to be included in the ruling group. The *ulama*, the scholars and jurists of Islam, are not always clearly distinguished from the sufis (many were in fact members of sufi orders), and in any case different sufi orders had different attitudes toward involvement with the state. Some sufis, such as the Bukhari Sayyid Suhrawardi group, were at times actively engaged in court politics, while others were simply ecstatic, unworldly saints. But there was a distinction between a *pir* and an *alim*. *Pirs* often received royal patronage in the form of what were known under the Mughals as *madad-i ma'ash* grants, or grants for subsistence. Some *ulama* also were given these grants, but most, if they were patronized at all, received a *mansab* salary similar to that given to a noble.[15] An *alim* was often *employed* by the state, but a *pir* never was: sometimes he was *supported* in his activities by the state. Thus a great *alim*, Malik-ul-Muhadessin, who died in 1522, was a scholar and a jurist and well-versed in Hadith. He received his title from Mahmud Bigarh, and was tutor to Sultan Muzaffar. A sufi *pir* could have done all of these things too, but in addition this *alim* was *employed* by Mahmud Bigarh in the *jizya* department, and was paid by means of a *jagir*.[16] Here he parted company with the sufis. Similarly, the *qazi* of Broach mentioned above found discipleship to Shah Alam incompatible with the holding of a *qazi's* position. Employment and payment by a *mansab* clearly distinguished an *alim* from a *pir*.[17] But men could move from one to the other. In 1642 the head of the Bukhari Sayyids was made *Sadr-us-Sadur* of the Mughal Empire, with a *mansab* of 4,000.[18] This man thereby crossed the line and became an *alim* instead of a *pir*.

Other religious leaders occupied positions as heads of their groups similar to those of the various Muslim saints and to the merchant heads. The Parsis had their own leaders, who represented the community before local officials when this was necessary. Usually internal disputes were handled within the community. Around 1500 the leader of the main Parsi group, at Naosari south of Surat, was Changa Asha. He "enjoyed very considerable administrative authority in and near Navsari," and also was the head of Parsis living elsewhere, such as in Surat, Broach and Cambay. In the seventeenth century the religious heads of the group still lived at Naosari; the economic

---

[15] See Irfan Habib, *The Agrarian System of Mughal India* (Bombay, 1963), pp. 298-316.
[16] *Arabic History*, p. 106.
[17] *Ibid.*, pp. 106-7.
[18] M.S. Commissariat, *History of Gujarat*, II, 112-13.

importance of the Parsis increased greatly in this century, especially in Surat, and their head there, Rustam Manock, was their leader in both religious and secular matters.[19]

Various Jain saints and reformers also occupied positions similar to the sufis and their *pirs*. Under the tolerant Akbar these heads even had a vertical function, for he was prepared to listen to them and redress their grievances. Akbar acknowledged that in all religious and most secular matters these saints had full jurisdiction over their disciples. At one time he wanted to honor a Jain ascetic, who had impressed him at court, with a religious title, but he was informed that only the head of the ascetic's order could do this. Akbar accordingly obtained the necessary authorization.[20] Other Jain leaders at Akbar's court got considerable concessions from the emperor. These leaders acted on behalf of their fellow Jains, and were their representatives at court.[21] The intermediary function of these leaders virtually ended under Awrangzeb, for he restricted his attentions rather closely to orthodox Muslims.

Shantidas Jawahari, the *nagarsheth* of Ahmadabad, was also the head of an important Jain group in the town. As such, he sometimes acted as an intermediary between the government and the constituents of the religious group which he headed. In 1625 he completed the great Jain temple called Manatunga in Ahmadabad. Twenty years later the intolerant Awrangzeb was governor of Gujarat, and he had the temple desecrated. Shantidas complained to Awrangzeb's father, the emperor Shah Jahan, and in 1648 Shantidas received a *farman* restoring, with restitution, the temple to him. This was, incidentally, a pyrrhic victory, for the temple was considered to be irrevocably polluted, and was abandoned by the Jains. In his role as intermediary, Shantidas received royal *farmans* bestowing on him a village and a sacred hill. These he held in trust for the Jain community he represented.[22]

For most of the vast rural population the heads were *zamindars*.

---

[19] J.J. Modi, *Asiatic Papers*, vol. IV (Bombay; 1929), pp. 162, 198; J.J. Modi, *A Few Events in the Early History of the Parsis* (Bombay, 1905), pp. 60-62, 71; W. H. Moreland, "A Dutch Account of Mogul Administrative Methods," *Journal of Indian History* III (April 1925): 83; M.S. Commissariat, *History of Gujarat*, I, 182-83.

[20] Artur Viegas, ed., *Relação Anual das Coisas que Fizeram os Padres da Companhia de Jesus nas suas Missões*, by Fernão Guerreiro, 3 vols. (Lisbon, 1930-42), II, 394-95; Siddhicandra, *Bhanucandra Carita* (Calcutta, 1941), pp. 5-6, 26-27, 30, 34-37, 41. For this specific incident, see *ibid.*, pp. 32-33.

[21] M.S. Commissariat, *History of Gujarat*, II, 229-43.

[22] M.S. Commissariat, *Studies in the History of Gujarat* pp. 55-60, 64-68, 74-75.

The term is only now being more strictly defined; I use here S. Nurul Hasan's classification of them into three divisions—chieftains, intermediary *zamindars* and primary *zamindars*.[23] The first included the great Rajput rulers of Rajasthan, and the numerous petty Rajput rajas of Gujarat. Like the *mahajans*, these local power figures had considerable autonomy in matters affecting themselves and the constituents of the groups which they headed. Their areas have recently been called "little Kingdoms," ruled by members of a lineage or clan.[24] Just as merchants could ignore a declaration of war by their ruler, so in these "little Kingdoms" sizable battles occurred, and villages changed hands, without the administration taking any notice.[25] Nor were these people necessarily Hindu. The Afghan rulers of Daman were in a similar position, as was Musa Khan Fawladi, the "absolute ruler" of Patan around 1560.[26]

The intermediary *zamindars* were primarily the local revenue collectors, usually hereditary and variously called *chaudhuris, desmukhs, desais,* or *despandes*. Among these were numbered the mass of Rajputs and Kolis in Gujarat, although the most powerful of these are best seen as chieftains.[27] The role of a *desai* in Gujarat was well described by Alexander Walker: "This is the head of a district: A local Chief. He has generally charge of the revenues, and is the principal landholder. He is the agent for the Ryots, and medium between them and the Government. They are Zamindars, and may be either Hindoos or Musselmen, although for the most part Hindoos ... There is commonly a managing Dessoy in each Village who settles the Iumma [*Jama:* standard assessment of land revenue demand], who receives so much percent for his trouble—1 percent and upwards as may be agreed on."[28]

[23]S. Nurul Hasan, "Zamindars under the Mughals," in R.E. Frykenberg, ed., *Land Control and Social Structure in Indian History* (Madison, 1969), pp. 17-31.
[24]B.S. Cohn, "Urbanization and Social Mobility in 'Early Modern' India: An Exploration," mimeographed paper, 1972, p. 3 *et seq.*, and see also the references in f.n. 6 of this paper.
[25] As, for example, in A.K. Forbes, *Ras Mala*, 2 vols. (London, 1924), I, 275, 369, 432-34; II, 270-71. For an excellent account of the great power of *zamindars* in the heartland *subah* of Allahabad, see S.N. Sinha, *Subah of Allahabad under the Great Mughals* (New Delhi, 1974), especially pp. 106-15, 135.
[26]For Daman, see chapter III; for Patan, Mirat, p. 78.
[27]See pp. 61-62.
[28]Walker of Bowland Papers, National Library of Scotland, 184 c 11, pp. 153-54. Walker wrote around 1800, but his accounts are based on oral tradition and some reading in Persian sources, and as such are useful for the pre-British period.

Below the *desais* and others were the primary, land-holding, *zamindars*. The structure here, and the potential connections between its levels, were enormously complex. Thus, in a Rajput state the raja was the link to the administration, and normally directly to its center, the sultan. Below the raja were whole mini-structures, consisting of many semi-autonomous groups and sub-groups, all of which could be connected both to the administration and to each other by their heads. Similarly, a peasant, or a primary *zamindar*, could have as his intermediary either a chief or an intermediary *zamindar*, but he in turn might not have access to the state. He could go through another chief, acting as his intermediary, to reach this. The power of the various *zamindars*, and so the level, if any, to which they related in the ruling group, varied greatly.

Within a village there were again groups and sub-groups. A village usually had several caste *panchayats*, handling the affairs of the various *jatis*. Each, or at least most, of these *jati panchayats* would gear in to other *panchayats* of the same *jati* in contiguous areas. Within the village, however, was a headman and sometimes a village *panchayat*, usually virtually identical with the head and *panchayat* of the dominant *jati*. This village headman, as a primary *zamindar*, was the intermediary for the whole village in some matters, such as the payment of land revenue. But in other matters of a social, religious, caste, or economic nature, the various *jati panchayats* were more likely to be dominant. Again Walker describes well the role of the headman in Gujarat: "The Patell or Pateil are the Heads of Villages ... The Patells are the Agents of the Ryots and manage their Transactions. The Amine or head and managing Patells are commonly elected by the Villagers, but the office is hereditary and it is sometimes divided amongst many ... There is generally however one or more Amine Patells who are considered the Head of the Village and the Managers of its concerns."[29]

Other determinants of groups could be distinguished almost indefinitely. Two more must suffice here. One was place of residence in a city. Many areas of a city were inhabited by members of a particular trade or craft, and coterminously with this members of a particular *jati*. In these cases the main criterion for a group was occupation, not residence.

Other quarters in Gujarati cities were however not defined by

[29] *Ibid.*, pp. 154-56.

occupation. In many cases, a quarter was founded by a noble or saint or other prominent person. In Ahmadabad, Ali Muhammad Khan tells us there were 360 or 380 quarters, each focused on the house of a noble, each containing a palace and a mosque, and each constituting a city in itself, with all classes of inhabitants represented.[30] Another of the suburbs of Ahmadabad, Rasulabad, was founded by the great sufi *pir* Shah Alam. Here lived his descendants, and others, and "these people lived comfortably, and gradually made fine houses and gardens. None of the Nazims or officers troubled the inhabitants, owing to the respect paid to the Saint and the Seyyid. From olden times the Saint's successors have been empowered to decide cases and settle the disputes of the inhabitants and traders. A separate Qazi was also appointed and attached to the Dargah."[31]

Here then are two sorts of divisions within the city — the occupational quarter, and the suburb built by a great man. The two were of course not clearly defined; thus within Rasulabad, for example, there were occupational quarters. A third division was also intertwined with the other two. This division consisted of the streets themselves. There apparently were appointed heads of each street. These street chiefs were subordinate to the *kotwal*, the official responsible for law and order in the city.[32] Thus in residential matters, and especially those relating to security and crime, a man would be part of a group comprising the residents of his street. His head for these matters, and his intermediary to the administration, in this case represented by the *kotwal*, would be his street chief.

One final example is that of groups of foreigners resident in Gujarat and other parts of the Mughal Empire, both merchants and others. The Gujarati army included many foreigners, who apparently always had thier own heads according to their country of origin.[33] The merchants, whether English, Dutch, Turkish, Armenian or Persian, usually lived in their own areas — a factory, a suburb or a *sarai* — had their own head, settled their own disputes and buried their own dead in their own cemeteries.[34]

[30]Mirat, supplement, pp. 10-11.
[31]*Ibid.*, pp. 14-15.
[32]Mirat, pp. 144-45, for a *farman* of Akbar's setting out the duties of a street chief.
[33]ANTTSV, XI, 108-8v; Arabic History, I, 27, 243, 439; Sikandar, p. 363.
[34]See pp. 17-18, and Lopo de Sousa Coutinho, *Historia de Cerco de Diu* (Lisbon, 1890), p. 84; Factories, 1665-67, p. 61; Lwon Khachikian, "Un merchand armenien en Perse, en Inde, et au Tibet (1682-1693)," *Annales. Economies, Sociétés, Civilisations* (March-April 1967): 237-39; ANTTSV, XI, 94v; John Fryer, *A New Account*

RULERS AND SUBJECTS

The semi-autonomy of the various groups within medieval Gujarati society must be stressed. The main role of a *sheth* or a *pir* was as head of his group, not as a link to the administration. Negotiations with officials were extraordinary for most of them most of the time. They were needed only in exceptional crisis situations when the group was unable to solve its own problems, or when abuse from a member of the administration could only be redressed by someone higher in the administrative hierarchy.

It was noted in chapter V how seldom merchants had contact with the state. Even taxation payments were channeled through head merchants, so that ordinary traders did not connect directly to any member of the administration. Yet these payments of customs duties and transit dues were significant, for only here did the administration and a head of a group have a routine connection. This applied to other groups also. Thus land revenue was collected annually, but in most of Gujarat most of the time not from individual peasants but from their heads, the *zamindars*. It was only in this matter of paying taxes that a head had also a routine connection to the administration. Apart from this, heads acted as intermediaries only in exceptional circumstances.[35]

What sorts of numbers are involved in these groups? Here, as usual, one is confronted with the problem of deficient statistics: the tombs of *pirs* are too often revered by nothing more specific than "thousands" or "numbers" of devotees, or "many people."[36] As regards the ruling group, Athar Ali quotes a figure for the whole Mughal Empire of 14,449 *mansabdars*, *ahadis*, gunners and attendants for late in Awrangzeb's reign.[37] One should probably double this figure to reach a total for all the group, as one must include the workmen of the *karkhanahs*, various entertainers, and artists, and a host of hangers-on. But at the

---

of East India and Persia, 3 vols.(London, 1909-15), I, 252-55. For *sarais,* see Fray Sebastian Manrique, *Travels of Fray Sebastian Manrique,* 2 vols.(Oxford, 1926-27), II, 152-190; S.N. Sen, ed., *Indian Travels of Thevenot and Careri* (New Delhi, 1949), pp. lvi, lvii, 48; Factories, 1661-64, p. 308; 1670-77, p. 195; Mirat, supplement, p. 69.

[35]Only here did the ruling group sort out all its subjects. All who paid revenue were, from the administration point of view, subjects of their state. From the peasant point of view, however, payment of revenue was simply an annual burden which had to be borne, but which signified little except an annual, and apparently arbitrary, exaction.

[36]For example, Mirat, supplement, pp. 48, 61, 62, 77.

[37]M. Athar Ali, *The Mughal Nobility under Aurangzeb* (New York, 1966), p. 7. He thinks the total for an earlier period was smaller.

outside, this group in Mughal India cannot have numbered over 50,000 men. Add in families and other dependents of these men bound by patronage to the emperor, and there would be at most 500,000 out of a total population for the Mughal Empire of 60-70,000,000.[38]

For lower groups, the following statistics give at least some indications. In the early sixteenth century a *kaka* of one group within the schismatic Imam Shahi sect led 18,000 converts. This *kaka* collected religious dues from these people and forwarded them to the *pir* who headed the whole sect. The *pir* was thus the head of a much larger number than 18,000.[39] In 1936 the sect was in decline, but still had about 200,000 adherents. Around 1700 some members of the sect revolted and were able to capture and hold Broach for some time.[40] In 1665 a Jain saint's body was accompanied to the cremation ground by 2,000 followers.[41] Twelve years earlier a European traveller had met over 2,000 pilgrims near Daulatabad. They were taking their idol from Sind to North Arcot.[42] Late in the fifteenth century the later leader of the Mahdavi movement in northern India, Sayyid Muhammad, took 360 followers with him on *hajj*.[43] The significance of this figure in estimating his following is seen when one remembers that at this time he had not yet declared himself to be the Mahdi. Further, only wealthy followers could afford to go on *hajj*. Early next century the *daira*, or establishment, of one of his disciples was inhabited by 1,400 people.[44] The total number of followers of the Sayyid himself, or of other important religious leaders, would be several times this figure.

There are also some indications of the size of one merchant group. Within the Portuguese empire in 1646 there were 30,000 *vanias*. They had heads in each major area—Goa, Div, Hurmuz (at least until the Persians took this port in 1622)—and the head at Div was considered

---

[38] Note that I do not include here the whole army, for I have noted how the army incorporated many semiautonomous groups, based on ethnic and kin criteria. See also Rafi Ahmad Alavi, "New Light on Mughal Cavalry," *Medieval India: A Miscellany*, vol. II (Aligarh, 1972), pp. 70-98. On the population of the Mughal Empire, see W. H. Moreland, *India at the Death of Akbar* (Delhi, 1962), pp. 18-21, and two new, interesting, and conflicting articles: A.V. Desai, "Population and Standards of Living in Akbar's Time," *Indian Economic and Social History Review* IX (1972), and Shireen Moosvi, "Production, Consumption and Population in Akbar's Time," *ibid.*, X (1973).

[39] W. Ivanow, "The Sect of Imam Shah," p. 43.
[40] *Ibid.*, pp. 68, 53-54.
[41] M.S. Commissariat, *History of Gujarat*, II, 149.
[42] Jean Baptiste Travernier, *Travels in India*, 2 vols. (London, 1925), II, 191.
[43] S.A.A. Rizvi, *op. cit.*, p. 85.
[44] *Ibid.*, p. 111.

to be the head of the whole group.[45] Including dependents, this group must have numbered close to 150,000.

There is no doubt that cities in medieval India were important in societal and political terms. Most members of the elite[46] lived in cities and towns. In terms of absolute numbers, however, cities were less important. H. K. Naqvi estimates the populations of Agra, Delhi, and Lahore at about 500,000 each early in the seventeenth century.[47] The two largest towns of Gujarat, Surat and Ahmadabad, cannot have been far behind. But as the total population of the empire was 60 or 70 million, the proportion of urbanites was clearly small. B. S. Cohn finds 9.3 per cent of India's population in 1881 in towns over 5,000, and thinks this may mark a slight decline from earlier.[48] Even so, 15 per cent seems to be the outside limit for urban dwellers in Gujarat or Mughal India.

In many of these groups patron-client connections were important in forming solidarity ties. These were the crucial determinants in the ruling group. They were also of prime significance in some lower groups. The English merchants included in their group their older-established Indian employees. There is a recorded instance of a ship belonging to an Indian broker being treated as an English vessel, and flying the English flag. Similarly, the English tried their Indian employees themselves, and claimed that these Indians should share in the privileges given to the East India Company's servants by the emperors. In 1636, on the other hand, one of their Indian brokers was imprisoned by the local officials when the English were accused of piracy.[49] Clearly, the tie here was patronage. Similar ties were important in other groups, perhaps in all groups, but they were probably outweighed by other factors in most of them. Occupation (in this Indian context often associated with *jati*), kin groupings, or racial origin were decisive.

The relations between these groups was made more complex, but also more harmonious, by the fact that one man could have several roles, for each of which he had a different head. Thus, a merchant could also be a disciple of a *pir*, as could a member of the ruling group from the sultan on down. Consider a hypothetical *vania* merchant called Tulsi Parekh living in Surat. This merchant came to

---
[45]AHU, Caixa 18, letter to king of January 25, 1646.
[46]See f.n. 3 of this chapter for the term "elite."
[47]H.K. Naqvi, *Urban Centres and Industries in Upper India, 1556-1803* (New York, 1968), pp. 81-82.
[48]B.S. Cohn, "Urbanization and Social Mobility," p. 32.
[49]Factories, 1630-33, pp. 328-29; 1633-36, p. 278; 1655-60, pp. 83, 313, 368.

Surat from the village of Haldaru, where his father had been the local money lender. His widowed mother still lives in Haldaru, supported by Tulsi Parekh's elder brother, who succeeded to the father's business. After he moved to Surat, Tulsi became a disciple of the great Jain reformer Hira Vijaya Suri. Tulsi thus has at least four heads, and membership in at least four groups. If his house is robbed, he goes to see the street chief. If his mother or brother are oppressed by a fellow villager, Tulsi Parekh, as a good son who retains close ties with the family village, will join his family and *jati* fellows in the village in complaining to the *zamindar* who controls Haldaru. In matters concerning his occupation in Surat, his head is a *patel* or *sheth*, and in religious matters Hira Vijaya Suri or one of his subordinates. These four heads are also potential links to the administration, but for most of the time Tulsi's problems are settled within one of his groups by its head or others, without there being any need for recourse to the ruling group in the state.

Similarly, one man could be a head and an intermediary for two different, although perhaps overlapping, groups. Shantidas Jawahari was both head of a Jain sect in Ahmadabad and the *nagarsheth* of the town. Virji Vorah also was the head of a *mahajan* and of a Jain sect. "Those who wanted to take *diksha* [renounce the world to become a Jain monk] had to seek his permission, and without it they were not allowed. Virji Vorah constantly checked the knowledge of *agam* [Jain religious] literature in those seeking *diksha*, and if he as well as the order was satisfied he would give his assent for *diksha*."[50]

This society was not completely localized. Some horizontal integration was provided by economic and religious ties. Important merchants, such as again Virji Vorah, had agents all over India, and even as far away as Iran and the Philippines. The *vania* group in Portuguese India was scattered from the Persian Gulf to Goa, and probably also had members further south in the Malabar ports. Ethnic groups within the army obviously travelled widely over India.[51]

---

[50] K.H. Kamdar, "Virji Vorah, Surat Millionaire Mahajan," *Journal of the Gujarat Research Society* XXX (October 1968): 279.

[51] It may be noted that the merchants belonged to a social group which was not coterminous with the bounds of a particular state, as also did various religious groups. Military leaders also seem to have felt free to move from state to state. To these people, what was of most importance was not the state in which they happened to be domiciled at any particular time but rather their social group, and this was bounded not by frontiers but by what Clifford Geertz calls "primordial attachments": "Primordial Sentiments and Civil Politics in the New States," C. Geertz, ed., *Old Societies and New States: The Quest for Modernity in Asia and Africa* (Glencoe, Ill., 1963), p. 109.

Religious ties were especially important in fostering contact over wide areas. Sayyid Muhammad's followers came from all over northern and western India. When Sivaji had himself legitimized as a kshatriya in 1674, he imported a Brahman from far away Benares to perform the ceremony.[52] In 1653 Tavernier met a group of pilgrims near Daulatabad. They were travelling from one corner of the subcontinent to the other, from Tatta, in Sind, to Tirupati, in North Arcot. The group numbered over 2,000, men, women and children, and they carried their idol with them in a palanquin.[53]

Nor was this society completely particularistic; rather, men were tied in many different ways with other men of different occupations, religions and residences. There is evidence of several groups combining to face a common threat. Faced with a massive challenge, Sivaji's raid of 1664, three men acted on behalf of all the inhabitants of the town of Surat. Shantidas as *nagarsheth* occasionally acted as an intermediary for the whole town of Ahmadabad.[54] In Portuguese Div all the inhabitants of the town, presumably excluding the Portuguese, on occasion petitioned jointly to Goa.[55] But such unity was probably exceptional. More common was action by one group, as in 1669 when the *vanias* of Surat alone shut up shop and closed down the town.[56]

On the other hand, there could be conflict both within groups and between two or more groups. I noted in chapter III the existence of factions engaging in political, and sometimes military, maneuvering among the Gujarati nobles. Similarly, there are hints of discord over the choice of a new *pir* for a sufi group.

Political disputes between lower groups are less well recorded. Clearly they occurred, but the best examples come when the government was involved, for then the chroniclers took notice. An excellent case study concerns the fifteenth-century dispute over the unofficial but very real position of "top saint" in Gujarat.

The first person to occupy this position was a leader in the Chishti *silsilah*, Shaikh Jalaluddin Ahmad Khattu. By repute he lived from 1337 to 1445. Late in the fourteenth century in Delhi he met and impressed a noble called Zafar Khan. In 1391 Zafar Khan was made governor of Gujarat and in 1407, as Muzaffar Shah, he became formally independent of Delhi. He then invited Shaikh Ahmad to join him in

---

[52]Jadunath Sarkar, *Shivaji and his Times* (Calcutta, 1920), pp. 240-41.
[53]J.B. Tavernier, *op. cit.*, II, 191.
[54]See p. 127.
[55]For example, AHU, Caixa 2, no. 252; Caixa 16, petition of January 15, 1644.
[56]See p. 122.

Gujarat. The saint agreed, and until his death in 1445 received very heavy patronage from the sultans in return for being their spiritual guide.[57] Following the Chishti's death, the position fell to a member of the Suhrawardi *silsilah*, Sayyid Burhan-ud-din Qutb-i Alam. He was descended from the great fourteenth-century Suhrawardi *pir* Makhdum-i Jahanian, or Sayyid Jalal-ud-din Bukhari, who was seen by the ruling dynasty in Gujarat as their patron saint.[58] But the newfound dominance of the Suhrawardis was soon challenged by another *pir*, Shaikh Kamal of Malwa, whose order is unknown. The struggle between Shaikh Kamal and Burhan-ud-din in 1451 was a fascinating one, particularly valuable for the way in which it reveals the interconnections with the sultans, which finally decided the outcome of this struggle.

Shaikh Kamal had close ties with Sultan Mahmud of Malwa. The sultan wrote the *shaikh* that if he could conquer Gujarat he would give the *shaikh* a free refectory for the poor, and a stipend of Rs. 3,00,000, equal to that of Shaikh Ahmad Khattu. The first part of the offer was at least as valuable as the latter, for a large refectory would attract many men. This in turn would increase the number of the *shaikh's* patronage clients, and so his power. The *shaikh* responded by issuing a public invitation to the Malwa sultan to invade Gujarat. As the sultan prepared his forces, the new sultan of Gujarat, Qutb-ud-din (1451-59), asked Shaikh Kamal to try and stop the threatened invasion. The *shaikh* refused, but the invasion was repulsed and the *shaikh* died. Death may have been due to mortification or pique, for the defeat of his Malwa patron left him with no chance to replace Burhan-ud-din as the spiritual advisor to the sultan of Gujarat.[59] These events were decisive, for the Suhrawardi dynasty of Burhan-ud-din, the Bukhari Sayyids, remained dominant during the rest of the sultanate period. Burhan-ud-din died in 1453, but his son, the great Shah Alam, went from strength to strength. He and his successors were enormously influential in Gujarat with both commoners and sultans, Hindus and Muslims.[60]

There is no need to embrace Indian nationalist myths about the glories of life in pre-colonial India, or to join the romantics (usually urban liberals) who extol the untramelled freedom of the simple

---

[57] Muhammad Mujeeb, *The Indian Muslims* (London, 1967), pp. 278-79, 290.
[58] K.A. Nizami, "The Suhrawardi Silsilah," pp. 144-49.
[59] Sikandar, pp. 64-81.
[60] K.A. Nizami, *op. cit., passim*.

peasant. There was plenty of oppression and crude use of power in medieval Gujarat. I have already noted tyranny from the administration: Awrangzeb's desecration of Shantidas' temple, Malik Ayaz's suspiciously rapid raising of Rs. 6,50,000 from the merchants of Div in 1509, Murad Bakhsh's forced loans in Surat and Ahmadabad, the tyranny of the *qazi* in 1669, Virji Vorah's unjust imprisonment by an avaricious noble. True, in these cases redress was later gained, yet this cannot have always happened, and in any case it was sometimes useless. Shantidas' temple remained polluted and unusable.[61]

Nor was there much chance of redress within any one group if the oppressor was powerful. Jahangir's *Memoirs* narrate several instances of arbitrary punishments of members of his court, both noble and commoner. Here an emperor could on occasion be autocratic. At a lower level, the usual practice of settling disputes within a group rather than by appealing to the government meant that a powerful figure could act relatively unchecked. The merchants, and Virji Vorah, again provide an illustration. In 1634 the English factors in Surat wrote home that they had decided to sell some coral to Tapi Das. This decision they took with some trepidation, for by it they risked offending Virji Vorah. As they explained,

The potency of Virgee Vorah (who hath been the usual merchant, and is now become the sole monopolist of all European commodities) is observed to beare such sway amongst the inferior merchants of this towne that when they would oftentymes buy (and give greater prices) they are still restrayned, not dareing to betray their intents to his knowledge and their owne sufferance, insomuch that the tyme and price is still in his will and at his owne disposure.

On this, and other occasions, Virji Vorah could not be flouted; two years later Tapi Das had still not dared to admit that he had bought this coral, for he was terrified of offending Virji Vorah. The coral still lay in the East India Company's warehouse.[62] Nor had the situation changed by 1643; lesser merchants, including the English, were still in thrall to his wealth and influence:

Virge Vora, by reason of our continuall mighty ingagements, must not be displeased in any case. I confess him to bee a man that hath often supplyed our wants in Suratt with moneys, for his owne ends. Notwithstanding, I hould him to have bynn the most injurious man to your trade in all the

[61] See f.n. 22 of this chapter.
[62] Factories, 1633-36, pp. 24, 218.

Mogulls dominions; for what ordinary Banian merchant dare come to the English Howse to look uppon corrall or any other comodity, hee by his potencye and intimacy with the Governour forgeth somewhat or other against the poor man, utterly to ruine him; so that no merchant in the towne dare displease him by comeing to our house to look uppon any comodity, except some or other sometymes whome hee sends purposely to bid for a comodity (that hee is about) little or nothing, onely to make us weary of our comodities. Hee knoweth that wee (in regard of our extreame ingagement) must sell, and so beats us downe till wee come to his owne rates; and this hath bynn his proceedings this many yeares.[63]

In one sense this sort of conduct was exceptional, for Virji Vorah was exceptionally wealthy. Because of this he apparently was able to get the governor of Surat to back up his exploitation of other merchants. But more generally these examples of very powerful men oppressing their inferiors provide yet another, and final, example of the large degree of autonomy held by different groups, and leaders within groups, in medieval Gujarat.

Several factors were responsible for this sort of loosely-integrated state. On the practical level, it was simply not possible for a pre-modern state like Gujarat to control closely its inhabitants. Anyone who reads the contemporary European travellers' accounts will be impressed by the difficult, laborious, and dangerous nature of travel in India. Akbar's feat in 1573 of covering nearly 600 miles in eleven days, from Fathipur Sikri to Ahmadabad, is rightly considered to be a considerable achievement, yet today the journey is a comfortable one day by train. In the sixteenth century poor roads, periodic local disorder, reliance on animals for transportation, and the difficult terrain of much of Gujarat simply made close control from the center over much of the state a physical impossibility.[64]

Other factors also militated against close control. One is the conception of the duties of a Muslim ruler. Talcott Parsons in his interesting discussion of advanced intermediate societies distinguishes between India and China, where full membership was granted only to an upper group, and Islamic societies, where in theory all Muslims were full members. He then modifies this by pointing out the basic dualism present in all the Islamic empires, as a result of the "lasting anchorage of the Islamic masses in traditional or nomadic

[63] *Ibid.*, 1642-45, p. 108.
[64] See Jean Deloche, *Recherches sur les routes de l'Inde au temps des Mogols (Etude critique des sources)* (Paris, 1968).

societies . . . ."⁶⁵ In similar fashion, H. A. R. Gibb shows how there developed a concept of an Islamic polity in which there was an overriding law, the *shariah,* but beneath this was a fair degree of elasticity according to different situations in different areas. The essential duty of an Islamic governor was only to protect the land and Islam, and respect general principles of Muslim conduct.⁶⁶ In no Muslim state was a ruler required or encouraged by the *shariah* or traditional Muslim concepts of the duties of a governor to interfere extensively or intensively in the lives of his subjects.

A crucial element was the extreme heterogeneity of the population of Gujarat. Statistics are lacking, but it is sufficient to point to the presence of *vaishnavite vaisyas, shaivite brahmans*, Jains, sunni Muslims, several sects of shia Muslims, Christians, and Parsis. In racial terms, there were Gujarati-born people, but also a host of Muslim foreigners, who were dominant in military and administrative roles.⁶⁷

The nature of the Gujarati and Mughal armies was in part a mirror image of the groups into which the polity was divided, and in part a cause of these groups. It was noted in chapter III the way in which the absence of a large centrally-controlled army decreased the effective power of a sultan vis-à-vis his nobles; it also made it impossible for a sultan to control closely his subjects. In Gujarat only Mahmud III tried to form a body of troops based at court and loyal to him alone. This attempt failed, and in any case the number concerned was apparently only 1200 men.⁶⁸ More typical is a description of the Gujarati cavalry in about 1560, in which the 12,000 men are divided up into eight racial groups, each under its own leader.⁶⁹ The Mughal army also consisted largely of contingents raised by nobles. The cavalry

⁶⁵Talcott Parsons, *Societies: Evolutionary and Comparative Aspects* (Englewood Cliffs, 1966), p. 85, and generally pp. 82-86.

⁶⁶H.A.R. Gibb, "Religion and Politics in Christianity and Islam," in J. Harris Proctor, ed., *Islam and International Relations* (London, 1965), pp. 7-15. See also S.R. Sharma, *The Religious Policy of the Mughal Emperors* (New York, 1972), pp. 9-23, and A.H. Hourani, *The Islamic City* (Philadelphia, 1970), pp. 18-20.

⁶⁷See, for example, S.C. Misra, *Muslim Communities in Gujarat* (Bombay, 1964), and N.A. Thoothi, *The Vaishnavas of Gujerat* (London, 1935).

⁶⁸E.C. Bayley, *The Local Muhammadan Dynasties: Gujarat* (London, 1886), p. 449. The Misra and Rahman text of the Mirat-i Sikandari also describes these troops as being solely accountable to Mahmud III, but gives no number (pp. 377-78). The Arabic History, I, 243, stresses their independence of the nobles, but gives their number as 12,000. Sikandar is generally better informed than Hajji al Dabir, and in any case 12,000 men seems to be too many to be brought into this sort of relationship to the sultan in a short period of time.

⁶⁹Arabic History, I, 460; see also *ibid.,* pp. 27, 243, 439; Sikandar, pp. 112, 363.

was again the main arm of the army, and this was recruited by minor leaders, who in turn attached themselves and their group of men to a higher chief. Each soldier tended to follow his immediate chief, with little regard for the interests of the whole army.[70] In such a situation a sultan could move only with the at least tacit consent of most of his nobles.

The scope of the legal system in Gujarat reflects both the limited aims of the sultans and these various practical restrictions on any extension of their control. Judicial officers were called *qazis,* there being a chief *qazi* at court, another for each province, and others at the district level. Other officials in Mughal India, and presumably in pre-Mughal Gujarat as well, also exercised some judicial functions; at the level of the *subah,* the *subahdar* and *divan,* and in the districts the *fawjdar* and the *kotwal.* The *qazis* handled cases covered by the *shariah,* the sacred law of Islam. Civil cases involving non-Muslims were judged according to their own customary law, which was administered by pandits, or by caste and village *panchayats.* Minor criminal cases were also in practice settled locally, without the state-appointed *qazi* being involved. In this respect a *farman* of Awrangzeb's of 1671 is revealing, for it codifies in thirty-three sections various crimes and their punishments. The listed crimes are all major offenses against the *shariah.* Petty criminal cases, and those covered by customary law, are not included. It should also be noted that not even all Muslims were under the jurisdiction of the *qazis.* In Gujarat Muslims who were converts from Hinduism were not always governed by the *shariah;* in succession matters they retained their Hindu customary law. In fact, in Gujarat very few cases, except serious criminal offenses, ever came before a *qazi.* He would occasionally be called on in intercommunal disputes, but civil cases were nearly always settled within the community or communities concerned, and not necessarily according to Muslim law.[71]

---

[70] V. A. Smith, *Akbar, the Great Mogul* (Delhi, 1966), pp. 261-62; William Irvine, *The Army of the Indian Moghuls* (London, 1903), pp. 57-58. A recent article by Rafi Ahmad Alavi (cited *supra,* f.n. 38) brings out the importance of kin and racial connections in forming solidarity ties among the Mughal cavalry. Alavi also shows that a contingent was not always of the same race as its head.

[71] N.J. Coulson, *A History of Islamic Law* (Edinburgh, 1964), pp. 16-17, 97-98, 136-37; S.C. Misra, *op. cit.,* pp. 162-63; M.B. Ahmad, *The Administration of Justice in Medieval India* (Aligarh, 1941), pp. 71-75, 78, 85-86, 91-92, 142-66; A.S. Altekar, *History of Village Communities in Western India* (Bombay, 1927), pp. 34-38; J.D.M. Derrett, "The Administration of Hindu Law by the British," *Comparative Studies in Society and History* IV (1961): 17. Awrangzeb's *farman* of 1671 is in

The Hindu law to which most of Gujarat's inhabitants were subject was itself kaleidoscopic. Leaving aside the major criminal cases of which the Muslim legal authorities took cognizance, all other cases were decided not with reference to some unitary omnicompetent code but according to the *varna* of the people concerned. This situation has only changed, and perhaps even now not completely, since India became independent. More specifically, J. D. M. Derrett finds four types of decision making and decision enforcement operating in pre-colonial times. Trade and professional groups, agriculturalists, and many other groups handled most cases for themselves, and virtually all in the area of personal law. Thus the beheading of the Hindu legal system resultant on the arrival of Muslim rule was of only theoretical importance for most people.[72]

For all these reasons, inhabitants of Gujarat enjoyed considerable autonomy within their groups. The state did not want to, and could not, interfere deeply in most of their activities. The explanation of the response to the Portuguese from Gujarat's merchants and rulers focused on this same matter of connections between groups in medieval Gujarat. Before the arrival of the Portuguese, Gujarat's merchants conducted their overseas trade free from any political interference. Portugal's vainglorious attempt to control trade was a laughable failure in most parts of Asia, but in Gujarat they came close to success. This they were able to achieve because of the context of relations between merchant and ruler in the area, which dictated that their system could be accepted by the merchants. I argued that the rulers could have responded effectively to the Portuguese had they wanted to, but instead most of Gujarat's nobles ignored Portuguese control of their subjects' sea trade. A few whose interests were threatened challenged the Portuguese, but on their own were able to achieve little.

This attitude did not apply only to the merchant response to the Portuguese, but rather to most activities of all lower social groups. Thus, merchants could oppress each other, trade with the Portuguese

---

Mirat, pp. 248-52; good general surveys are those by M.B. Ahmad, *op. cit.*, Ibn Hasan, *The Central Structure of the Mughal Empire* (London, 1936), pp. 306-44, and B.S. Jain, *Administration of Justice in Seventeenth Century India* (Delhi, 1970).

[72] J.D.M. Derrett, *op. cit., passim;* Marc Galanter, "The Problem of Group Membership: Some Reflections on the Judicial View of Indian Society," *Journal of the Indian Law Institute* IV (1962): 331-58, and especially pp. 342-43; J.D.M. Derrett, *Religion, Law and the State in India* (London, 1968), pp. 152, 161-62, 188, 211-12.

in time of war, set prices and holidays, and pay customs duties at Diu. None of these activities affected the rulers and so the rulers took no notice of them. Similarly, *zamindars* could fight sizable battles, villages could change hands, the Imam Shahis and the Parsis could govern themselves almost completely autonomously, and Indian employees of the English East India Company could fly the English flag on their own ships; again, the limited prerogatives and interests of the rulers were not involved and so they ignored all this. Thus my description of the response to the Portuguese is really only a detailed illustration of the general nature of relations between rulers and subjects in medieval Gujarati society.

This society seldom achieved close relations between ruler and subject. Nevertheless, there were institutionalized mechanisms available. These were provided by the second, and minor, role of the heads of the social groups. In their intermediary capacity these heads could and did provide this society with vertical integration when this was seen to be desirable.

It seems clear, however, that horizontal integration within a social group was comparatively greater and more frequent than vertical integration between a social group and the rulers. Indeed, the ruling group itself should be seen as a relatively integrated unit, spread thin over the whole state, but connected horizontally by common allegiance, based on patronage, to the emperor or sultan. The lower social groups were much more localized, yet even here different members of some groups could be widely scattered and yet maintain contact and continue to feel primordial attachment to their group. Two examples are the merchants, who were diffused even beyond India, and some religiously-based groups. In capsule form, Gujarati society consisted of two layers. The upper one made up one group, and was comparatively closely integrated. The lower was composed of many diverse groups; *within* each group the degree of integration paralleled that of the upper ruling group, but solidarity *between* the lower groups was minimal. Nor was there much contact between most of the lower groups and the upper one. In this disaggregated society attachment was felt to a social group or groups rather than to the state of Gujarat.

APPENDIX

MONEY AND VALUES

The standard study of coins and money is contained in Vitorino Magalhães-Godinho's massive work *L'Economie de l'empire Portugais aux XVe et XVIe siècles* (Paris, 1969), pp. 287-531. My problem was to find one unit of currency for use throughout this monograph. As my work is concerned with Indian history, I finally settled on rupees, and on divisions into *lakhs* and *crores* (100,000 and 10,000,000). In conversions from other currencies I have taken R. 1 as being equivalent to 200 Portuguese *reis;* thus a Portuguese *xerafim* is taken as being worth 50 percent more than a rupee. In this respect I have relied on C. R. Boxer, *The Great Ship from Amacon* (Lisbon, 1959), Appendix, "Currency, Weights and Measures," pp. 335-42. For rates of conversion from Portuguese to Gujarati currency, see f. n. 56 of chapter I, *supra*. Sometimes a specific rate of conversion is noted in the sources, and in such cases this has of course been used, but most often I have been unable to adjust for the very considerable fluctuations in the price of bullion in sixteenth-century India.

Occasionally in the text I give a modern U.S. dollar equivalent. Here I use C. G. F. Simkin's claim that one *cruzado* in the sixteenth century was worth £ 2/17/0 today, at the 1968 price of gold of $35 per troy ounce, and taking £1 at $2.80. (C. G. F. Simkin, *The Traditional Trade of Asia* [London, 1968], p. 163, f.n.) Hence, R.1 in the sixteenth century was worth nearly $4.00 today. Here again conversions from gold *cruzados* to silver *xerafins* and rupees are obviously perilous. Further, many of my statistics are only slightly more specific than the "thousands and thousands and *lakhs* and *crores*" which a sultan of Gujarat once paid to the Portuguese. Still, in a work touching on economic history something had to be decided on; I have tried to be cautious in my use of the sources, and it behooves the reader to treat my statistics in a similarly gingerly way.

GLOSSARY

This glossary is intended solely for the convenience of readers of this monograph. Fuller definitions and derivations for most of these words will be found in the following texts: H. H. Wilson, *A Glossary of Judicial and Revenue Terms* (Delhi, 1968); Sir Henry Yule and A. C. Burnell, *Hobson-Jobson: A Glossary of Anglo-Indian Words and Phrases* (Delhi, 1968); and S. R. Dalgado, *Glossário Luso-Asiatico*, 2 vols. (Coímbra, 1919-21).

Alim	A Muslim religious scholar or jurist.
Baneane	Portuguese corruption of *vania*, q.v.
Banyan	English corruption of *vania*, q.v.
Benjan	Corruption of *vania*, q.v.
Bohrah	Member of an Ismaili shia sect.
Cafila	A land caravan, usually of camels; used by the Portuguese to refer to the convoys of small trading ships which sailed under their auspices.
Cambay	In this monograph always used to refer to the town of this name at the head of the Gulf of Cambay, except in quotations, where Gujarat may be meant.
Cartaz	Pass issued by the Portuguese to a merchant ship.
Chauth	Demand for one-quarter of the land revenue of an area.
Crore	10,000,000. Cf. *lakh*.
Divan	Financial official.
Farangi	Frank, European. Slightly perjorative.
Farman	Order or decree issued by a Muslim ruler.
Fawjdar	Administrative head of a *sarkar*, q.v.
Fidalgo	A Portuguese gentleman or petty noble—literally "son of a somebody."
Fusta	Single-masted oared boat, with about forty oarsmen and of about forty tons. In English, "foist."

Ismaili	A much divided group within the Muslim shia community.
Jagir	An allotment of territory to provide for the support of a noble and his troops and retainers.
Jagirdar	Holder of a *jagir*.
Jati	A relatively homogeneous Hindu or Jain endogamous group, based mostly on occupation. Loosely used interchangeably with the term "caste."
Khanqah	A hospice for *sufis*, q.v.
Khojah	Member of the Ismaili shia sect which today recognizes the Agha Khan as its head.
Kotwal	Urban police official.
Lakh	Indian term for 100,000. One hundred *lakhs* make one *crore*, q.v.
Mahajan	A body governing in commercial matters people engaged in a particular occupation. Also a city-wide body regulating all commercial matters.
Nagarsheth	Head, elected or hereditary, of a city-wide *mahajan*, q.v.
Panch	Body regulating trade matters for a group of artisans.
Panchayat	A governing council in general.
Patel	Head of a *panch*, q.v.; headman in general.
Pir	Head of a *sufi* group; a Muslim mystic in general.
Qazi	Muslim judge.
Sarkar	A territorial and administrative unit in sultanate Gujarat and Mughal India.
Sarraf	A banker; a merchant.
Sheth	Head of an occupational *mahajan*, q.v.
Shahbandar	The head of a group of foreign merchants in a port; in Surat and occasionally elsewhere, a port official.
Silsilah	A *sufi*, q.v., order.
Subah	Province.
Subahdar	Governor of a province.
Sufi	A Muslim mystic, a member of a sunni Muslim religious order.
Ulama	Plural of *alim*, q.v.
Vania	A Gujarati Hindu or Jain merchant.
Varna	The four (Brahman, Kshatriya, Vaisya, Sudra) ritual divisions of Hindu society.

Xerafim	The standard Goan silver coin, consisting of 300 *reis*, and roughly equal to Rs. 1½
Zamindar	A holder or controller of an area of land, its products, and its population.
Zamorin	Title of the Hindu rulers of Calicut.

BIBLIOGRAPHICAL ESSAY

Chronicles

My main sources for the sixteenth century were Portuguese and Persian chronicles. Both have profound limitations for the sort of subject covered in this monograph. One of the former once dismissed what had happened during a particular year as not worth recording, "since what they did chiefly related to trade, a subject unbecoming to a grave history such as this." These chronicles were written for kings and sultans by their dependents. They aim to glorify their masters. They reflect the courtly ethos, whether of the *fidalgo* or of the *khan*. The Persian ones especially do not dwell on, nor sometimes even mention, occasions when their patrons were discomfitted. Thus, Malik Ayaz's defeat off Div in 1509 is described in detail in the Portuguese chronicles, but goes unmentioned in the Persian accounts. Merchants are but dimly perceived, emerging infrequently to offer defiance or a very large bribe, and retreating speedily to their world outside the cognizance of the chronicler.

The best guide to the Portuguese chronicles is C. R. Boxer's *Three Historians of Portuguese Asia (Barros, Couto and Bocarro)* (Macau, 1948), in which he deals with these three most important chroniclers of Portuguese India. Others include Gaspar Correa's lively but often unreliable *Lendas da India*, 4 vols. (Lisbon, 1858-64) and Manuel de Faria e Sousa's *Asia Portuguesa*, 6 vols. (Lisbon, 1945-47), originally written in Spanish and adding little to the Portuguese chronicles it is based on; Fernão de Mendes Pinto's colorful and largely fictitious *Peregrinação de Fernam Mendez Pinto*, 4 vols. (Lisbon, 1908-10); and Fernão Lopes de Castanheda's *História do descobrimento e conquista da India pelos Portugueses*, 9 vols. (Coímbra, 1924-33), which is extremely valuable for the earlier sixteenth century. J. B. Harrison's "Five Portuguese Historians," in C. H. Philips, ed., *Historians of India, Pakistan and Ceylon* (London, 1961) is particularly helpful for anyone interested in the Portuguese chroniclers' coverage of sixteenth-century India.

There are several studies of Persian chronicles. Peter Hardy's

Historians of Medieval India: Studies in Indo-Muslim Historical Writing (London, 1960) is an excellent study of the preconceptions and preoccupations of these medieval historians. Jean Aubin has performed a valuable service in elucidating the various recensions of the Persian chronicles of Gujarat: "The Secretary of Mahmud Gavan and his Lost Chronicle," *Journal of the Pakistan Research Society* I (October 1964). S. C. Misra used the invaluable *Mirat-i Sikandari* in his own work, and has published two accounts of its use, importance, and antecedents. The first was the Introduction to his edition of this text (S. C. Misra and M. L. Rahman, eds., *The Mirat-i Sikandari* [Baroda, 1961], pp. 1-56), the second under the title of "The *Mirat-i Sikandari* of Shaikh Sikandar and its Predecessors," in Mohibbul Hasan, ed., *Historians of Medieval India* (Meerut, 1968). Two essential guides to Persian sources for Indian history are C. A. Storey's *Persian Literature: A Bio-bibliographical Survey*, section II, fasciculus 3, M. "History of India" (London, 1939), and D. N. Marshall's *Mughals in India: A Bibliographical Survey*, vol. I, Manuscripts (London, 1967). A detailed guide to the literature on Muslim India is currently under preparation at the University of Wisconsin, edited by John Richards and Jack Wells.

A note to the wary concerning the Persian chronicles and their translations is in order here. Of the seven most important chronicles dealing specifically with Gujarat, four have not been translated: Mir Abu Turab Vali, *A History of Gujarat*, ed. E. Denison Ross (Calcutta, 1908); "Tarikh-i Mahmud Shahi" and "Dhamimah-i-Mathir-i-Mahmud Shahi," corrected copies of both of which are in the Library of the Department of History of the M. S. University of Baroda; and the shorter *Tarikh-i-Salatin-i-Gujarat*, published by A. A. Tirmizi in *Medieval India Quarterly* V (1963). The three other most important chronicles have been translated. M. F. Lokhandwalla's recent translation of Abdullah Muhammad al-Makhi al-Asafi al-Ulughkhani hajji ad-dabir's *Zafar ul Walih bi Muzaffar wa Alihi*, vol. I (Baroda, 1970), is far from perfect, at times indeed incomprehensible. But for those like myself who know no Arabic (the language of this chronicle) it is the only alternative available. It should be noted that this volume is a translation of *daftar* I of the text. This is the most important part of this work; the rest, *daftar* II, is simply a rehash of Islamic history in other areas of India. Scholars reading volume I are advised to use E. Denison Ross's invaluable index and introduction to his publication of the text: Abdallah Muhammad bin Omar al-

Makki al-Asafi Ulughkhani, *An Arabic History of Gujarat: Zafar al-Walih bi Muzaffar wa Alih*, ed. E. Denison Ross, 3 vols. (London, 1910-28).

The translators of the Persian *Mirat-i Ahmadi*, Syed Nawab Ali and C. N. Seddon for the supplement, and M. F. Lokhandwalla for the chronicle—2 vols. (Baroda, 1928-65)—did a much better job, especially for the supplement. Even so, there is really no alternative to checking their translations with the original text, which has been well edited—3 vols. (Baroda, 1927-30). At times certain words are of crucial importance, and here the text must be used.

For reasons cogently set out by S. C. Misra in his already cited studies, for the fifteenth and sixteenth centuries the *Mirat-i Sikandari* is the most valuable of all. There are two translations, but neither is satisfactory, partly as neither is of a good copy of the Persian text. Apart from this, Fazlullah Lutfullah Faridi's translation is really a paraphrase, useful only for getting the sequence of events: Sikandar ibn Muhammad urf Manjhu ibn Akbar, *Mirat-i Sikandari*, trans. Fazlullah Lutfullah Faridi (Dharampur, n.d.). E. C. Bayley's effort is fuller (E. C. Bayley, *The Local Muhammadan Dynasties: Gujarat* [London, 1886], pp. 59-455), but goes only up to the death of Sultan Mahmud III in 1553. The actual text ends in 1591-92. Moreover, Bayley sometimes dismays the reader with footnotes such as these: "The following stories, told at tedious length in the original, are reproduced here in abstract to illustrate the character of the Sultan, and the manners of the day;" "The description of the beauties of Ainpurah is omitted. It is prolix and uninteresting;" "This expression may be accepted as showing that the writer did not publish wilfully anything which he considered coarse or indecent. Nevertheless, there are a few passages which, on this score, are necessarily omitted or modified in translation." In fact, for Sikandar there is no choice but to use the already-cited Misra and Rahman text. The Baroda printers did a less than perfect job, but it is still eminently usable, especially as the editors provided a detailed introduction and index.

Other Portuguese Material

For Portuguese sources other than chronicles, the best place to start is in the excellent bibliographies and footnotes of C. R. Boxer's many works. A recent example of the service he has done for all students of the Portuguese empire is the bibliography in his *The Portuguese*

Seaborne Empire. 1415-1825 (London, 1969), pp. 392-413. For the Portuguese in India, and sixteenth-century Indian history, an important category of Portuguese sources is descriptions of Asia, or of Portuguese Asia, at particular times. For the early sixteenth century the Book of Duarte Barbosa is most useful. A translation of this was published by the Hakluyt Society as *The Book of Duarte Barbosa*, 2 vols. (London, 1918-21), but I used the manuscript version in the Biblioteca Nacional de Lisboa, "Descrição das terras da India Oriental, e dos seus usos, costumes, ritos e leis por Vasco da Gama [*sic*]," Mss. 9163. A second, and very detailed, such work is António Bocarro's "Livro das plantas de todas as fortalezas, cidades e povações do Estado da India Oriental," which was written in the 1630s. This is much more exclusively focused on the Portuguese than is Barbosa's work. It was published, very carelessly, by A. B. de Bragança Pereira as tome IV, vol. II, parts 1-3 of his *Arquivo Português Oriental*, 3 vols. (Bastorá, Goa, 1937-40). Bocarro's Book is very closely based on the work of his contemporary, Pedro Barreto de Rezende, called "Descripçoens das Cidades e Fortalezas da India Oriental." I used two copies of this work, the first in the Biblioteca da Academia das Ciências de Lisboa, Mss. Azuis, 266-68, and the second a very fine copy with beautiful illustrations in the British Museum Library (Sloane Mss., no. 197). Both these copies also include Barreto de Rezende's account of the governorships of Portuguese India up to the 1630s. A well-edited publication of this important work would be a great service. F. P. Mendes da Luz's "Livro das Cidades e Fortalezas que a Coroa de Portugal tem nas partes da India, 1582" was published in photostat form in *Studia* no. 6 (1960), and Tomé Pires' *Suma Oriental*, invaluable for early sixteenth-century trade, was published as *The Suma Oriental of Tomé Pires*, 2 vols. (London, 1944), this edition including both the text and a translation.

A great many other Portuguese documents have been published, usually in unedited and untranslated form. Among the more useful are two extended first-hand accounts: Francisco Rodrigues Silveira, *Memórias de um soldado da India*, ed. A. de S. S. Costa Lobo (Lisbon, 1877) and the diaries of the viceroy of Portuguese India in 1629-35, *Diário do 3rd Conde de Linhares: Vice-Rei da India*, 2 vols. (Lisbon, 1937-43). Several ephemeral Goan journals published documents from the Goa archives: *Boletim do Instituto Vasco da Gama* (1926-53); *O Chronista de Tissuary: Periódico Mensal* (1866-69); *O Gabinete Litterário das Fontainhas* (1846-48); *Instituto Vasco da Gama*

(1872-75); *O Oriente Português: Revista da Commissão Archeologica da India Portugueza* (1904-20, 1931-41); and even the official government gazette, *Boletim do governo do Estado da India*, from 1857 to 1877. For the history of Gujarat, the most notable document published in any of these journals is Ethel Pope, ed., "Chronica Geral dos Sucessos do Reyno de Gusarate a qm. chamão Cambaya," *Boletim do Instituto Vasco da Gama*, nos. 22-23 (1934). Francis A. Mendonça translated and edited this account, retaining the original title, in his M.A. thesis (as yet unpublished) for the M.S. University of Baroda in 1963.

The two most notable Portuguese journals which continue to publish documents of colonial interest are *Studia: Revista Semestral* (1958-) and *Boletim da Filmateca Ultramarina Portuguesa* (1954-). Both these journals are sponsored by the munificent Calouste Gulbenkian Foundation, which also is subsidizing other printings of documents. These include *Documentação Ultramarina Portuguesa*, 5 vols. to date (Lisbon, 1960-), which prints Portuguese-related documents held in libraries outside Portugal; *As Gavetas da Torre do Tombo*, 8 vols. to date (Lisbon, 1960-), the Gavetas being one of the most important collections in this Lisbon archive; and two continuing collections of missionary documents (whose interest is far from being exclusively ecclesiastical): Artur Basilio de Sa, ed., *Documentação para a história das Missões do Padroado Português do Oriente. Insulíndia*, 5 vols. to date (Lisbon, 1954-), and António da Silva Rego, ed., *Documentação para a história das Missões do Padroado Português do Oriente. India*, 12 vols. to date (Lisbon, 1947-). Another run of equally valuable missionary documents, in this case Jesuit, is José Wicki's editing of *Documenta Indica*, 11 vols. to date (Rome, 1948-). A comparable source is Padre Fernão Guerreiro's *Relação Anual das Coisas que Fizeram os Padres da Companhia de Jesus nas suas Missões*, ed. Artur Viegas, 3 vols. (Lisbon, 1930-42).

Other publications of Portuguese documents are legion: only a few more can be listed here. The letters of Affonso d'Albuquerque, governor from 1509 to 1515, are a vital source for the early sixteenth century and are available as *Cartas de Affonso de Albuquerque, seguidas de documentos que se elucidam*, 7 vols. (Lisbon, 1884-1935). A modern edition of Albuquerque's Commentaries, by his son Braz de Albuquerque, is an urgent need. A rather unsatisfactory English version was published by the Hakluyt Society as *Commentaries of*

Afonso Albuquerque, 4 vols. (London, 1875-84). Elaine Sanceau has edited the letters of a later viceroy: *Cartas de Dom João de Castro* (Lisbon, 1955). J. H. da Cunha Rivara edited *Archivo Português Oriental,* 10 vols. (Nova Goa, 1857-77), especially valuable for its late sixteenth- and early seventeenth-century documents from the Goa archives. A. B. de Bragança Pereira's successor series, *Arquivo Português Oriental,* 11 vols. (Bastorá, Goa, 1936-40), is much less useful, except that it did publish Bocarro's already-described Livro. This series is full of inaccuracies, misprints, and unnecessary interpolations from Bragança Pereira.

A prime source is the letters exchanged between the governor in Goa and the king in Portugal or (after 1580) Spain. For the years 1605-19 these letters are available in R. A. de Bulhão Pato's *Documentos Remettidos da India ou Livros das Monções,* 5 vols. (Lisbon, 1880-1935). R. J. de Lima Felner published some important sixteenth-century documents in *Subsídios para a história da India Portugueza* (Lisbon, 1868). The late archivist in Goa, P.S.S. Pissurlencar, published several fine runs of documents, including *Regimentos das Fortalezas da India* (Bastorá, Goa, 1951) and *Agentes da Diplomacia Portuguesa na India (Hindus, Muçulmanos, Judeus e Parses).* (Bastorá, Goa, 1952). His last and greatest publication was *Assentos do Conselho do Estado,* 5 vols. (Bastorá, Goa, 1953-57), which contains minutes and correspondence from the Council of State in Goa in the seventeenth century.

Given that I have listed here only a brief selection of published Portuguese documents, it may seem that the archives have little left to offer. It is true that a large selection of Portuguese sixteenth-century materials, so valuable for Asian history and strangely still so neglected, have been published. Yet much remains in manuscript; the archives in Goa and Lisbon cannot be ignored. For the Goa archives, the fullest guide in English is C. R. Boxer's "A Glimpse of the Goa Archives," *Bulletin of the School of Oriental and African Studies* XIV (June 1952). There is a short survey of their value for Indian history by M. N. Pearson, "The Goa Archives and Indian History," *Quarterly Review of Historical Studies,* forthcoming. But the basic guide for these archives is P.S.S. Pissurlencar's invaluable *Roteiro dos Arquivos da India Portuguesa* (Bastorá, Goa, 1955). Throughout this monograph I have followed his usage as regards numbering and titles of the volumes of documents in the Goa archives. The source I used most was the long series "Livros das Monções do Reino," nos. 4-52, which contains letters exchanged between the governor and the king from 1595 to the 1680s. Other material of value for this monograph was scattered throughout more than 100 other 300-page volumes of documents in Goa. Despite the value of these archives, their limitations must also be noted. The bulk of documentation begins in the mid-seventeenth century, too late for my needs. As regards the letters sent home to Portugal, it cannot always be assumed that the governor wanted the king to know the truth, the whole truth, and nothing but the truth. What one really needs are letters sent from Div and other forts to Goa, or the accounts of the factor in Div, or lists of *cartazes* granted in Div. With pitifully few exceptions, these are no longer extant. One can only wish for the account books or reminiscences of a Portuguese merchant living in Cambay.

For Portuguese archives, the best guide is still Virgínia Rau's "Arquivos de Portugal: Lisboa," in *Proceedings of the International Colloquium on Luso-Brazilian Studies* (Nashville, 1953). In Lisbon the most important archive was the Arquivo Nacional da Torre do Tombo, for it contains a large volume of sixteenth-century material. For my purposes, and for those of anyone working on the Portuguese in India, the most valuable runs were the published *Gavetas*, and the very bulky "Corpo Chronologico," for which there is a manuscript index available. The early volumes of the series "Documentos Remetidos da India (ou Livros das Monções)," 62 vols., contain the originals of R. A. de Bulhão Pato's already-cited *Documentos Remettidos da India ou Livros das Monções*, and the later volumes supplement (sometimes duplicate) the Goa "Livros das Monções do Reino." The two other main collections in the Torre do Tombo, both mainly sixteenth century, are the "Colecção de São Vicente," 26 vols., and the "Colecção de São Lourenço," 6 vols. Some other material was found in the Biblioteca Nacional de Lisboa, and the Biblioteca da Academia das Ciências de Lisboa. The Biblioteca da Ajuda was useful, and could have been much more so were it not so poorly catalogued and organized.

The prime location of Portuguese colonial documents in Lisbon is the Arquivo Histórico Ultramarino. I used there the first twenty-four *caixas* (boxes) of Indian material, although this is nearly all seventeenth century. Finally, some more seventeenth-century documentation was found among the Additional Manuscripts of the British Museum Library. A guide to these sources is C. R. Boxer, "More about the Marsden Manuscripts," *Journal of the Royal Asiatic*

Society (1949). Two general guides to Portuguese material in England are: Frederico Francisco de la Figanière, *Catalogo dos manuscriptos portuguezes existentes no Museo britannico* (Lisbon, 1853), and Conde de Tovar, *Catálogo dos manuscritos portugueses no Museu britânico* (Lisbon, 1932).

Other European Sources

The English sources on Gujarat in the seventeenth century are relatively well known. They include the long series of publications of documents from the India Office: William Foster and F. C. Danvers, eds., *Letters Received by the East India Company from its Servants in the East, 1602-1617*, 6 vols. (London, 1896-1902), and William Foster and Charles Fawcett, eds., *The English Factories in India, 1618-1684*, 17 vols. (London, and Oxford, 1904-1954). Traveller's accounts are legion; among the more interesting are M. S. Commissariat, ed., *Mandelslo's Travels in Western India (A.D. 1638-9)* (London, 1931); Niccolao Manucci, *Storia do Mogor, 1653-1708*, trans. and ed. William Irvine, 4 vols. (London, 1907-8); Surendranath Sen, ed., *Indian Travels of Thevenot and Careri* (New Delhi, 1949); John Ovington, *A Voyage to Surat in the Year 1689* (London, 1929); William Foster, ed., *Early Travels in India, 1583-1619* (London, 1921); *The Itinerary of Ludovico di Varthema* (London, 1928); Jean Baptiste Tavernier, *Travels in India*, ed. Vincent Ball, 2 vols. (London, 1925). Also included are accounts by the following, all published by the Hakluyt Society: Thomas Best (London, 1934); Pietro Della Valle (2 vols., London, 1892); Nicholas Downton (London, 1939); Dr. John Fryer (3 vols., London, 1909-15); Richard Hakluyt, ed. (12 vols., Glasgow, 1903-5); John Jourdain (Cambridge, 1905); J. H. van Linschoten (2 vols., London, 1885); R. H. Major, ed. (London, 1857); Fray Sebastian Manrique (2 vols., Oxford, 1926-27); Peter Mundy (6 vols., London, 1905-36); Friar Domingo Navarrete (2 vols., Cambridge, 1962); Samuel Purchas, ed. (20 vols., Glasgow, 1905-7); François Pyrard de Laval (2 vols., London, 1887-90). Finally, the Walker of Bowland Papers in the National Library of Scotland, Edinburgh, contain some valuable ethnographic material which, although compiled around 1800, is based on oral tradition and some reading in the Persian sources. I described some of these materials in the *American Philosophical Society Year Book, 1973* (Philadelphia, 1974), p. 646.

The other source of information by Europeans on seventeenth-century Gujarat is the Dutch records. Lack of time, and a certain linguistic hesitancy, dictated that I not work in the archives in The Hague. The India Office Library, London, includes among its Records a series of manuscript translations from the Dutch archives. I used the run I/3/2 to I/3/100, but with caution, as these translations are not completely reliable. But despite a strong plea from M. A. P. Meilink-Roelofsz for scholars to use The Hague more ('Note to "Ahmadabad in the XVIIth Century,"' *Journal of the Economic and Social History of the Orient* XIII [1970]: 100-102.), it is my impression that Dutch records are less useful than those in Persian, Portuguese, and English, at least for the earlier seventeenth century. W. H. Moreland published many translations of Dutch sources for this period of Indian history, and these are conveniently listed among Margaret Case's complete bibliography of his writings: "The Historical Craftsmanship of W. H. Moreland (1868-1938)," *Indian Economic and Social History Review* II (July 1965): 254-58.

Other Local Sources

The quantity of indigenous records from Gujarat is far inferior to those in European languages. For the period up to 1650, at least, all that is available is the Persian chronicles on Gujarat which I have already described, and scattered information in other, all-India, Persian chronicles. Among the latter, the following may be mentioned: Abu'l Fazl Allami, *The A'in-i Akbari*, trans. H. Blochmann, D. C. Phillott, H. S. Jarrett, and Jadunath Sarkar, 3 vols. (Calcutta, 1939-49); Abu'l Fazl Allami, *Akbar Nama*, trans. Henry Beveridge, 3 vols. (Calcutta, 1902-39); Muhammad Qasim Firishtah, *Gulshan-i Ibrahimi, or Tarikh-i-Firishtah*, trans. by John Briggs as *The Rise of the Muhammadan Power in India*, 4 vols. (Calcutta, 1908-10); *Tuzuk-i Jahangiri*, trans. Alexander Rogers and Henry Beveridge (New Delhi, 1968); Khwajah Nizam-ud-din Ahmad, *Tabaqat-i-Akbari*, trans. B. De, 3 vols. (Calcutta, 1927-39); Nawwab Samsam-ud-daula Shah Nawaz Khan, *Maathir-ul-Umara*, trans. Henry Beveridge and Baini Prashad, 2 vols. (Calcutta, 1941-52). Two Arabic works contain useful data. Ibn Batuta, *The Rehla of Ibn Batuta (India, Maldive Islands and Ceylon)*, trans. Mahdi Husain (Baroda, 1953) is valuable for trade and shipping in the fourteenth century, while Shaikh Zeen-ud-Deen, *Tohfut-ul-Mujahideen*, trans. M. J. Rowlandson (London, 1833), is excellent for an indigenous account of the Portuguese in the sixteenth century.

Five other publications of shorter contemporary Persian documents relating to Gujarat may be mentioned here: M. S. Commissariat, ed., "Imperial Mughal Farmans in Gujarat." *Journal. Bombay University* IX (July 1940); Diwan Bahadur Krishnalal M. Jhaveri, ed., *Imperial Farmans (A. D. 1579 to A. D. 1805) Granted to the Ancestors of His Holiness the Tikayat Maharaj* (Bombay, 1928); J. J. Modi, ed., "A Petition in Persian by Dastur Kaikobad to Emperor Jahangir," *Journal of the K. R. Cama's Oriental Institute*, no. 13; J. J. Modi, ed., "Rustam Manock and the Persian Qisseh," *Journal of the Royal Asiatic Society, Bombay Branch*, series VI, nos. 1 and 2 (1930); K. A. Nizami, ed., "Faizi's Masnavi on Akbar's Conquest of Ahmadabad," *Medieval India Quarterly* V (1963).

It is possible that there will be further small finds of Persian documents relating to medieval Gujarat, but the other main potential source appears to be Jain temple records. These are going to be extremely difficult to get access to, let alone read, and they may turn out to be of little use anyway, but one short article based on them was most interesting: K. H. Kamdar, "Virji Vorah, Surat Millionaire Mahajan," (in Gujarati) *Journal of the Gujarat Research Society* XXX (October 1968). Finally, Alexander K. Forbes' *Ras Mala, Hindoo Annals of the Province of Goozerat in Western India*, ed. H. G. Rawlinson, 2 vols. (London, 1924), based on oral tradition alive in the mid-nineteenth century, does something to redress, in favor of the Hindu majority of the population of Gujarat, the Muslim bias of the Persian chronicles.

Secondary Literature

Much of the secondary literature has been discussed in passing in the footnotes. In general, it has to be said that this literature is sparse and of uneven quality. Historians of modern India sometimes complain of the lack of reliable monographs dealing with aspects of their period of study. True, their landscape is only sparsely dotted with such works, but for the sixteenth century it is virtually a desert. This paucity has meant that many topics related to the main theme of this monograph had to be investigated from the original sources; very seldom has it been possible to say, for example, "For Portuguese trade between Asia and Europe, see Professor X's standard monograph," or "Religious reform movements in medieval Gujarat are definitively described in Dr. Y's recent work."

Given the large, and accessible, bulk of documentation on the Portuguese colonial empire, the existing literature is disappointing. It is earnestly to be hoped that the recent political changes in Portugal will lead to a new, and more critical, assessment by Portuguese of their country's colonial past. In the meantime, the many works of C. R. Boxer hold the field as the place in which to begin any study of the Portuguese empire. The best survey is his *The Portuguese Seaborne Empire, 1415-1825* (London, 1969), which summarizes a lifetime of study on the subject. It is relevant, however, to note here that Boxer's main specialized interests concern Portuguese activities in East Asia and Brazil. Three other valuable studies by Englishmen appeared in the *New Cambridge Modern History*: J. B. Harrison, "Colonial Development and International Rivalries outside Europe: Asia and Africa," vol. III (Cambridge, 1968); J. B. Harrison, "Europe and Asia," vol. IV (Cambridge, 1970); I. A. MacGregor, "Europe and the East," vol. II (Cambridge, 1958). In sum, these three studies make up by far the best survey of Portuguese activities in Asia in the sixteenth century.

Among Portuguese historians, two stand out. The late Virgínia Rau, although primarily a medievalist, published some solid colonial studies. Two examples are *O "Livro de Razão" de António Coelho Guerreiro* (Lisbon, 1956) and "Regimento da casa das Contos de Goa de 1589," *Revista do Centro de estudos económicos* IX (1949). More directly relevant to my interests was Vitorino Magalhães-Godinho's massive study *L'Economie de l'Empire Portugais aux XVe et XVIe Siècles* (Paris, 1969). For reasons of accessibility I used this French version. Although the Portuguese edition, *Os descobrimentos e a economia mundial,* 2 vols. (Lisbon, 1963-71), is fuller, its extra material was not of direct importance for my interests. This work sets a new standard of diligence and scholarship in the whole field of Portuguese colonial historiography.

The literature on the Portuguese in India is relatively sparse. F. C. Danvers' *The Portuguese in India,* 2 vols. (London, 1894), although recently (and expensively) republished, is so slipshod and boring as to be a caricature of what an historical work should not be. Much better is R. S. Whiteway's *The Rise of Portuguese Power in India, 1497-1550* (London, 1899), an old but still valuable survey. Ronald Bishop Smith has recently published *The First Age of the Portuguese*

Embassies, Navigations and Peregrinations to the Ancient Kingdoms of Cambay and Bengal, 1500-1521 (Potomac, Md, 1969), an engagingly antiquarian survey of value mostly for its translations of Portuguese accounts of these two areas. A recent and very impressive monograph is Niels Steensgaard, *Carracks, Caravans, and Companies: the Structural Crisis in the European Asian Trade in the Early 17th Century* (Copenhagen, 1973). Two Portuguese studies of value for the Portuguese in India are Alfredo Botelho de Sousa, *Subsídios para a história militar marítima da India*, 4 vols. (Lisbon, 1930-56) and Júlio Gonçalves, *Os Portugueses e o Mar das Indias* (Lisbon, 1947). Germano da Silva Correia's large *História da colonização portuguesa na India*, 6 vols. (Lisbon, 1948-56) contains masses of rather undigested information on the Portuguese population of Goa in the sixteenth to eighteenth centuries.

Much recent research first appears in the very important Lisbon journal *Studia: Revista Semestral* (1958-   ). A comparable series is Jean Aubin's *Mare Luso-Indicum*, of which two volumes have so far appeared. This series focuses directly on Portuguese activities in the Arabian Sea area, and so far has been notable for Aubin's own outstanding contributions and for the scrupulously edited documents which he publishes in it.

Turning to literature on medieval India, the works of W. H. Moreland (listed in the already-cited article by Margaret Case) are still useful economic studies, but the reader needs to remember that Moreland retained his Indian Civil Service bias throughout his life. His scholarship was impeccable, yet whether consciously or unconsciously his books were designed to show that India was better off under British rule than it had been under native rule in the seventeenth century. His modest and low-key approach should not be allowed to disguise the fundamentally polemical tone of his work. Nearly all the best recent work on Mughal India comes from scholars associated with, or trained at, Aligarh Muslim University: Satish Chandra, M. Athar Ali, A. Jan Qaisar, M. P. Singh, S. Nurul Hasan, and many others. Most immediately important is Irfan Habib. Apart from his many brilliant articles on economic and political subjects, his *Agrarian System of Mughal India* (Bombay, 1963) is a most notable achievement. The most interesting shorter or preliminary work on medieval India is likely to be found in the excellent journal *Indian Economic and Social History Review* (Delhi, 1963-   ), and in *Medieval India: A Miscellany* (Aligarh, 1969-   ), of which two volumes have so far appeared, and which supersedes *Medieval India Quarterly*, 5 vols. (1950-63). Readers desiring a tedious chronology of rulers and battles in medieval India should consult the *Cambridge History of India*, vols. III and IV (Cambridge, 1928-37), or the various "Lives" of the Mughal emperors, most of which are listed in U. N. Day, *The Mughal Government* (New Delhi, 1970), pp. 245-46.

The outstanding scholar of medieval Gujarat is S. C. Misra, whose *The Rise of Muslim Power in Gujarat: A History of Gujarat from 1298 to 1442* (London, 1963) is by far the best work available on the history of Gujarat. Much useful information, good chronologies of events, and useful bibliographical data can be found in M. S. Commissariat's *History of Gujarat*, 2 vols. (Bombay, 1938-57), and his *Studies in the History of Gujarat* (Bombay, 1935). S. A. I. Tirmizi has recently published a volume of interesting essays, *Some Aspects of Medieval Gujarat* (Delhi, 1968), while Muhammad Ibrahim Dar's little *Literary and Cultural Activities in Gujarat under the Khaljis and the Sultanate* (Bombay, n. d.) breaks new ground in this neglected area of research. Older ethnographic studies of some use include: N. A. Thoothi, *The Vaishnavas of Gujarat* (London, 1935); R. E. Enthoven, *The Tribes and Castes of Bombay*, 3 vols. (Bombay, 1920-22); Govindbhai H. Desai, *Hindu Families in Gujarat* (Baroda, 1932); Anant Sadashir Altekar, *History of Village Communities in Western India* (Bombay, 1927); S. H. Hodivala, *Studies in Parsi History* (Bombay, 1920); S. K. Hodivala, *Parsis of Ancient India* (Bombay, 1920); and C. B. Sheth, *Jainism in Gujarat, A. D. 1100-1600* (Bombay, 1953). S. C. Misra's *Muslim Communities in Gujarat* (Bombay, 1964) is a more recent and more sophisticated study of a religious group in Gujarat.

INDEX

Aden, 10, 11, 48-49
Ahmadabad: products, 20; mahajan of, 123, 125, 127; quarters in, 63, 142
Ahmadnagar, sultan of, 44
Akbar, 44, 57, 58, 61; ships of, 57, 58, 101; conquers Gujarat, 83; relations with Portuguese, 83-84; and Jains, 139
Albuquerque, Afonso, 31, 33; policies of, 55; and Malik Ayaz, 71
d'Almeida, Francisco, 31; policies of, 55; and Malik Ayaz, 70-71
d'Almeida, Lourenço, 70
Arabs, trade of, 8, 10, 12-14, 53-54
Army: Gujarati, 65, 90, 142, 151-152; Mughal, 144 n. 38, 146
Asian trade: structure at 1500, 7-18; routes, 10-13; control of, 14-16
Awrangzeb, 122, 127, 130, 139, 152

Bahadur, Sultan: conquests, 61, 73-74; and Malik Is-haq, 74; and navy, 75, 90, 91; and Portuguese, 75-77; death, 77; and merchants, 129, 130
Bassein, 57; ceded to Portuguese, 76
Bijapur: sultan of, 44; attacks Goa, 81; cloths from, 97
Bohrahs, 27, 28; as social group, 136, 137
Bukhari Sayyids, 136, 137, 138, 147-148
Burhan-ud-din Qutb-i Alam, Sayyid, 148

Cafilas, 45-47; to Cambay, 86, 93-94, 97, 107, 110, 120
Calicut, 10, 12, 80 n. 72; Portuguese and, 53-54, 98
Cambay: port of, 10, 16, 17, 95, 111, 115; sultanate of, 19-20, 89; revenue of, 23; Portuguese in, 38-39, 86, 97 n. 25, 110
Capital: English, 4; Dutch, 4-5; on Gujarati ships, 5, 100-101; provision of, in Gujarat, 21-22; on trade to Portugal, 36; in Gujarat, 108-110, 128-130. *See also* Red Sea
Cartazes, 40; justification for, 40-41; described, 40-43; "free," 44, 83-84, 99; and Gujarati traders, 76-77, 79, 93-95, 99-100; and Akbar, 83-84
Caste, 145, *See also* Jati panchayats; Nagar Brahmans; Saraswat Brahmans; Vanias

Castro, D. João de, 80, 81, 115; raids in Gulf of Cambay, 95-96
Changa Asha, head of Parsis, 138
Chaul: battle of 1508, 70; Portuguese fort at, 71; trade of, 99-100; vania of, 109
Cities: quarters in, 63, 141-142; size of, 145
Cochin, 30, 49, 54, 112
Communications, 150
Copper, 36, 51-52
Cotton cloths, Gujarati trade in, 10, 12, 20-21, 97-98, 107
Customs duties and revenues, 13, 18; Gujarati, 23-24, 87, 88-89, 109; collection of, 107, 131, 143; Portuguese, 32, 43-44, 49-50; in Lisbon, 36, 89; in Div, 79, 82, 84, 97, 106-107, 113, 114; in Cochin, 49, 112; in Hurmuz, 109

da Cunha, Nuno, 74-76 *passim*; attacks in Gulf of Cambay, 95
Daman, 49-50, 57-60 *passim*; captured by Portuguese, 82-83
Danishmand Khan, 129
Darya Khan, 64
Daud, Sultan, 65
Desais, 140
Div (Diu), 10-11, 16; Portuguese factory at, 69, 73; battle of 1509, 70-71; attacked by Portuguese 71-72, 75; Portuguese fort at 76-77; sieges of, 77-81; Portuguese conquer completely, 81-82; prosperity of, 97, 112-113; merchants of, 103, 121; an elite group, 104-105; becomes City, 104; captain of Gujarati merchants in, 105, 113; merchants of, and customs duties, 106-107; Portuguese abuses in, 113-114. *See also* Malik Ayaz; Malik Is-haq.
Dutch East India Company, 42, 49 n. 75, 94, 100; early years in Gujarat, 4-6; seize Mughal ships, 121-122

East Africa, 12, 97-98, 113
Egypt, 11, 12-13; fleet battles Portuguese, 70-71; revenue of, 70, 89, 90-91
English East India Company, 42, 100; early years in Gujarat, 4-6, 118; seize Gujarati ships, 118-120; and Mustafa Khan, 121;

175

trade to Red Sea, 125; employees of, 145, 149; and Virji Vorah, 149-150
Foreigners: merchants, 17-18; in Gujarat, 142

Goa, 31, 32, 33-34, 35, 45, 46, 47; trade of, 97; Gujarati merchants in, 105
Gogha, 11
Goridas Parekh, 105
Gujarat: trade of, 10-14; value of trade, 22-24; to Red Sea, 94, 98-99, 100-101, 103, 110, 125; area of, 19-20; products of, 20; conquered by Mughals, 75-77, 83; wealth of, 108-109; population of, 151. *See also* Army; Gujarati merchants; Gujarati nobles; Portuguese-Gujarati wars; Sultans
Gujarati merchants, 11, 21; divisions within, 25-29, 102-103; and Muhammad Qulij Khan, 58, 60, 93; initial response to Portuguese, 92-93; accept Portuguese control, 93-98, 115-116; and pepper trade, 98-99; evade Portuguese system, 99-100; trade to Red Sea, 100-101; trade to Malacca, 101-102; importance to Portuguese, 103-104; captains of, 105; cooperate with Portuguese, 106-108, 112-113; wealth of, 108-109; investments, 109-110; and wars, 111, 115-116; and English East India Company, 118-119; relations with Gujarati officials, 119-123, 125-132; and Jahangir, 120; and Portuguese officials, 121; and hartals, 122
Gujarati nobles: definition of, 61, 133-134; relations with sultans, 61-67; bases of power, 62-64, 88-90; origins, 66; factionalism among, 67; response to Portuguese, 86-91; ethos of, 90-91, 132; trade of, 112; relations with merchants, 119; financial links with merchants, 127-130. *See also* Ruling group
Gulf of Cambay, 10, 115; Portuguese raids in, 74-75, 81, 95-96

Hajima Ahmad Ali, 128
Headman, 141, 146
Hira Vijaya Suri, 28, 146
Horse trade, 13, 33
Humayun, 75, 76, 77
Hundis, 21
Hurmuz, 10, 12, 31, 46; trade of, 13; customs duties in, 109. *See also* Horse trade

Imad-ul-Mulk, 67, 82
Imam Shahi sect, 137, 144
Indigo, 20
Intermediaries, 126; role of, 134-137, 138-143, 146

Jagirs, in Gujarat, 63-64, 65-66
Jahangir, 118, 119, 120, 149; ship of, 101

Jains, 25-27, 28; heads of, 125, 139, 146; as social group, 139
Jalaluddin Ahmad Khattu, Shaikh, 147-148
Jalal-ud-din Bukhari, Sayyid, 148
Jati panchayats, 123, 135, 141

Kakas, 137, 144
Kamal, Shaikh, of Malwa, 148
Kanara: rice trade of, 13, 45, 46-47; merchants of, and war, 112 n. 85
Khan Jahan, 65
Khanqahs, 135-136
Khojahs, 27-28
Khwaja Hasan Ali, 128
Khwaja Jala-ud-din Mahmud, 128
Khwaja Safar, 42, 67 n. 26, 78; and sieges of Div, 78, 79-81; and Portuguese, 87-88
Kolis. *See* Rajputs and Kolis

Land revenue: value of, in Gujarat, 23-24; collection of, 61-62, 130 n. 34, 143
Legal system: Muslim, 152; Hindu, 153
Lopes de Sequeira, Diogo, relations with Malik Ayaz, 71-72

Mahajans: described, 123-124; in Gujarat, 122, 125-6, 127, 131, 135
Mahmud Bigarh (Mahmud I), 65, 68, 70 n. 38, 136, 138; ship of, 8 n. 4; conquests, 61; navy of, 90
Mahmud III, 64-65, 77-78, 79, 80, 82
Malabar: "pirates" of, 46, 47, 107, 126; rulers of, 49; pepper trade of, 98-99; traders of, 126
Malacca, 8-22 *passim*, 53; Gujaratis in, 92-93, 101-102
Malik Ayaz, 53, 66, 67-68, 93; relations with Portuguese, 68-73, 87; trade of, 68-69; military strength, 69-70; early conflicts with Portuguese, 70-72; relations with sultans, 72-73. *See also* Div
Malik Gupi, 66, 67, 73, 129
Malik Is-haq, 73-74
Malwa, sultan of, invades Gujarat, 116, 148
Manatunga, Jain temple at, 139
Mascarenhas, D. João, 79, 80
Merchants, *See* Arabs; Dutch East India Company; English East India Company; Foreigners; Gujarati merchants; Portuguese private traders
Mir Jumla, 129
Monetization, 21-22
Money, 155
Monsoons, 7, 45, 78
Muhammad, Sultan, 116
Muhammad Qulij Khan: and the Portuguese, 57-60, 84-85, 112; and Gujarati merchants, 58, 60, 93

INDEX

Muhammad Zahid Beg, Haji, 127-128
Muhammad Zaman Mirza, 77
Mukarrab Khan, 85
Murad Bakhsh, 126, 127
Mustafa Khan, 121
Muzaffar Shah I, 100
Muzaffar Shah II, 73, 138; and Malik Ayaz, 72-73

Nagar Brahmans, 130
Nagarsheth, head of Ahmadabad mahajan, 123. *See also* Shantidas Jawahari
Naosari, and Parsis, 138-139

Ottoman Turks, 69; besiege Div, 78

Panch, 123
Parsis, 28 n. 94; as social group, 138-139
Patel: head of panch, 123, 125, 135, 146; in villages, 141
Patronage, 133, 145
Pepper trade. *See* Spice trade
Portuguese: arrival in India, 30; conquests, 30-31; ethos of, 31 n. 3, 54, 55; revenues of, 32-33, 43-44, 56; administration, 33-35; "corruption" in, 50-51, 87, 113-114; fleets, 44-49, 100; relations with Muhammad Qulij Khan, 57-60; relations with Malik Ayaz, 67-73; relations with Bahadur, 73-77; relations with Mughals, 83-85; analysis of Gujarati response to, 85-91. *See also* Portuguese trade
Portuguese-Gujarati treaties: of 1534, 76; of 1535, 76; of 1537, 77-78; of 1539, 79; of 1549, 81; of 1559, 82
Portuguese-Gujarati wars, 74-75, 78, 80, 81, 83, 85, 111, 120
Portuguese private traders, 35, 36, 37-39, 46, 51, 97, 112; in Cochin, 49. *See also* Cambay
Portuguese trade: to Portugal, 35-36; within Asia, 36-37, 39; control of Asian trade, 39-47; success of system, 48-52, 98-100, 115; aims analyzed, 52-56; system assessed, 114-117. *See also* Cafilas; Cartazes; Portuguese private traders

Qazis, 122, 125, 152; of Broach, 136, 138
Quarters, in cities, 63, 142
Qutb-ud-din, Sultan, 148

Rajputs and Kolis, 61-62, 66, 140
Rander, 11, 129; attacked by Portuguese, 75
Rasulabad, 142
Red Sea, 10-14 *passim*, Portuguese and, 48-49, 51; Gujarati trade to, 94, 98-99, 100-101, 103, 110, 125
Rice trade, 13, 43-44, 46-47

Ruling group, 149; described, 133-134; relations with social groups, 134-135, 143, 153-154; size of, 143-144; role of, 150-151. *See also* Gujarati nobles; Social groups
Rustam Manock, head of Parsis, 139

Safi Khan, 119
Saints, Muslim: role as intermediaries, 135-137; disputes between, 147-148
Saraswat Brahmans, in Goa, 105
Sayyid Muhammad of Jaunpur, 137, 144, 147
Shah Alam: as intermediary, 136; founds suburb, 142; head of Bukhari Sayyids, 148
Shahbandar, 17-18; of Surat, 121, 127-128, 135
Shah Jahan, 121-122, 126, 139
Shantidas Jawahari: nagarsheth of Ahmadabad, 125; activities of, 126, 127, 130; role of, 135, 146, 147; as Jain head, 139
Sheth: head of mahajan, 123, 125
Ships: Arab, 7-8; sizes, 8. *See also* Portuguese fleets; Malik Ayaz; Bahadur
Shroffs, 21, 130
Sidi Muhammad, 111
Silk trade, 20
Sivaji, 126, 128, 147
Social groups: role in medieval Gujarat, 134-143, 153-154; role of heads, 134-135; size of, 143-145; multiple membership in, 145-146; cooperation between, 147; disputes between, 147-148; oppression within, 148-150; reasons for autonomy, 150-153. *See also* Intermediaries; Ruling group
Sources, historical, 3-4, 161-73
Spice trade, 10-13 *passim*, 52, 98-99
Street chiefs, 142, 146
Sufis, as social group, 135-136, 138, 147-148
Sultans of Gujarat: revenues of, 23-24; relations with nobles, 61-67; nature of control, 61-64; ethos of, 61-62, 90-91, 150-151; weakness after 1537, 62; weakness on accession, 64-65; legitimacy, 65; and Div, 72-74; response to Portuguese, 85-91; navy, 90; and merchants, 130-132. *See also* under individual sultans
Surat, 4, 11, 57, 58, 60, 78, 80; revenue of, 23; fort of, 42, 79; merchants of, 58, 60, 84; attacked by Portuguese, 74-75, 83; English seize ships of, 118-119: hartal in, 122; mahajan in, 125

Thamim Malik Yakub, 129
Trade. *See* Asian trade; Gujarati merchants; Portuguese private traders, Portuguese trade; and under particular places and products.
Tribute, 61-62

INDEX

Ulama, contrasted with sufis, 137-138

Vanias, 26-27, 28, 146; of Div, 103, 104, 113; of Mocha, 103; of Goa, 105; of Chaul, 109; ethos of, 110; of Surat, 122; and officials, 129; number in Portuguese areas, 144-145. *See also* Gujarati merchants

Virji Vorah: head of mahajan in Surat, 125; activities of, 125-127, 146; wealth of, 125; role of, 135; head of Jain sect, 146; power of, 149-150

V.O.C. *See* Dutch East India Company

War: and Portuguese trade, 97; and Gujarati merchants, 111-112, 116, 120; and officials, 112; and Kanara merchants, 112 n. 85

Zamindars, 139-141, 146

www.ingramcontent.com/pod-product-compliance
Lightning Source LLC
Chambersburg PA
CBHW021709230426
43668CB00008B/771